EVANGELISM EXPLOSION

D. JAMES KENNEDY

FOREWORD BY BILLY GRAHAM

Revised by D. James Kennedy and Archie B. Parrish

TYNDALE HOUSE PUBLISHERS
Wheaton, Illinois

This book
is affectionately dedicated
to the hundreds of laymen and laywomen
of the Coral Ridge Presbyterian Church
and to the tens of thousands of others
throughout the world
who have faithfully over the years
put into practice the principles
and methods of this program.

REVISED EDITION
LIBRARY OF CONGRESS CATALOG CARD NUMBER 71–116480
ISBN 0–8423–0780-X, CLOTH
ISBN 0-8423-0782-6, PAPER

PRINTED IN THE UNITED STATES OF AMERICA.

THE AUTHOR

Dr. D. James Kennedy was born in Augusta, Georgia, was reared in Chicago, and has spent most of his life in Florida. He received his B.A. degree from the University of Tampa and his B.D. Cum Laude from Columbia Theological Seminary, and his Master of Theology, Summa Cum Laude, from the Chicago Graduate School of Theology. He received the Doctor of Divinity Degree from Trinity College and Trinity Evangelical Divinity School. He is presently engaged in completing his dissertation for the Ph.D. Degree from New York University.

Dr. Kennedy has lectured and taught in more than a dozen seminaries and colleges and the general assemblies of a number of denominations. He has spoken to over 50,000 ministers and seminary students on the subject of lay evangelism. He is a regular member of the faculty of the Billy Graham Schools of Evangelism.

THE RESULTS OF THIS PROGRAM

The Evangelism Explosion program has been in continuous operation in the Coral Ridge Presbyterian Church of Fort Lauderdale, Florida, for the past fifteen years. Up to 500 people have gone out weekly to share the Good News of Christ with others. God's gracious working through this effort has been exciting to observe. The church has grown from seventeen to about 4,500 members and from one minister to eleven. Of more importance than membership figures is the actual attendance on Sunday. For the past four years the peak attendance has increased by more than 1,285 per year, bringing the top attendance on a Sunday morning to about 8,000. In the area of stewardship the church has gone in this time from home mission support to a budget of over $3.25 million. About eighty-five families have left the church to go into full-time Christian service. These are just some of the many startling results that can take place when a church takes seriously the command of Christ to equip the saints to do the work of ministry.

July 1, 1977

TRANSLATIONS OF EVANGELISM EXPLOSION

It has been properly said that language is the matrix of culture. To move from one language to another is to move from one culture to another. One of the reasons God became man in the person of Jesus Christ in the Jewish culture was to communicate to man as completely as possible. Since the purpose of Evangelism Explosion is to accurately communicate the good news of life through faith in Christ, we feel it is imperative that translations be culturally relevant. Straight, literal, wooden translations have a limited capacity for communicating.

Furthermore, there is a personal dimension to Evangelism Explosion ministry that cannot be placed on paper. For these reasons we have some very specific requirements for anyone desiring to undertake the translation of this work.

Concerning the translator:

1. We need to know his relationship to the evangelical community in his country.
2. We need to know his background in the language and culture of his people and his understanding of the English language.

Regarding the translation:

1. Copies of the translated portions as they are completed, together with the English equivalent, indicating any cultural adaptations, are to be provided to the International Center.
2. Initial production is to be in small quantities so that field testing can be adequately done before much money is invested.
3. After approximately a year of field testing, the material may be produced in larger quantities for use in local churches.
4. We need to know where the book will be printed, in what quantity, how it will be distributed to the churches, and whether or not the distributor is willing to work with Evangelism Explosion III International to promote solid local church-based ministries of evangelism in conjunction with the book.

All these things must be agreed upon before permission will be granted for translation.

Continuous dialogue is expected during the time of translation and field testing. When the final manuscript of the translation has been completed, a full copy, together with the English equivalent showing any cultural adaptations, must be submitted to E.E. III International.

Final permission for printing and distribution of the translation will be granted if the manuscript is linguistically correct, if the content is true to the fundamental concepts of E.E. III, and if there has been proper cultural adaptation.

If you are interested in making a translation or assisting the funding of a translation, write to E.E. III International, P.O. Box 23820, Fort Lauderdale, Florida 33307.

CONTENTS

FOREWORD

by Dr. Billy Graham

The Reverend Dr. D. James Kennedy is minister of the Coral Ridge Presbyterian Church of Fort Lauderdale, Florida, and I have known him for several years and followed his ministry closely. So enthusiastic have I become over his program for evangelizing a parish that I have asked him to come regularly and address our Crusade School of Evangelism, where he has been before many thousands of theological students, ordinands, young clergy and other Christian workers.

Dr. Kennedy was not always a preacher. Indeed, he was a dancing instructor, par excellence, with the Arthur Murray Dancing School and rapidly rising into prominence in that profession. Then one day his clock radio brought him a disturbing question from Dr. Donald Gray Barnhouse, the Philadelphia preacher, concerning where he would spend his eternal destiny. He could turn off his radio, but he could not turn off the eternal implication of this all-important question. The result was a revolutionary conversion. He subjected himself to the disciplines of being trained for and ordained into the ministry.

Christianity Today magazine correctly describes his congregation as the fastest growing in the Presbyterian Church in the U.S. In nine years it has grown from none to more than two thousand members and this at a time when churches everywhere are complaining of dwindling memberships. There are doubtless a number of reasons for this phenomenal growth but I would like to cite two. The first is the unwavering devotion of Dr. Kennedy, as a man, to Jesus Christ his Lord, a devotion that counts no sacrifice too great, no cost too high to pay to give Jesus Christ his best. The second is the fact that Pastor Kennedy has recaptured the biblical concept that the Church's primary task is "every-member evangelism." The Church, having come to Christ, is to go for Christ. In this book, Dr. Kennedy outlines how a whole congregation can be motivated and mobilized to perform this task of evangelism. The pastor himself must provide the example and leadership in this task. He chooses trainees and in four months of engaging them an evening a week, trains them in the science and art of house-to-house evangelism. He teaches them the course. He goes with them and demonstrates how it is done. Then the trainees graduate into trainers and, in turn, train others. In the words of a Canadian pastor who saw 103 members added to his church in the first eight months of effecting this program, this plan of Dr. Kennedy's is "the most revolutionary technique for personal evangelism to mobilize the sleeping giant of our laity to be discovered in the twentieth century."

Unworthy as I may feel at times, it has been my privilege for twenty years to see many of the world's largest stadiums crowded to hear the claims of Christ presented from the Bible. Equally important in New Testament evangelism, however, is this basic principle of one-to-one evangelism.

June 1970

PREFACE

to the Revised Edition

"I will build my church and the gates of hell shall not prevail against it!" (Matthew 16:18).

Never in the history of the world has it been more evident that Jesus is building his Church. In Africa the Christian church is growing thirty-two times faster than the birth rate. In Korea the Christian church is growing four times faster than the population increase. George Gallup has called 1977 in America "the year of the evangelical." More than fifty million American adults claim to have been "born again."

Perhaps the most significant factor generating this growth is the mobilizing of the laity. Increasingly Christians are realizing that *the Great Commission has been given to the whole Church for the purpose of evangelizing the whole world.* Realizing this, Jim Kennedy began sharing what God was doing at Coral Ridge Presbyterian Church with church leaders from across the world. The more God's blessing at Coral Ridge was shared, the more God blessed Coral Ridge. And the Discipleship Training Ministry that was developed and is still functioning in the local church, has now grown into an interdenominational international fellowship. During this time of "maturing" we have made some mistakes and some dramatic improvements. There have been three phases of development and so we now call this ministry Evangelism Explosion III International.

I. EVANGELIZING

From the beginning of E.E., it was clear that evangelism was not an end in itself . . . but the beginning. Though the basic purpose of E.E. was (and still is) evangelism, we realized that this could best take place in a loving, discipling relationship. And . . . we knew that new believers could not be left to themselves, but needed concerned follow-up.

II. DISCIPLING

The more E.E. worked in the area of evangelizing, the more it was evident that effective evangelism best takes place within the context of three levels of discipleship.

(1) TRAINER AND TRAINEE

On-the-job training makes more and better lay evangelists. On-the-job training means that an experienced lay evangelist takes someone with less experience with him when he shares the gospel. Over a period of months the less experienced person is drawn into the presentation little by little, until finally the less experienced one is able to lead the entire conversation.

(2) E.E. PARTICIPANTS AND OTHER MEMBERS IN THE CHURCH

The entire church family is discipled through the E.E. ministry via the Prayerpartner Program. Each E.E. participant asks two adult church members to uphold him in prayer during the semester of training. Needs are shared and prayed for each week. Evangelism contacts are mentioned and brought before the Lord. In this way, more people in the church have direct involvement with the evangelism ministry.

E.E. participants in the prayerpartner relationship with other workers in the church are helped to see that bringing people to Christ is only the beginning. The teachers and leaders of the church are there to help them build up the new Christians.

Every congregation has a high percentage of people who are only attenders. As these attenders enter into prayerpartner relationships with participants in the E.E. ministry, they grow in their desire to be spiritual reproducers. The discipling that takes place through the Prayerpartner Program eliminates a pharisaical elitism among those who are in the evangelism program. It provides channels for developing stronger disciples throughout the church.

(3) NEW BELIEVERS AND SPIRITUAL PARENTS

The Great Commission instructs us to make "disciples of all nations." To properly disciple another, one's life must be shared. It is not enough simply to know the content of the gospel. Individuals who are functionally mature in their own lives have the responsibility to disciple their spiritual children into responsible reproducing mature disciples.

III. CHURCH NURTURING

The local church is the family of God. It is composed of those who from a human standpoint are young and old, and from a spiritual standpoint are mature and not so mature. For a disciple to develop to proper functional maturity he has to know how to relate, not only to other mature disciples, but also to those who are not mature and to the non-Christian in the world.

Some churches have entered into evangelism programs without considering their spiritual health. Tragedy can be the result. Leaders need to constantly work on the health of the local congregation so that there can be responsible reproduction and growth in the local church.

Jesus said, "By this shall all men know that you are my disciples because you love one another." He said as we are one in him, "the world will know that God has sent him." The loving unity of God's people, living in a disciplined relationship with each other under the authority and the love of God, become a demonstration to the world of the power and the truth of the gospel. Though the precepts of the gospel may be proclaimed to an individual in a few minutes, their reality must be lived out in a lifetime of relationship within the body of Christ. This has been properly called **body evangelism.** The corporate witness to the life-transforming truth of the gospel in the local church becomes the backdrop for individual proclamation. Individual proclamation without this reality will always be somewhat limited. Also the individual proclamation is to build up the local body in spirit and size. Christ is not interested in proclamation for its own sake. He is building his Church.

Not long after the first Leadership Clinic in Fort Lauderdale, Florida, in 1967, church leaders from other countries expressed interest in this work. Those who were functioning in basically healthy churches with cultural sensitivity found great benefit.

Now an international center has been established for this ministry in Fort Lauderdale, Florida. Regular communication is maintained with ministries throughout the world. More than 80 percent of the people to be evangelized now living are not in the Western world. Within the next ten years we believe God will have Evangelism Explosion ministries operating in an indigenous fashion in virtually every nation in the world.

One thing needs to be emphasized: Evangelism Explosion III International considers itself the servant of the local church. We believe the responsibility for evangelization rests in the local church. Having been developed in the context of a congregation, we desire to function only within the God-established order that exists in each church. In this way we hope to mobilize local congregations to do the task of world evangelization.

In this Third Revised Edition of *Evangelism Explosion* Dr. Kennedy has revised the section on training laymen and refined the content of the presentation of the gospel. The analysis of the introduction has been greatly enlarged. Many new insights have been added in the gospel, the commitment, and the section on testimony. The material providing answers to common objections is significantly increased. Some very effective new illustrations have been added to the chapter dealing with this subject.

I have completely rewritten the material dealing with follow-up. It forms a composite of effective follow-up activities taken from many churches of different denominations with effective Evangelism Explosion programs. Also I have written material on Enlistment for Enlargement, Questionnaire Evangelism, The Gospel for the Secular Mind, Relational Evangelism, The Occasional Witnessing Situation and The Chain of Command. Though this material is new to the Evangelism Explosion textbook, it has been taught in Leadership Clinics and field-tested in a great number of local churches.

I would like to express great appreciation to Jim Kennedy, not only for the contribution he has made to the church of Jesus Christ, but also to my personal life. He is a scholar, prophet, and man of great vision. To work with him has been one of the greatest challenges of my life. Also I feel I would be remiss if I did not acknowledge my deep indebtedness to Dr. Donald MacGavran of The School of World Mission, Fuller Theological Seminary. His concepts of church growth have radically altered my perspective. I have been exposed to these concepts through hours of discussion with Peter Wagner and John Wimber of the Church Growth Division, Fuller Evangelistic Association, Pasadena, California. I wish that all church leaders could be exposed in depth to the dynamic concepts God has given to these men.

Much of the formalizing of the material I have contributed to this volume would not have been possible without the faithful work of Mrs. Gladys Israels. She began as one of Dr. Kennedy's first trainees more than thirteen years ago at Coral Ridge Presbyterian Church. Now the Board of Directors of E.E. III International has appointed her as Coordinator of the International Center.

The participants in the E.E. ministry at Coral Ridge have been a constant source of information and inspiration. Especially Mrs. June Baughman, our evangelism secretary.

Her heart for souls and head for details have added much to this ministry.

Mr. David Schwausch and Reverend Robert Carl read much of the manuscript and, from their wide experience in Evangelism Explosion, provided significant insights.

A special word of appreciation must be given to those who tirelessly typed for so very many hours the thousands of words that are now before you. Especially to Mrs. Jean Murray, Mrs. Karen Robeson, Mrs. Ruth Rohm, I express my gratitude; also to the many volunteers who worked in preparing this manuscript.

July 1977

Archie B. Parrish
Minister of Evangelism
Coral Ridge Presbyterian Church
Executive Director
Evangelism Explosion III International

PREFACE

to the First Edition

There is something new in the life of the Christian church today! It is the "Evangelism Explosion."

In recent years we have heard much about the "population explosion"—the burgeoning of masses of people at rates hitherto undreamed of. The population has been increasing at a far greater rate than the church. The reason for this is simple. While the world has been multiplying we have been making "additions to the church." It is patently obvious that if the church is adding while the world is multiplying there is no hope of our ever catching up.

The only answer to this dilemma, humanly speaking, is "spiritual multiplication." This involves the laity. In fact, it involves everyone who names the name of Christ.

An Evangelism Explosion is God's answer to the population explosion. Thousands of laymen and ministers, trained and equipped to graciously and effectively present the gospel of Christ, provide the fissionable material. The Holy Spirit working through the gospel, which is the **dunameis** or "dynamite" of God, provides the explosive power, and the result is not chaos but the creation of a vast host of new Christians who are in turn being trained to carry on this spiritual chain reaction.

At the World Consultation on Mobilization Saturation Evangelism held in Switzerland in mid-1969, it was noted that the decade of the sixties had been the decade of the emergence of the laymen in the church. About the year 1960 a number of different groups and movements arose spontaneously in various parts of the world, all having the same vision: the mobilizing and equipping of the vast lay army of the church to do the work of ministry. It seems that after centuries of a clergy-oriented ministry the Holy Spirit is finally breaking through our man-made molds to create the type of church that he meant should exist from the beginning, and which did exist for the first three centuries of this era of our Lord.

That this is the movement of the Spirit of God in our time is further evidenced by the tremendous eagerness with which thousands of ministers are responding to the opportunities and potentiality of lay multiplication evangelism.

Laymen can not only be trained to witness but they can be trained to train others to witness and thus multiply their labors. It has been well said, "He is best employed who is involved in multiplying the workers."

The results of such a lay evangelism program in our own church have been so astonishing that they would appear unbelievable to those who do not understand the spiritual power engendered by such a ministry. We are awed and humbled as we become almost observers to the mighty works of God, and we know that this is his doing and it is marvelous in our eyes.

The aim of this book is to help other churches, pastors, and laymen to learn better how to do person-to-person evangelism and also how to train others to do the same.

I would like to acknowledge my gratitude to the many others now long forgotten and untraceable who nevertheless have been the source of many of the thoughts and illustrations in this book. In addition I would like to express my thanks to the Rev. Kennedy Smartt who patiently took me with him on home visitation and instructed me in the fine art of personal evangelism.

I would also like to express my appreciation and acknowledge my indebtedness to the many who have helped to make this book a reality. I would like to thank the Rev. Harry Miller who first gathered all our material together into notebook form; and the dedicated group of men and women in our church who put this together as a notebook over and over again through the years for use in our church and clinics; to my personal secretary, Mrs. Mary Anne Bunker, for her constant assistance; and a most special word of appreciation and thanks to Mrs. Ruth Rohm, our publications secretary, for her faithful labors in typing, retyping, and editing the work.

D. James Kennedy
Fort Lauderdale, Florida
1970

HOW TO USE THIS BOOK

BRIEF OVERVIEW

For a brief overview of the principles and results of the E.E. III ministry, read "Training Laymen for Evangelism."

The balance of the book provides core curriculum for at least four semesters of training in the local church. A semester is usually about four and one half months long. Thus the content of this book is designed to provide training for two to three years.

CHURCH-ORIENTED PROSPECTS

A church concentrating on church-oriented prospects should begin the first semester with the standard gospel presentation, a minimum amount of follow-up, handling objections and enlistment.

In the second semester, for those operating as trainers, emphasis is placed on proficiency and flexibility in presenting the gospel, with special emphasis on introduction and commitment. Additional information is presented concerning enlistment and follow-up, and trainer responsibilities are dealt with in detail.

After a person has successfully completed the basic course for trainers, emphasis in the next semester is on handling objections and problem situations.

"The Gospel for the Secular Mind" can be studied for a semester. This will give additional flexibility in dealing with difficult people.

PAGAN PROSPECTS

If you are dealing primarily with pagans—people with no familiarity with the Christian faith, then trainees should begin with "The Gospel for the Secular Mind," the questionnaire introduction, and brief exposure to enlistment and follow-up.

When the person becomes a trainer, the course content concentrates on developing proficiency with the questionnaire introduction, variations in the commitment, trainer responsibilities, and more detailed information concerning follow-up and enlistment.

The second semester content concentrates on difficult situations and objections.

During the third semester, a trainer's concentration should be on the gospel for the church-oriented person. This will give additional illustrative material and insights into sharing the gospel.

For information on Learning Kits that provide weekly study assignments and supplemental material and Leaders' Manuals that provide weekly lesson plans for each semester of training, write to Evangelism Explosion III International, P.O. Box 23820, Fort Lauderdale, Florida, 33307.

ONE
TRAINING LAYMEN FOR EVANGELISM

A. SURVEYING THE PROGRAM

This is not theory, but fact! These are not the idle speculations of the ivory tower but the tested results of hard experience. First in the congregation of the Coral Ridge Presbyterian Church of Fort Lauderdale, Florida, and then in thousands of other churches throughout the United States and much of the rest of the world, these principles and procedures have brought new life and vitality and have resulted in the conversion of multitudes of people.

READILY TRANSFERABLE TECHNIQUES

This program of training laymen for the task of evangelism grew out of the specific problems and opportunities faced by our congregation. Yet the program contains readily transferable techniques which have been used by numerous other congregations in cities and towns, in ghettos and rural areas, and in many languages and cultures throughout the world. We believe that the principles contained in the program represent some of the basic principles of the New Testament concerning the matter of evangelism, though by no means does this program exhaust all of the biblical teaching and possibilities of evangelism. This is a program of personal lay evangelism and does not begin to encompass many of the other sound and biblical methods of evangelism, such as crusade evangelism, pulpit evangelism, literature evangelism, etc.

LAYMEN—THE STRATEGIC KEY

Realizing that laymen are the most strategic and also the most unused key to the evangelization of the world, we have endeavored to build a program which will motivate, recruit, and train men and women and boys and girls to do the job of evangelism—and then keep them doing it! This, of course, is not an easy task, as most pastors can testify. And yet it would seem that the basic principles of New Testament evangelism require that this mobilization of the laity take place. We are not talking about the "flash and ash" type of program of which there have been numerous examples on the evangelical scene, but we are talking about a type of mobilization and recruitment which will insure an ongoing program of lay evangelism year after year in the local church. Let us look at some of these principles through which this may take place.

B. EXAMINING THE PRINCIPLES

EVERY CHRISTIAN A WITNESS

Christ's first instructions to his new followers in the first chapter of Mark were, "Come ye after me, and I will make you to become fishers of men." His last instructions on this earth to his disciples were, "But ye shall receive power, after that the Holy Ghost is come upon you: and ye shall be witnesses unto me both in Jerusalem, and in all Judaea, and in Samaria, and unto the uttermost part of the earth." Christ thus began and ended his ministry with the command to be witnesses and fishers of men! This thrust of his teaching is summed up in the Great Commission where Jesus commands his followers to go into all of the world and preach the gospel to every creature. **The first and most obvious principle, then, is that the Church is a body under orders by Christ to share the gospel with the whole world.** But the question then arises, how is this to be done and by whom?

THE WILES OF SATAN

The Apostle Paul said that we are not ignorant of the wiles of the devil. But I wonder how true that is today? I wonder how many times we have been deceived by him? I am sure it has been often. What is the greatest strategic victory that Satan has ever achieved? What would you suppose it to be? The most signal victory for Satan would obviously be the worst defeat for the Church. What might it be?

SATAN'S GREATEST VICTORY

Surely a number of his devious stratagems leap to mind. I would like to suggest one thing which, in my opinion, is his greatest victory. Let me present it to you in the way of an analogy. Suppose that in our modern, secular world, the center for propaganda in Moscow dreamed up a new idea. They polished it very carefully and then began to spread it abroad. It appears first of all in some avant-garde publications, coming to surface in magazine and newspaper articles. Perhaps a play is made out of it, and then a motion picture, and finally a television production. Groups would be formed to push the movement, protests would be made, and finally the idea prevails and is accepted by the American people, almost unanimously. What is the idea? It is this: that wars are very dangerous, complicated operations and ordinary persons could get hurt needlessly, therefore they should go home and let the generals and admirals fight wars. I don't think there is any doubt in our minds as to what would be the outcome of the cold—or not so cold—war in which we are engaged.

LET THE GENERALS FIGHT THE WAR

Right away we say, "That is ridiculous! Such a ludicrous idea could never be put over on any people." Yet in the Church this, in essence, is exactly what Satan has done! I am certain that for the vast majority of Christian church members the idea has firmly taken root in their minds that it is primarily the task of the minister to fight the battles of Christ—especially for the souls of men. In the minds of most, the work of evangelism is the work of professionally trained men. "After all," they say, "I'm just a butcher, or baker, or candlestick maker, and what do I know about theology? I've never been to seminary; leave it to the trained ecclesiastical generals!" This I believe has been the greatest tragedy that has befallen the Church of Jesus Christ. Its results are so far reaching, so vast in scope, that we have little concept of what damage has been done.

THE EARLY CHURCH

But it wasn't this way in the early church! Examine again that passage in Acts 8:4 where it says, "All they that were scattered abroad went everywhere preaching the word." That is a great text to preach. But some people might say, "Well, just a minute, preacher, not so fast. You have turned that corner a little too rapidly. You see, the people that went everywhere spreading the Word and preaching the Word were the apostles. You remember, Jesus chose these twelve and they were trained, and they went out and spread the Word."

EVERYONE EVANGELIZING!

Well, we all know that a standard exegetical axiom is, "A text without a context is a pretext," and this has been a pretext long enough for letting ecclesiastical George do it! The significant context of that verse is found in Acts 8:1 where we read that "they were all scattered abroad except the apostles." And (Acts 8:4) "they that were scattered abroad went everywhere preaching the word." The word translated "preaching the word" is the Greek word *euangelizo* which means "evangelizing." That is, everybody *except the apostles* went everywhere evangelizing! Now we know that the apostles did their share. But the point that the inspired writer is emphasizing here is that everyone besides the apostles also went and evangelized.

EARLY RESULTS OF LAY EVANGELISM

This is how the Church of Jesus Christ in 300 years accomplished the most amazing results. The whole pagan Roman Empire was undercut and overthrown by the power of the gospel of Christ which, on the lips of Christ-conquered disciples, crossed seas and deserts, pierced the darkest jungles, seeped into every city and town, and finally into the senate and the very palace of Rome itself—until a Christian Caesar was placed upon the throne. How? Because *everyone* was evangelizing.

The Christian church was burgeoning with such rapidity that by the middle of the second century one of the great apologists could say, "We are everywhere. We are in your towns and in your cities; we are in your country; we are in your army and navy; we are in your palaces; we are in the senate; we are more numerous than anyone." Constantine knew very well (whether or not he was truly converted I will leave for the historians) that he had no chance of unifying the Roman Empire or holding power in that empire without the help of the Christians.

CLERGY-LAITY SPLIT

By A.D. 300 the church had shown such tremendous strength and virility, and was spreading so swiftly, that it appeared the entire civilized world could be evangelized by A.D. 500. But something happened. Emperor Constantine in the year 313 issued the Edict of Toleration by which the long agonizing persecution of the Christians was at last brought to a halt. In the following decades numerous other edicts favoring the Christians were passed, until at last the whole Roman Empire was declared by fiat to be Christian. Thus millions of barbarians flooded into the church, bringing with them all of the pagan superstitions and heresies. They didn't even know the gospel. They had never experienced its transforming power and, of course, they could not go out and tell others about it. So, little by little, the idea arose that there was a division between the clergy and the laity, and that this task of evangelism was the job of the professionally trained individuals. So they decided to let ecclesiastical George do it. The Dark Ages followed! With only a few bright spots in the history of the church since that time, this deplorable condition has continued down to our day.

LET CLERICAL GEORGE DO IT

So successful has Satan been with this stratagem that it has been estimated that probably 95 percent of American church members have never led anyone to Christ. Thus the army of Christ has been more than decimated and the response from the pew has been, "Let clerical George do it." I am thankful that today there is an obvious reversal of this trend as more and more laymen and churches are realizing and accepting their responsibility to witness.

IMPORTANCE OF LAYMEN

The second important principle, then, is that it is the task of the ministers to train their laymen to evangelize. Over 99 percent of the church is made up of laymen. If they are A.W.O.L. (absent without official leave) there is little doubt that the battle will be lost.

PURPOSE OF MINISTERS

If the laity has been deceived, I think it is equally true that the ministers have also been deceived by the subtlety of Satan concerning the basic purpose of their ministry. In the fourth chapter of Ephesians we read that Christ has given to the Church "some apostles; and some, prophets; and some, evangelists; and some, pastors and teachers; for the perfecting of the saints, for the work of the ministry, for the edifying of the body of Christ." This is the way it reads in the King James translation. This, however, is not a very accurate rendering of the Greek text. Instead of the preposition "for" being repeated three times, the Greek would be better rendered: "for," "unto," "unto." A more literal translation, then, would be that Christ has given pastors and teachers to the Church "*for* the equipping of the saints *unto* the work of ministry, *unto* the upbuilding of the body of Christ."

REVOLUTIONARY CONCEPT

Such a concept, once grasped, would completely revolutionize many ministries. A basic criterion for determining the successfulness of a pastorate would then become: "How many saints have I equipped to do the work of ministry?" As ministers, then, we need to see ourselves not as the star performers or virtuosos, but rather as the coach of a well-trained and well-coordinated team.

We have seen what needs to be done and by whom; now let us ask: How are we going to get them to do it?

MISSING KEY—ON-THE-JOB TRAINING

There have been hundreds of thousands of messages preached on the responsibility of Christians to witness, and yet there is a striking absence of any formidable army of lay witnesses. Something, therefore, must be missing. This brings us to our third important principle, namely: *"Evangelism is more caught than taught."* This oft-repeated cliché rather accurately describes what is missing in most attempts at teaching laymen to evangelize, and it also describes fairly well the method that Christ used to teach his followers.

I have asked thousands of ministers whether they have preached sermons on the need to witness and have taught classes on this subject. Most of them have raised their hands, but when I have asked how many of them make a habit of taking their people with them when they go out to evangelize, only three or four percent will usually respond. I questioned a group of ministers, missionaries, and teachers and found that only 1½ percent of their members were regularly engaged in leading people to Christ, and only three of these people took their laymen with them when they went to evangelize.

The average person can no more learn to evangelize in a classroom than he can learn to fly an airplane in the living room. The missing link of modern evangelistic training, which was so thoroughly provided by Christ, is "on-the-job" training.

TRAIN SOUL-WINNERS

The fourth principle of this program is that *it is more important to train a soul-winner than to win a soul.* Spiritual multiplication will not take place unless converts are turned into evangelists, disciples into disciplers. Since about 95 percent of converts never win anyone to Christ because they are not equipped to do so, it is obvious that training a person to evangelize effectively will be more fruitful than merely winning someone to Christ.

The Lord Jesus did not say to go and make converts, but to go and make disciples. *It is because winning a person to Christ is so important that training someone to win 10 or 100 or 1000 people to Christ is so much more important.* One of the wonderful parts of this program is that these two tasks are combined and people are trained to evangelize by observing as others are being evangelized. Thus one is not done to the exclusion of the other.

These are the basic principles that we feel need to be understood and accepted if a church is to have an effective program of evangelism.

C. REVIEWING THE HISTORY

FEAR OF WITNESSING

This program grew out of the experiences I had in the Coral Ridge Church, which started as a home mission project in 1960. I came directly to this work from seminary, and though I preached evangelistically and I had taken all the courses offered at seminary on evangelism and read many books besides, I found that the sophisticated people of Fort Lauderdale did not respond to my message from the pulpit. I was totally lacking in both confidence and know-how in regard to confronting individuals face to face with the gospel. After eight or ten months of my preaching, the congregation had dwindled from forty-five to seventeen, and I was a most discouraged young minister. About that time I was invited to Decatur, Georgia, to preach for ten days of evangelistic services. Happy to get away for a while from my Fort Lauderdale fiasco, I accepted the invitation.

LIFE-CHANGING EXPERIENCE

When I arrived the pastor told me that I would be preaching each night, but more importantly, he said, we would be visiting in the homes each day—morning, noon and night—to present the gospel to people individually. I was petrified, for I knew I had no ability whatsoever to do this. However, the next morning we went out. After about a half hour of my stumbling attempts at evangelism, the pastor took over the conversation and in about fifteen or twenty minutes led the man to Christ. I was astonished but did not realize even then the impact that this was to have on my life. For ten days I watched this pastor lead one person after another to Christ for a total of fifty-four individuals during those ten days.

I went back to Fort Lauderdale a new man, and I began to do just what I had seen done. People responded in the same way. Soon dozens, scores, and then hundreds accepted Christ. The principle of "on-the-job" training had been applied to my life, and had produced its results.

FAILURE OF CLASSES

I then realized that there was a definite limit to the number of people that I myself could see, and that I ought to train others to do what I was doing. What I then foolishly did is the same thing that thousands of others no doubt have done: I organized a class on witnessing. I gave them six lessons and sent them out. They all went home terrified! I waited a few months and tried again. This time I gave them twelve lessons—again no success. A few more months and another series, more elaborate, more complex: fifteen weeks—again no results. I do not know of one single adult that was brought to Christ by any one of these laymen as a result of these witnessing classes.

THE MISSING LINK

Finally it struck me like a bolt of lightning—I had taken classes for three years and had not learned how to witness. It was not until someone who knew how had taken me out into people's homes that I finally got the confidence to do it myself.

Thus I began the program which has continued for the past seventeen years. It began by my taking out one individual until he had confidence to witness to others, and then another, and another. And so it has grown. After the people are trained, they in turn can train others.

D. MOTIVATING THE CHRISTIANS

PROBLEMS OF MASS RECRUITMENT

Often when an evangelism program is envisioned, a pastor will begin by preaching on the subject and then inviting everybody who is willing to take part to come on a specified night to begin the program. This is the way we tried at first to motivate people and recruit them, but we found it was not very successful. The basic motivation will no doubt begin from the pulpit with sermons on the responsibility, privilege, and necessity of witnessing for Christ. The great texts already mentioned, and others, should certainly be preached with clarity and forcefulness. However, our experience teaches us that the actual recruiting should not be done from the pulpit, but rather should be done on a person-to-person basis, first by the pastor and then by the trained laymen.

E. RECRUITING THE WORKERS

INDIVIDUAL INVITATION

When Christ called his apostles, he first prayed all night and then called them specifically by name. Now an apostle *(apostolos)* was "one sent forth with a commission." The term has both a narrow and a wider meaning. In its narrow sense it refers only to the twelve apostles whom Christ first called. In its broader sense it refers to every Christian who has been sent forth by Christ with the Great Commission. We would therefore recommend that after much prayer the minister select several people whom he would like to take with him to learn how to evangelize.

REPORT-BACK SESSIONS

We have selected Wednesday morning from 9 to 12 and Thursday evening from 7:15 to 10:30 as our time of visitation. In each case we have a report-back meeting which I feel is quite important to prevent discouragement. During these sessions we provide Sanka and doughnuts. At these times we hear the reports of the work of the day. A person from each team gives the report for that day's visit. This not only encourages those who are listening but also gives each trainee additional opportunities to stand before others and speak, thus encouraging them in their ability to speak to others. A results form is filled out. Statistical results of the day's calling are also indicated on a specially prepared chalkboard. Problems or objections encountered during the visit may be brought up at this time and the pastor may wish to make some comment about them, thus helping the entire group to more effectively deal with the obstacles that are confronted in the homes. These report sessions help reduce dropouts due to discouragement, as evangelists have an opportunity to have their spirits lifted by returning to hear others whom God has blessed that night or morning.

How the report sessions are conducted is described in detail later in this book (see First Week Follow-up).

GETTING STARTED

Not three men. I would suggest that the pastor begin by selecting two people for one morning and two others for one night. As long as we do not have three men together, which seems a bit heavy, we have not found that the three individuals constitute much of a problem. One reason for going out by threes was that it solved the problem of what to do with women in the program. Someone might say, "But doesn't the Bible tell us that we should go out two-by-two?" Well, let us take a closer look at that passage.

There is no doubt that Christ sent out the Seventy, two-by-two. But the question arises, "Whom did he send out?" I believe there is little doubt that he sent out seventy men. If, however, he had had thirty-five men and thirty-five women, what would he have done then? This, of course, was not feasible in that day. Today it is. In our time, to send out two women into a modern metropolis at night is exceedingly dangerous. To send out a woman with somebody else's husband is also dangerous, but three is still a crowd under any circumstances. Sending them out by threes has the double advantage of including women in the program and also doubling the speed of training. Someone might ask, "Can't you send out a husband and wife together?" Yes, you can, but this is a dead-end street, for the whole purpose of this program is to continually expand the number of people trained and you cannot do this without dividing the husband and wife team.

Length of training. We have two training programs a year, the first beginning early in October and running about four and a half months until the middle of February. Then we begin our next training class, which runs till the beginning of summer. All of these details will vary according to local customs and circumstances.

Rapid multiplication. I did not want to begin a program in this small way with only one or two individuals, but wanted rather to train a whole class of evangelists at one time. The result was that I ended up with none. However, if you begin with a few, you can grow in not too much time into a large body of witnesses. At the end of the four and a half month training program, each of these four trained individuals would recruit two more workers, and the minister also would recruit four more. Now there would be the original four plus their eight, making twelve plus the minister's new four, making sixteen, plus the minister, or a total of seventeen. After the next class the sixteen laymen would get thirty-two more, making forty-eight, plus the minister's four, which makes fifty-two, plus the minister, making fifty-three. And soon it could grow to a hundred, two hundred, etc.

Recruitment banquets. The people are recruited by personal visits at which time the program is explained by the trained individual in detail and they are invited to a dinner* where there will be a fuller explanation of the goals and principles and

---

* The program may grow in a church until it reaches a point at which a dinner is no longer feasible, in which case a rally may be held. This is what has happened at Coral Ridge. These rallies are generally held on Friday nights.

reasons for the program, plus testimonies of what has been accomplished. Then they are asked to commit themselves to the entire four and a half month training program or else not to start. Paul said, "I am afraid of you, lest I have bestowed on you labor in vain."

F. TRAINING THE EVANGELISTS

Our program consists of three types of training.

TYPES OF TRAINING

1. Class instruction. These classes, lasting about forty-five minutes each, are held one a week on the day the people come to the church for visitation. They meet together for class instruction and then go out into the field. During this class instruction there is a brief lecture on the topic of the week, assignments are given for study during the following week, and the class is divided into three-person teams in which they practice what has been learned during the previous week. The details for the class instruction and the homework assignments are given in the Learning Kits which have been mentioned before.

2. Homework assignments. This detailed textbook contains instructions on how to present the gospel logically and interestingly. Assignments are given each week, consisting of portions of the gospel presentation to be learned. These are checked and recited each week at the class.

3. On-the-job training. The third and most important part of the training is "on-the-job." Here each trainee goes out with a trained individual and listens as this trained person endeavors to lead someone to Christ. *This is the vital, almost indispensable, element of training.*

It is here that the trainee overcomes the greatest obstacle that he faces in learning to witness—the fear of what others will say. During the sixteen weeks of training he will see the gospel presented a good many times and see a number of people come to profess their faith in Christ. This will have a transforming effect upon him and will do more than anything else to assuage his fears.

An important principle to keep in mind here is the *gradual transferral of responsibility.* In the same way that a student learning to fly an airplane would gradually assume more responsibility for the overall task of taking off, flying, and landing, so the evangelistic trainee gradually assumes increasing responsibilities.

The three parts of flying, namely: take-off, flight, and landing, may be likened to the three parts of a gospel presentation, namely: introduction, gospel, and commitment. As a student of flying first handles the plane in the air, so the trainee begins by handling increasingly larger parts of the gospel. Then he includes also the introduction and the commitment.

In this way the overall task is broken down into manageable assignments for the student. The part of the gospel presentation that the student is to give on a particular night has been assigned the week before, studied by the student, and first recited in class before he goes out.

In the home the trainer, when he reaches that point, will say something such as the following: "Well, John, I've been doing most of the talking so far. Why don't I let Mary share with you something about the grace of God and what it means to her."

Mary will then pick up the presentation at the assigned point and present as much as she has learned, and when she hesitates the trainer will pick up the conversation again by saying something such as, "Thank you, Mary, that was very well said." And then the trainer concludes the presentation.

G. OBTAINING THE PROSPECTS

It is important if we are going to effectively train our people that we provide them with the best possible source of prospects. To deal consistently with only the most difficult type of individuals is most certainly going to discourage the average beginner. We have found from our experience that the best sources of prospects are the following:

THE BEST PROSPECTS

People who have visited our worship services. Generally speaking, I would say that these are the easiest people with whom to deal. Their hearts are further prepared by a few weeks of sitting under the ministry of the Word.

Some will say, however, "We do not have many visitors come to our church." This objection was raised by a minister in one of the evangelism schools that I was conducting. I asked him how many visitors he did have. He said, "We may have two or three on any given Sunday." I then asked him how many people he had going out to present the gospel to them. He said, "Oh, I have no one doing that," to which I responded, "Well, then, you already have two or three visitors too many."

There was a time when we had only a handful of people coming to church and very few visitors, but you can begin with the visitors that you do have. We have found that the number of visitors has increased as the enthusiasm engendered by this program has increased.

HOW TO GET MORE VISITORS

In seeking to increase the number of visitors coming to church, we may ask ourselves the question: "What causes people to visit a church?" In a survey conducted at our church we asked about 1,000 people why they came to our church for the first time. The overwhelming majority said that some member of the church had invited them. This, then, is one of the big secrets of getting people to come to church—encouraging your members to invite them.

Periodic "Visitors' Sundays" with perhaps some coffee served afterward and a special emphasis on inviting friends for several weeks beforehand is a fruitful source of prospects. An enthusiastic congregation will provide more than enough people to talk to about Christ.

RELATIVES AND FRIENDS

After those who come to your church, the second most responsive source is the **relatives and friends** of new believers. Each of us is the center of a network of relationships. The longer you are a Christian, the fewer non-Christians remain in your "network." The new Christian usually has many non-Christian friends and relatives. As the Lord begins to change the new Christian's life, those near him notice. The witnessing team can be of great assistance in sharing the gospel. Relational evangelism will be discussed later in this book.

SUNDAY SCHOOL

A third source of prospects would be the parents of children who attend Sunday school. This source, however, will not prove very fruitful unless Sunday school teachers have had an active program of visiting in the homes and showing an interest in the children's progress in their Christian education. If this has been done, however, the parents will be generally open to the gospel.

NEW RESIDENTS

A fourth source of prospects is the weekly or biweekly or monthly listing of those who have bought new homes in the area. This can be obtained from some source in almost every city. Any real estate salesman in the congregation can usually tell you where to obtain it. In Fort Lauderdale it costs seventy-five dollars per year, but it is worth many times that to any church.

We begin by sending a friendly letter to these people, welcoming them into the community and offering our services in any way possible. We conclude the letter by stating that someone from the church will drop by in the near future and welcome them personally to our area and to our church. A card is then made out for the visitation team showing the date the letter was mailed and indicating that the people are new residents in the area. They are then processed in the visitation program.

RELIGIOUS QUESTIONNAIRE

A fifth source of prospects, if the first three fail to provide an adequate number, is a religious questionnaire. For more than six years we have worked with a small "assurance questionnaire." It can be used in residential and public places. Five questions are raised that let you know if the person contacted is responsive or resistive. The questionnaire must be used wisely—no blitzing, or you will generate resistance. How to use the assurance questionnaire is discussed later in this book.

These questions will sift the general population and help you to find the people who have a genuine interest in spiritual matters. As has been said many times, "There is no sense in tugging at green fruit."

H. PRESENTING THE GOSPEL

POSITIVE APPROACH

Our basic approach is neither apologetic, defensive, nor negative. It is a simple, positive statement of the Good News of the gospel. We have found that most Christians do not know how to make an intelligible, forceful, and interesting presentation of the gospel. This is basically what we are trying to teach them to do.

WRITTEN PRESENTATION

We feel that a very useful tool which is often omitted from texts on evangelism is an actual presentation of the gospel itself. Such a presentation is included in the training materials, and the people are encouraged to learn it and use it as a guide as they begin to present the gospel of Christ. Later it is no doubt adapted to the individual personality with many additions or subtractions, as the case may require. But most people need something with which to start.

BASIC TRAINING

The essential things which we are trying to teach our people are: how to get into the gospel and find out where the person is spiritually, how to present the gospel itself, how to bring the person to a commitment to Jesus Christ at the conclusion, and how to vitally relate the new convert to the family of God.

THREE PARTS OF GOSPEL

In teaching the trainees the presentation of the gospel (II in the outline), we proceed in the following manner. First, we have them learn the Outline of the Gospel, which might be considered as the skeleton. Second, we have them learn Scripture verses which give muscle, so to speak, to the outline. Third, we have them learn illustrations which flesh out and make clear and understandable the Outline of the Gospel.

BUILD ON OUTLINE

In having the trainees learn the gospel, we do not have them memorize the entire presentation but rather have them learn the outline and then gradually build onto it. First we have them learn just enough so the "bones" of the outline don't rattle. Then we have them give a three-minute presentation of the gospel. And then we enlarge it to five minutes and then to eight. We continue to enlarge the presentation until they are able to present the gospel in one minute or one hour, depending on what the particular situation warrants. We provide them with the long presentation of the gospel, as well as the short one, which is used as resource material for building their presentation on the basic outline.

MAKE IT THEIR OWN

In this way it becomes their own. We encourage them to work on it, practice it, give it, until indeed they own it and can give it with authority.

NOT A "CANNED" APPROACH

This raises the question of our basic philosophy of training others to present the gospel. A careful study of the New Testament will show that Jesus used a different method in presenting the gospel himself than he did in training his followers. When he sent them out he told them where to go, what to do, what to take with them, and what to say upon entering and leaving the home.

In teaching a large group of people anything, it is inevitable that a certain degree of stereotyping will take place. However, we have tried to avoid the two extremes that exist in training others to present the gospel. These extremes are, on the one hand, the completely "canned" approach whereby the person memorizes a presentation, or reads it to someone, or gives him a tract or a tape or a book. In every instance the layman has simply taken the product of the "expert," that is, the clergyman, and is passing it on mechanically to others. This method we reject because of its "canned" flavor and also because it short-circuits the creativity of the layman.

The other extreme is called the "spontaneous expansion of the church." Under this theory all we need do is get people soundly converted, filled with the Spirit, and they will go out and just naturally win the world for Christ. Unfortunately it doesn't seem to work this way. Obviously Christ didn't think too highly of this method, for he spent three and a half years training his apostles.

We have tried to select a method intermediate between these two. We give the layman some help, some guidance, some direction, but also allow him to express his own creativity. We do this by giving him an outline plus some Scriptures and illustrative material. But we urge him to continually add to this his own illustrations which he discovers in his own reading or from his own experience, as well as other Scriptures which speak strongly to him concerning one of the points of the gospel. In this way he builds his own gospel presentation on the skeleton which we provide for him and continually personalizes it more and more until it becomes "his own."

I. PRESERVING THE FRUIT

IMPORTANCE OF FOLLOW-UP

A program of evangelism such as this generates a tremendous need for follow-up. It has produced a need for a follow-up secretary and also a follow-up minister on our staff. However, the main responsibility for follow-up rests with the individual who has led the person to Christ. In this training workbook we have a rather elaborate section on follow-up principles and procedures. In essence the follow-up procedure involves the spiritual parent using the total services of the local family of God. In the past we have used a variety of printed materials. Now we have produced our own. The "Forever Family Follow-up Series" consists of a number of small booklets such as *Welcome to the Forever Family, Prayer in the Forever Family, Your Personal Influence and the Forever Family.* These materials are tailored to the local church and the context of the Evangelism Explosion Discipleship Training.

The first week of the new convert's life is the most critical. Therefore, I have prepared a series of six cassettes which are loaned to the convert the day he makes a profession or brought to him as soon as possible. He is encouraged to listen to one of these messages each day for the first week of his Christian life. The subjects covered are: Knowing You Are Going to Heaven; Staying Right with God; Getting into the Bible; Practicing the Art of Prayer; Continuing in Fellowship (Koinonia); Transforming the World. A study booklet has also been prepared to go with these so that they may be used in a classroom session as well. This has been very profitably done in some churches.*

The first Sunday after one professes faith, he should be encouraged to attend a Sunday school class. The best arrangement is to have a three-week class on three basic elements for Christian living—Feeding on the Word of God, Cleansing, and Relating to the Forever Family of God. Each unit should be self-contained and a new believer can start with any one of the topics. This helps get him off to a good start.

After the new believer completes these three classes he should start in the eight "This Is the Life" classes. With these nine weeks of study behind him, he can go into almost any class in your adult education program.

SPIRITUAL GRANDCHILDREN

Follow-up procedures are not completed until the convert has been taught to study God's Word, to pray, to live the Christian life, and to walk with Christ. Then he is encouraged to come into the evangelism program to learn how to win others to Christ. Yet at this point the follow-up still is not complete, for he must be taught not only how to reproduce but also how to disciple his new convert until he has matured to the place where he also is able to bring someone else to Christ. This emphasis of spiritual multiplication, looking past the first generation to the second, third, and fourth, is the secret of an expanding and multiplying evangelistic ministry. In just a few years this has produced instances of great, great, great, great, great, great, great grandchildren in the faith. The acid test of any follow-up procedure will ultimately be: Is it producing spiritual grandchildren and great grandchildren? If not, then something is amiss and somewhere the process is breaking down.

J. MULTIPLYING THE RESULTS

A VISION FOR THE WORLD

Christ said, *"The field is the world."* I believe that our field should be the world; that every church, every individual has a worldwide responsibility. I do not believe that any church can settle for anything less than worldwide evangelism as its own responsibility. Is it utterly unrealistic? I think not. Eleven men, indeed a very small church, have succeeded in carrying the gospel to most every nation on the earth. And the march of those eleven men goes on today.

I do not believe, however, that it necessarily must take hundreds or thousands of years for the impact of the gospel to spread around the world. The process of spiritual multiplication can grow with the rapidity of the physical population explosion that we are seeing today. Our goal then is to reach the world for Christ. How can this be done?

MULTIPLYING YOUR MINISTRY

First we must realize that our responsibility extends beyond our church, our city, our state, or our country. But how are we to meet this responsibility? We have

* D. James Kennedy, *This Is the Life* (Glendale, Calif.: Gospel Light Publications, 1973), p. 102. D. James Kennedy, *This Is the Life Cassettes* (Glendale, Calif.: Gospel Light Publications, 1973).

proceeded in this manner. In addition to training an increasing number of people in our own church, we have also trained a good many other churches in the city and in the immediate area.

In 1967 we began having clinics for church leaders. Only thirty attended that first clinic. However, in 1970 attendance leaped to 350 and we had to turn away an additional 1,500 because we could not accommodate them. We tried to increase to five Leadership Clinics per year at Coral Ridge Church, but this was too disruptive to the local church life. We encouraged other churches to have similar clinics. A few were able to do this well, but most were not successful at conducting Leadership Clinics. I spoke to many church leaders and our minister of evangelism conducted numerous small area clinics. The more we became involved, the more we understood the ingredients necessary for successful Leadership Clinics. The emphasis of content of the clinics is very properly on evangelism technique. But evangelism is for the purpose of producing disciples and healthy disciples are produced only in reasonably healthy churches. Therefore, to insure maximum responsible multiplication of this ministry the process of certification was established in 1973. Certification gives uniform minimum standards of excellence with maximum potential for communication and multiplication. We feel it is an essential element in strategy for effective evangelization of the world. As a result of years of experience, we now are seeing very effective Certified Leadership Clinics conducted throughout the United States, Canada, England, Scotland, and Australia. In West Germany, Holland, Ireland, Switzerland, India, Hong Kong, Korea, Taiwan, Japan, New Zealand, and Haiti culturally relevant equivalents of this ministry are in operation and our goal is to see them become totally indigenous national fellowships.

Because of wide interest in this ministry, Evangelism Explosion International was established as a nonprofit corporation. Its ministry is interdenominational and international. Our monthly newsletter, *Evangelism Explosion III UPDATE,* is available free upon request.

Laypeople certified as trainers in their local churches can function as missionary trainers on short or long-term bases in other churches in different parts of the world. A mighty army is being mobilized. The very gates of hell are being stormed and Christ is building his church!

Soli deo gloria.

TWO
A PRESENTATION OF THE GOSPEL

A. OUTLINE OF THE GOSPEL PRESENTATION

I. The introduction
   A. Their secular life
   B. Their church background
   C. Our church
   D. Testimony: personal and/or church
   E. Two diagnostic questions:
      1. Have you come to a place in your spiritual life where you *know for certain* that if you were to die today you would go to heaven?
      2. Suppose that you were to die tonight and stand before God and he were to say to you, "Why should I let you into my heaven?" What would you say?

II. The gospel
   A. Grace
      1. Heaven is a free gift
      2. It is not earned or deserved
   B. Man
      1. Is a sinner
      2. Cannot save himself
   C. God
      1. Is merciful—therefore doesn't want to punish us
      2. Is just—therefore must punish sin
   D. Christ
      1. Who he is—the infinite God-man
      2. What he did—he paid for our sins and purchased a place in heaven for us which he offers as a gift.
   E. Faith
      1. What it is *not*—mere intellectual assent nor temporal faith
      2. What it *is*—"trusting in Jesus Christ alone for our salvation"

III. The commitment
   A. The qualifying question: "Does this make sense to you?"
   B. The commitment question: "Would you like to receive the gift of eternal life?"
   C. The clarification of commitment
   D. The prayer of commitment
   E. The assurance of salvation
IV. The immediate follow-up
   A. Bible (seven-day call back appointment)
   B. Prayer HOLINESS
   C. Worship
   D. Fellowship
   E. Witness

B. A BRIEF PRESENTATION OF THE GOSPEL

I. INTRODUCTION (A–D)

(Condensed, ten-minute presentation starting with the two diagnostic questions and ending with the commitment question.)

E. Two diagnostic questions

QUESTION 1

Well, that's very interesting, Sue, but tell me, have you come to a place in your spiritual life where you can say you know for certain that if you were to die today you would go to heaven?

I didn't think anyone could really know that!

I didn't know myself for many years, but then I discovered something wonderful! I discovered it was possible to know for sure! I even discovered that this was the reason the Bible was written. The Scripture says, "These things are written that ye may know that ye have eternal life." **1 John 5:13**

Would you like for me to share with you how I came to know for sure I was going to heaven and how you can know it too?

Yes, I really would.

QUESTION 2

Fine! I'll be happy to. First, let me ask you another

question which I think really brings this whole matter into focus and which clarifies our thinking about it greatly. Suppose that you were to die today and stand before God and he were to say to you, "Why should I let you into my heaven?" what would you say?

I can't think of any answer.

I know you don't have a thesis prepared on the subject, but just offhand what comes to your mind? What do you *think* you would say?

Well, I've tried to do the best I can and I've tried to keep the Ten Commandments. I try to live by the Golden Rule.

GOOD NEWS

Well, that's interesting, Sue. Those things are all very commendable.

You know something, Sue, when you answered that first question I thought I had some really good news for you. And after hearing your answer to the second question I know that I do. *In fact I would go so far as to say that in the next sixty seconds you are going to hear the greatest good news that you have ever heard in your whole life!* That's quite a statement, isn't it?

It certainly is.

II. THE GOSPEL

A. Grace

1. HEAVEN IS A FREE GIFT

2. IT IS NOT EARNED OR DESERVED

Let's see if I can back it up. A large part of my life I felt exactly as you do. I thought if I was ever to get to heaven I'd have to earn it. I'd have to become good enough, and work for it and deserve it. And then I discovered something that absolutely amazed me. I discovered that heaven is absolutely a *free gift*—it is unearned, unmerited, and undeserved. It's free! Isn't that tremendous?

Let me show you a Scripture verse in the New

Testament. It's Romans 6:23. Here it is. Just read it for yourself.

> "The wages of sin is death, but the *gift of God* is eternal life through Jesus Christ our Lord." **Romans 6:23**

"The gift of God is eternal life . . ." Isn't that amazing?

You're probably thinking, "How can that be? Who gets it? How can we know that we have it?" Let me see if I can show you, not only that this is the way it is, but this is the only way it could be.

B. Man

1. IS A SINNER

The Bible teaches that all of us have sinned, that there is not one of us good enough to get into heaven because God's standard is perfection! If we have to be good enough, Jesus says we would have to be perfect. "Be ye therefore perfect, even as your Father which is in heaven is perfect. . . . But all have sinned and come short of the glory of God." In our thoughts, in our words, in our deeds—we have all failed to keep his commandments both by sins of commission and by sins of omission—that is, by the things we have done and the things that we have left undone.

Matthew 5:48

Romans 3:23

2. CANNOT SAVE HIMSELF

This is the reason that none of us can earn his way into heaven. We can't save ourselves. The Bible says, "By grace are ye saved through faith . . . *not of works,* lest any man should boast."

Ephesians 2:8,9

C. God

1. IS MERCIFUL—THEREFORE DOES NOT WANT TO PUNISH US

2. IS JUST—THEREFORE MUST PUNISH SIN

The problem of man trying to save himself becomes even more acute when we look at what the Bible says about God.

We know that God is merciful and loving, gracious

and kind, but *the same Bible says that the same God is also just and holy and righteous;* that he is of purer eyes than to look upon iniquity; that he must punish sin. The Bible says that God is angry with the wicked every day and that he has commanded all men everywhere to repent. Of course, we know the Bible teaches that God is loving and merciful and gracious. He doesn't want to punish us. He must deal with sin but he doesn't want to punish us because he loves us. Now what is the answer to this dilemma?

God in his infinite wisdom devised a solution. God sent his Son into the world to solve this problem for man.

D. Jesus Christ

1. WHO HE IS—THE INFINITE GOD-MAN

Now, who is Jesus Christ? According to the Bible, Jesus Christ is God, the second person of the Trinity, the Creator of the universe. The Bible says, "In the beginning was the Word and the Word was with God, and the Word was God . . . the Word became flesh and dwelt among us." God came down into human flesh.

John 1:1,14

2. WHAT HE DID—PAID FOR OUR SINS AND PURCHASED HEAVEN FOR US, WHICH HE OFFERS AS A GIFT

What did he come to do? The whole Bible is about one great transaction. Imagine this book in my right hand contains a minutely detailed account of our life: everything we've ever done, all of our sins, all of our thoughts, all of our motives, everything we've ever done in secret—all are recorded in this book. The Bible says that someday the books will be opened and everybody will know all about us. That's going to be a red-faced day for many! I am convinced of one thing: if any man is judged according to the things recorded in the book of his life he will be condemned.

This (hold up the book) is our problem, you see, our sin. Here is our sin upon us like a great burden. (Place the book on the palm of one hand.) This keeps us out of heaven. This prevents us from rising up to God. What's going to be done with that?

In the Old Testament God's provision for sin was

described in all the foreshadowings and types. John the Baptist announced that God's Lamb had finally come. Then Jesus Christ fulfilled the mission that was his. What was it? Simply, it is described in one text: "All we like sheep have gone astray; we have turned every one to his own way; and the Lord hath laid on him the iniquity of us all." **Isaiah 53:6**

Suppose my other hand here represents Jesus Christ. The Bible says God placed all our sins on Jesus. (Transfer the book to the "Jesus" hand.) He has laid to the account of Christ our guilt, our sin—the sin which God hates. God has imputed or laid upon Christ our sins. And then I read something which as a parent really astounded me. I read, "It pleased the Lord to bruise him . . ." He was "smitten of God and afflicted." God poured out all of his wrath for sin on his own Son. Christ in our place, as our substitute, paid the penalty for sin. **Isaiah 53:10,4**

And he says that he goes to prepare a place for us. He purchased a place for us in heaven. **(John 14:2)**

You know, Sue, the wonderful thing is that this place in heaven Christ purchased for us he offers to us freely as a gift. *"The gift of God is eternal life."* By his grace he freely offers to give to us this gift of heaven. **Romans 6:23**

E. Faith

1. WHAT IT IS NOT—MERE INTELLECTUAL ASSENT

How do we receive it?

"By grace are ye saved through *faith* . . ." Faith is the key that opens the door to heaven. Someone said that faith is the empty hand of a beggar receiving the gift of a king. **Ephesians 2:8**

Many people think they have faith but they really don't know what it is. Let's see what **faith is not.** Many people believe that Jesus lived and died and rose again. And they suppose that this is faith. But this is **merely an intellectual assent** to certain historical facts. The Bible teaches us that even the devil believes in Christ in this way. But that won't do.

(Nor temporal faith)

Other people think that they have faith in Christ, but when you ask them what they really mean, they are only trusting in Christ for the temporal things of life, such as health, or their children, or their finances, or strength, or guidance—the things that have to do only with this life that we live right here.

2. WHAT IT IS—TRUSTING JESUS CHRIST ALONE FOR SALVATION

But what the Bible means by faith is *trusting in Jesus Christ alone for our salvation*—resting our hope of eternal life in Christ.

Christ didn't come down here merely to get us through an appendicitis operation or to get us safely on a plane to New York! Christ came to get us to heaven that we might have eternal life.

Faith is trusting Jesus Christ **alone** for our salvation.

People trust in only one of two things—either in themselves or in Christ. And I was trusting in the same thing that you were—in my own efforts to try to live a good enough life. Then I realized that if I could get myself to heaven in this way, I would save myself; and if I could save myself I would be my savior; and if I were my savior then I would be in competition with Jesus Christ who claimed to be the Savior of the world.

What I needed to do was to cease trusting in myself and start trusting in Jesus Christ. And so, years ago, sincerely and repentantly, I did just that, and I received the gift of eternal life. I didn't deserve it then and I don't deserve it now, but by his grace I have it!

Let me illustrate this with this chair.

Do you believe this chair exists? (Point to empty chair.)

Yes.

Do you believe it will hold you?

Yes.

It is not holding you now. How could you prove you believe it exists and can hold you?

By sitting in it.

Let the chair represent Jesus Christ. For a long time

I believed he existed and could help me, but I did not have eternal life because I was trusting my own good works to get me into heaven. Remember what you said you would say to God if he asked why he should let you into heaven? You said, "I try to do the best I can . . ." Who is the only person referred to in your answer?

Me?

Who were you trusting to get you to heaven when you said that?

Me.

To receive eternal life you must transfer your trust from yourself to Christ.

(Motive for living a godly life)

What, then, is the motive for living a godly life? The motive for living a godly life is gratitude for what Christ has given to us. The Bible says that *"the love of Christ constrains us."*

A former president of Princeton put it this way. He said, "As a young man I accepted Christ and the gift of eternal life. All the rest of my life was simply a P.S. to that day, saying, 'Thank you, Lord, for what you gave to me then.' "

III. COMMITMENT

A. The qualifying question

Sue, **does that make sense to you?**

Oh, yes, that's wonderful!

You've just heard the **greatest story** ever told, about the **greatest offer** ever made, by the **greatest Person** who ever lived.

B. The commitment question

Now the question is this: **Do you want to receive this gift of eternal life that Christ left heaven and died on a cross to give you?**

Oh, yes, I do.

C. AN EXTENDED PRESENTATION OF THE GOSPEL

[The extended presentation of the gospel containing many additional illustrations and scriptural texts which may be used as a resource for building short presentations upon the basic outline.]

I. INTRODUCTION

A. Secular life

(A knock at the door.)

Good morning, Mrs. Tucker. I'm Dr. Kennedy from the Coral Ridge Presbyterian Church. May we come in and visit with you a while?

Why, hello. Please do come in.

Thank you. This is Mary Smith and George Simon from our church. We were so happy to have you visit with us and wanted to become better acquainted with you.

That's real nice of you.

May we sit over here?

Fine.

Thank you. This is a lovely home you have. That painting is most interesting. It seems to radiate peacefulness and contentment. Did you paint it yourself?

Oh, no. A friend did it for me just before we moved here. We have enjoyed it.

Where did you move from, Mrs. Tucker?

Virginia.

Virginia! I thought I noticed a bit of Virginia accent.

I don't doubt it.

Do they really say "aboot the hoouse" up there?

Yes, they do.

Do they really? Let me hear you say "about the house."

Lookoout, there's a moouse in the hoouse!

That's delightful. I've always enjoyed listening to people with Virginia accents. Tell me a little more about yourself. How did you happen to move down here?

> We vacationed in this area several times and just loved it. When my husband retired we came down and looked around one summer and settled in Fort Lauderdale. We just love it here.

It is a beautiful city, isn't it?

> Yes, it is.

B. Church background

What church did you attend back in Virginia?

> Baptist.

The Baptist church? Well, I knew there was something nice about you. I have many friends who are Baptists.

> Thank you. I was a charter member.

You had the joys of seeing a new congregation born and you helped it grow.

> Yes, some of those days were pretty trying but we got our problems ironed out and it is a large church now. I was president of the Women of the Church for two years and taught a Sunday school class for awhile.

Wonderful! It's good to meet someone who is really active in the life of her church. We are truly delighted to have you here in Fort Lauderdale with us now. **How did you happen to attend our church?**

C. Our church

> We were looking for a church in the neighborhood and while driving around we saw your building.

How did you like the service?

> Oh, we liked it very much. The people seemed so friendly and made us feel at home. The singing is just wonderful. You people seem to really enjoy singing. Somehow the spirit was different.

You noticed something different about the congregation?

> Yes, we did.

Do you have any idea what causes that difference?

No, but I'd like to know.

D. Testimony

1. **Church** (as here)

or

2. **Personal**

Let me share with you what I think it is. You know, many people have mentioned to me that they sense something different about our church. They noticed the singing, as you did. They saw something different about the expression on people's faces—as if they were happier. Is this the sort of difference you were thinking of?

Yes.

The secret of that difference is really rather simple when you look at it closely.

Jesus Christ came that we might have life and have it abundantly. The Scriptures were written that men and women might know that they have eternal life and yet we have found that a majority of people that go to church, even those who have gone all of their life, aren't really sure that they have this abundant life, and they're not really sure about what will happen to them when they die. They have hopes but they don't know for sure that they would go to heaven. For many years I felt that same way. I was striving but I wasn't really sure. How about you, Mrs. Tucker?

E. Two diagnostic questions

1. "Have you come to a place in your spiritual life where you know for certain that if you were to die today you would go to heaven?"

Why, I don't think anyone can really know.

You know, that's just the way I felt about it. For many years I didn't know. I wasn't even aware of the fact that anybody knew. But let me tell you some really good news: I discovered that *it is possible to know* and there are a great many people who do know.

Really?

That was an amazing discovery to me! In fact I even learned that that was the reason the Bible was written! The Bible says: "These things have I written . . . that ye may know that ye have eternal life" (1 John 5:13).

Why, I never knew that!

I didn't either. Isn't that a fantastic thing! Think how wonderful it would be if you could go to bed tonight and lay your head on your pillow knowing for certain that if you don't wake up in your bedroom, you will wake up in heaven with Jesus Christ. Wouldn't that be a wonderful thing to know?

Yes, it really would.

Would you like for me to share with you how I made that discovery and how you can know it too?

Yes, please do.

All right. I'll be happy to, for it is the greatest discovery that I have ever made. It really has changed my whole life. I wouldn't trade everything else in the world for this wonderful assurance and the joy of sharing it with other people. You know, it's amazing how many people are hungry to know! I talk to people in all strata of society and everywhere there are men and women eager to know, and yet no one has taken the time to explain these things to them.

I've never heard it.

Before I get into it, let me ask you another question which, I think, really crystallizes our thinking on the matter. This was a question that was very helpful to me. A minister asked me this one day:

2. Suppose that you were to die today and stand before God and he were to say to you, "Why should I let you into my heaven?" What would you say? That's a pretty good question, isn't it?

It certainly is.

It really makes you think. What would your answer be?

Well, I never thought of anything like that. I've gone to Sunday school and church all my life. And I try to be as good as I know how. Of course, I know that I haven't always been perfect, but I don't think I've ever intentionally hurt anyone. And I try to love my neighbor. I don't think I've been too bad.

All right. Anything else?

Well, I visit the sick and I do the very best I can to live according to the Golden Rule.

Well, thank you, Mrs. Tucker. It's Rene, isn't it? May I call you that?

Yes.

(Good news)

You know, Rene, when I asked you if you knew for sure if you had eternal life and you said that you didn't, I thought I had some really good news to tell you. And after your answer to that second question, *I know that I do!* In fact, I would say that in the next few minutes *you are going to hear the greatest good news that you've ever heard in your whole life.* That's quite a statement to make, isn't it?

It certainly is.

II. THE GOSPEL

A. Grace

1. HEAVEN IS A FREE GIFT

Well, let me see if I can back it up. You know, all my life I felt exactly like you did. I thought that heaven was something I had to earn; something that I had to merit by keeping the commandments and following rules and sometimes I almost despaired of the whole thing. Then I discovered something that absolutely amazed me. I discovered that heaven is not something that you earn, or that you deserve, or that you work for, but that, **according to the Scriptures, heaven—eternal life—is absolutely a free gift!**

Free?

Absolutely free! Isn't that amazing?

Yes, it is.

2. IT IS NOT EARNED OR DESERVED

It's unearned, undeserved, and unmerited. It's free. You know, we sort of think there's nothing in this life that's free. We always look for the price tag. And we are probably right. But thank God that the greatest thing that man could ever have—eternal life—is free! Of course the idea that we have to pay for everything is something which is ingrained in us from our earliest days. This is the way which seems right to every man. In fact, most people think they're going to get to heaven that way. It's the way that seems right to every man, isn't it?

Yes, it is.

(Man's ways are not God's ways)

The Bible says this: "There is a way which seemeth right unto man but the end thereof are the ways of death" (Proverbs 14:12). God says that his ways are not our ways and as high as the heavens are above the earth, so high are his ways above our ways and his thoughts above our thoughts. **God's way is the way of grace.** He is the God of all grace. Rene, let me show you a Scripture verse in the New Testament. This is found in **Romans 6:23.** You see what it says? "For the wages (wages, of course, are what we earn, what we deserve) of sin (and we're all sinners) is death (physical death, spiritual death, eternal death) BUT (and here's the good news) the gift of God is eternal life through Jesus Christ our Lord." "The gift of God is eternal life." Isn't that amazing, Rene?

That's wonderful!

Why, it's the most wonderful thing that I've ever heard in all my life!

I'm sure that this raises many questions in your mind. "How can these things be? How can God do this and still be just? And who gets the gift, after all? Everybody?" Not at all. In fact, **Christ said that few there are that find the way and many there are which go in to destruction (Matthew 7:13,14).** Well, if everybody doesn't get the gift, who does get it? How do we get it? And how can we know if we have it?

Now, Rene, let me see if I can answer these questions for you. In fact, I think I can show you not only that this is the way, but when you understand what the Bible teaches concerning man and concerning God, I think you will see that this is the only way it could be.

B. Man

1. A SINNER

The first thing I came to understand was what God says about man in the Bible—that is what God says about us, you and me. This is a practical place to begin because it brings us face to face with the predicament in which we find ourselves—and a real predicament it is! **According to God's Word, we have made a colossal mess out of everything we have our hands on.**

If we were to get away from this planet and look at it objectively, we would appreciate the truth of this statement. We have wars and riots; we have crime and delinquency; we have murder and hatred and envy and strife. According to the Bible, **all of these are the result of sin.**

This is the fatal malignancy which infects the soul of the entire human race. The Bible says, "There is none righteous, no, not one . . . for all have sinned and come short of the glory of God. There is not a just man upon the face of the earth that doeth good and sinneth not. We have turned every one to his own way" (Romans 3:10, 23; Isaiah 53:6). The Bible teaches that all of us have sinned, right?

I know that.

(Word, thought or deed)

This is a very black picture. In fact, the Bible paints it even darker. It is against this backdrop that we must see the glorious picture of the gospel. Sin is a cancer destroying the human race and cannot be dealt with effectively until it is openly acknowledged.

In thought, word, and deed we have all come short of the standard God has set for us. **Jesus said that sin in thought is the same as sin in deed.** "Ye have heard it said . . . whosoever shall kill shall be in danger of the judgment . . . but I say that whosoever is angry with his brother without a cause shall be in danger of the judgment. Ye have heard that it was said . . . thou shalt not commit adultery; but I say . . . whosoever looketh on a woman to lust after her hath committed adultery. . ."

Christ said further, "Ye have heard that it hath been said, thou shalt love thy neighbour . . . but I say unto you, love your enemies, bless them that curse you, do good to them that hate you, and pray for them that despitefully use you . . . that ye may be the children of your Father which is in heaven" (Matthew 5:21–48). Jesus made it very plain. He said, "Did not Moses give you the law, and yet none of you keepeth the law?" (John 7:19).

(Omission or commission)

The Bible teaches that we have not kept God's Commandments but have violated them all; if not in deed, at least in thought and word. We have not lived by the Golden Rule all the time. We have not really done the best we can. **There are not only sins of commission,** in word, thought and deed, but according to the Bible, **there are also sins of omission:** those things which we should have done that we have not—failing to pray or to read the Bible, or to truly love our neighbor, or to go to church. The Bible says these are all sins.

Sometimes I wonder just how many times a day the average person sins. I imagine it's fifty to one hundred times or even more. John Calvin said no one knows the one-hundredth part of the sin that clings to his soul. Today a psychologist would tell us that we have forgotten 99 percent of all those things we have ever done wrong. We suppress them because we don't like to think about the unpleasant.

Just suppose that a person sinned only ten times a day or even five—or even just three. Why, he would practically be a walking angel! Imagine if not oftener than three times a day did he think unkind thoughts, or lose his temper, or fail to do what he ought toward God and man—he would be a pretty fine person, would he not?

Even if he were this good, he would have over 1,000 transgressions a year! If he lived to the average age of seventy, then he would have 70,000 transgressions. Think what would happen to an habitual offender in a criminal court with 70,000 transgressions on his record!

2. CANNOT SAVE HIMSELF

This impresses us with man's predicament. **According to the Bible he is a sinner.** He has broken God's Law.

The Bible goes on to teach that our predicament is compounded by another factor that is understood by even fewer people. Because man is a sinner, **he cannot save himself,** he cannot earn his way into heaven. That is, he cannot merit eternal life by doing good things. The Bible states this clearly. "Not by works of righteousness which we have done, but according to his mercy he saved us" (Titus 3:5). "By grace are ye saved through faith . . . not of works lest any man should boast" (Ephesians 2:8, 9).

There was a time when I thought I could get to heaven by keeping the Ten Commandments, living according to the Golden Rule, and helping people less fortunate than myself. However, occasionally I would wonder just how well I would have to do all these things to get into heaven.

It was sort of like wondering in school, what is the passing grade in my classes?

Did you ever wonder about how good you would have to be to make it, Rene? Well, **God has told us how well we have to do these works to get into heaven.** He has revealed the passing grade in his class of life. **Do you know what it is?**

No.

All right. Hold on to your chair! Are you ready? Here it comes! Jesus said: "**Be ye therefore perfect,** even as your Father in heaven is perfect" (Matthew 5:48).

Perfect?

There it stands! That's the passing grade! The amazing thing I discovered is that **God doesn't grade on a curve.** God says, "Be ye . . . PERFECT" (Matthew 5:48).

This is not an isolated text that might be interpreted in some other way, but this is something that is taught throughout the Bible. For example, Paul said, *"Cursed is every one that continueth not in all things which are written in the book of the law to do them"* (Galatians 3:10). If we don't continually do everything that we are told to do, then we are under the curse of God.

James put it another way: **"If we offend in one point we are guilty of all"** (James 2:10). If we commit just one sin we step outside the realm of the law and become an outlaw. You don't have to break every law in the book to be a criminal and have the police looking for you; just one crime is all it takes to have a lot of policemen looking for us. One sin is all that it takes to make us guilty and to make us an outlaw. Just one sin! Satan thought just one evil thought and because of that he was cast out of heaven. (See Isaiah 14:12–15.)

Well, then, no one's going to be able to go to heaven!

It would look that way, wouldn't it? You see, what we have said is that your understanding (which is the same as mine used to be) is simply that a person gets to heaven by trying to be good enough. Now, boiling it all down, that is what you've come to understand all your life, right?

Yes.

(None good enough)

Just like I did. But the problem is: **What is good enough?** The Bible makes it plain that **good enough is perfect!** There is no doubt about that fact.

This presents a problem, doesn't it? It does look as though nobody is going to heaven.

That's right.

(Impossibility of salvation by works)

Well, that would be right—if this was the way that you get to heaven! Martin Luther said that *the most damnable and pernicious heresy that has ever plagued the mind of man was the idea that somehow he could make himself good enough to deserve to live with an all-holy God.*

We couldn't make an omelet out of five good eggs and one rotten egg and serve it to company and expect it to be acceptable! Well, even less can we serve up our lives to God, which may have many things in them that men would call good, and yet are filled with deeds and thoughts that are rotten, and expect them to be acceptable to God.

If we want to get to heaven by our good works, then all we have to do is be perfect. God's standard is complete obedience to him at all times—and all of us have fallen short of this. We just don't have the wherewithal to pay for eternal life.

Queen Elizabeth I of England offered her doctor half the British empire for six months of life when she was dying. Of course, the doctor couldn't give her six seconds. How much less, then, can we buy eternal life from God by our good works.

(An entirely different way)

If anybody is going to be in heaven then there must be some entirely different way of getting there.

The Bible, of course, says that there are going to be people in heaven. Might I add that Jesus seemed to indicate that the number of people in heaven will be a minority of those that have lived upon the earth. "Strait is the gate, and narrow is the way, which leadeth unto life, and *few* there be that find it . . . for wide is the gate, and broad is the way that leadeth to destruction, and *many* there be which go in thereat" (Matthew 7:13, 14). This "few" is a great multitude that no man can number, but seemingly it is the lesser part of mankind, which makes us realize that we can't just take it for granted.

Trusting in our own efforts to be good obviously will not get us to heaven. This was the religion of the Pharisees. Do you remember? Jesus described them in this way: "They trusted in themselves that they were righteous" (Luke 18:9). Many people have this belief today. In talking of these matters with literally thousands of people, we have found the vast majority indicate they intend to enter heaven on the basis of their own good works. The Bible teaches, "There is a way that seemeth right unto man" (Proverbs 14:12). It would appear that this is the way that seems right unto man. But the Bible continues, "the end thereof are the ways of death."

So then there must be another way. What is it? Well, to understand it we have to move on from our consideration of what God has said about us to what he says about himself. About us, he has said we are sinners and we can do nothing to remedy our sinful condition.

C. God

1. LOVING AND MERCIFUL

One of the most amazing and most difficult facts to learn about God is that *he loves us* in spite of what we are. He loves us, not because of what we are, but because of what he is. For the Bible tells us that "God is love" (1 John 4:8).

This love of God becomes all the more incomprehensible when we have come to see ourselves as we truly are. Then we feel like crying out with the great hymnist, Charles Wesley:

And can it be that I should gain
An interest in the Savior's blood?
Died He for me, who caused His pain?
For me, who Him to death pursued?
Amazing love! how can it be
That Thou, my God, shouldst die for me?

How vast! How measureless is this love of God for us!

2. JUST—THEREFORE MUST PUNISH SIN

But the same Bible that tells us that God is loving and gracious also tells us about this same God that he is just and righteous and must punish sin. God tells us, "I am holy and just and righteous. I am of purer eyes than to behold evil. The soul that sinneth it shall die" (Habakkuk 1:13; Ezekiel 18:4). We are looking at man's problems now through the magnifying glass of God—as they are seen by an all-holy, sin-hating God who says he is angry with the wicked every day. Because he is a just Judge, he must punish our sins. His law declares that our sins must be punished: "That will by no means clear the guilty" (Exodus 34:7b). He threatens to visit our transgressions with the rod and our iniquities with stripes. There is no doubt about this—**God will certainly punish all sin.**

In our hearts we would view with contempt a judge who is overly lenient with offenders. If one were to "slap the wrist" of his friend who was guilty of a heinous crime, we would cry, "Impeach him. Justice must be preserved." So it is with God. "Shall not the Judge of all the earth do right?" (Genesis 18:25).

I thought God was mostly love.

He is both holy and loving. It is interesting to note that for many centuries before he revealed the real height of his love in Jesus Christ, he established that his throne is a throne of righteousness. He is the thrice-holy One who will deal with sin. Throughout the Old Testament his justice and holiness are clearly manifested.

If he were only justice we would all be condemned. However, he is loving and merciful. **Although he must punish sin, he loves us and therefore doesn't want to punish us.** If he were only loving, there would be no problem. If he were the grandfather figure, as most Americans picture him, he could just take us all to heaven—all of us: Dillinger and Cappone, Nero and Judas, and the devil himself. He would simply say, "Come on, fellows, I didn't really mean it when I said, 'But every one shall die for his own iniquity' " (Jeremiah 31:30). No! *Any love dealings that God has with us must be consonant with his justice.*

The teachings that God emphasizes about himself are: **He is holy and just and must punish sin; but he is also loving and merciful and does not wish to punish us.** In effect, this created a problem which he has solved in Jesus Christ.

D. Jesus Christ

1. WHO HE IS—THE INFINITE GOD-MAN

Now, what is the answer to that problem? God in his infinite wisdom devised a marvelous solution. *Jesus Christ is God's answer to our predicament.* He sent him into the world and, as you know, we celebrate his birth every Christmas.

Rene, I would be interested in your opinion about Christ. Who do you think he is? What kind of a being was he?

> Well, he was probably the best man that ever lived. He was a wonderful teacher and I believe he is supposed to have worked miracles.

Fine! Jesus was a great teacher and miracle-worker. And he was good. Anything else?

> Well, he was the Son of God.

Yes, he was. But I am also a son of God. Is he any different from me?

> I don't really know.

The Bible teaches that Jesus Christ—Jesus of Nazareth, the Carpenter of Galilee—**was and is God!** He is the Creator of the world! He is the One who created the whole universe! Jesus is God Almighty, himself!

This comes as a real surprise to many people. They don't realize that he is God the Son—that God is Father, Son and Holy Spirit, and that the Trinity is one God. Yet we sing this truth every Sunday morning in the Doxology: "Praise God from whom all blessings flow . . . praise Father, Son and Holy Ghost." Or, as the Westminster Confession puts it, "In the unity of the Godhead, there be three Persons of one substance, power and eternity."

2. WHAT HE DID—PAID FOR OUR SINS AND PURCHASED HEAVEN FOR US, WHICH HE OFFERS AS A GIFT

God the Son became man! This is what we mean by incarnation. This is what we celebrate at Christmas. God became man for a grand and noble purpose. He left his home in glory and was born in the filth of a stable. He lived a perfect and spotless life. He taught the world's greatest teachings! He worked its mightiest deeds. Finally he came to the end of his life—to **that hour for which he had come into the world.** In that hour we see the **great transaction** about which the whole Bible is written—the great transaction which is the central fact of the Christian religion.

> What is it?

Let's imagine this book in my right hand is a minutely detailed account of my life. It includes everything I have ever done. Every word I have ever spoken, every thought that ever crossed my mind. Someday, the Bible says, the books are going to be opened and everything about our lives will be brought to light. "The hidden things of darkness will be made manifest. That which has been whispered in the ear will be shouted from the housetop" (1 Corinthians 4:5; Matthew 10:27, paraphrased). Everyone will know all about us—all we've thought or done; all our hidden motives; all the sins—most of which we have forgotten. How many thoughts can you remember from twenty years ago?

None!

(The multitude of our sins)

Psychologists tell us 10,000 thoughts go through the human mind in one day. That's 3,500,000 per year! To remember only 1 percent from 20 years ago you would have to come up with 35,000. Someone has well said that a clear conscience is quite often the result of a poor memory.

If we must give an account of every idle word, how many would that be? We speak millions every year. Who knows? God does! They are all written down in his book. And one day the books will be opened. I am utterly convinced of one thing: that **if any man is judged according to the things recorded in the book of his life, he will be condemned.** I am certain that this is true of my own life.

Here then (hold up the book) is the problem—my sin. God loves me (point at fingers of right hand) but he hates my sin (point at book) and must punish it.

To solve this problem he sent his beloved Son into the world (lift up left hand parallel to right hand). The Scripture says, "All we like sheep have gone astray; we have turned everyone to his own way; and the *Lord* hath laid on him the iniquity of us all" (Isaiah 53:6). (As you say the words "laid on him," transfer the book in one distinct motion from the right to the left hand and leave it there.) God has laid to the account of Christ all of my sin and guilt. All of my sin which God hates has been placed on his beloved Son. Christ bore our sin in his own body on the tree (1 Peter 2:24).

Then I read something which as a parent astounded me. It was that Christ was "smitten of God and afflicted. It pleased the Lord to bruise him; he hath put him to grief" (Isaiah 53:4b, 10a). What does it mean to suffer infinitely? Whatever that means I realized that Christ had done that for me.

We may not know, we cannot tell
What pains He had to bear,
But we believe it was for us
He hung and suffered there.

(It is finished)

On the cross Jesus endured the wrath of God, the infinite wrath of God. Even the sun hid its face as the God-man descended into hell for us. Finally, *when the last sin had been paid for, Jesus said, "It is finished!"* (John 19:30).

This is an interesting word in the original text. It is *"Tetelestai,"* a commercial word which means "It is paid; the debt is paid." "The wages of sin is death" (Romans 6:23), or the wrath of God. Jesus said, *"Tetelestai.* It is paid!" Further, he said, "In my Father's house are many mansions. If it were not so I would have told you. I go to prepare a place for you" (John 14:2). *"Tetelestai."* It is paid. It is purchased. With his own passion on the cross, Jesus secured a place in heaven for his own people. Christ then rose triumphantly from the grave, and through his incredible victory over death he now offers us life everlasting.

(The gift of God)

Most of my life I thought as you. If ever I was to go and dwell in heaven, I would have to deserve it. My life would have to be good enough. In other words, I would have to pay an admission price of good works to enter the door of heaven. I was amazed to learn that it's not so!

I don't have to pay for it. Jesus has already paid for it and I can have eternal life as a gift. Listen: "The wages of sin is death but the *gift of God* is eternal life through Jesus Christ our Lord" (Romans 6:23). That is the gospel, the good news of the Christian faith: **God offers heaven to us as a gift.** Heaven is free to us because it was paid for by Christ. The gospel is not "do," but it is "done." Jesus paid it all.

The Bible says, "By *grace* are ye saved . . . not of works lest any man should boast" (Ephesians 2:8, 9). What is the meaning of grace? The Chaplain to the Queen of England at a meeting of world leaders once gave this acrostic: G-R-A-C-E: **G**od's **R**iches **A**t **C**hrist's **E**xpense. God's riches: forgiveness, heaven, eternal life, peace, joy, and a sense of the love of God—**at Christ's expense.** The expense of the scourge, Gethsemane, the mocking, the plucking of his beard, the crown of thorns, the nailing of his hands, the piercing of his side, the wrath of God, and hell itself. "Jesus paid it all. All to Him I owe." He offers us eternal life as a gift by grace.

Who receives this gift? Everybody? No. The Bible says that few find the way to life and that many go to destruction.

How then can we have this gift?

E. Faith

This brings us to the fourth and last thing we need to understand: **We receive the gift of God by faith.** The Bible says, "By grace are ye saved *through faith*" (Ephesians 2:8).

Faith is the key that opens the door to heaven. You know, you could have a key ring with a lot of keys on it, like this; they all look somewhat alike. But I'll tell you something. If you go to the front door of my home, you could try all of these keys except the right one, and they would not open that door. The right key to heaven is called **faith, saving faith.** That is what will open the door to heaven. There is nothing else in the world that will open that door.

1. WHAT IT IS NOT—MERE INTELLECTUAL ASSENT

Let me tell you what saving faith is not. Many people mistake two things for saving faith. If you were to look at these keys you would find that several of them look very similar. In fact, you might not be able at first glance to tell which was which. So it is with faith.

Now, **the first thing that people mistake for saving faith is this: an intellectual assent to certain historical facts.** You believe in God, don't you?

Yes, I always have.

You always have believed in God. So have I. But that type of belief is not what the Bible means by saving faith. I believed in God all my life but for about twenty-five years I was not truly saved.

The Bible says the devil believes in God. Did you know that? The Bible says, "Thou believest that there is one God; thou doest well, the devils also believe, and tremble" (James 2:19). **So believing in God is not what the Bible means by saving faith.** The demons in the Gadarene demoniac said, "What have we to do with thee, Jesus, thou Son of God? Art thou come hither to torment us before the time?" Even the demons believe in the deity of Christ! But they evidently weren't saved! That's one thing people mistake for saving faith; an intellectual assent to the historicity of Christ, but that's not what the Bible means by faith.

. . . *(nor temporal faith)*

Let me give you one other thing that people mistake for saving faith. You have prayed to God many times, haven't you?

Oh, every day.

You've had problems that you've committed to the Lord, right? You've trusted him for some things.

Oh, yes. I couldn't have gotten through life without prayer.

Rene, for example, what did you trust him for?

Well, when my children were sick, when our finances were low and our business was bad—why, I've always prayed to the Lord for those things.

You see, you had more than intellectual assent. You have actually trusted him for some things, right?

Yes.

Your children were sick. Your financial situation and your business were bad. I could probably add other things. You probably trusted him for decisions which you had to make; you probably even prayed that he would keep you safe while you traveled on a long trip. Perhaps you had an operation. You prayed to him to bring you through that safely. Things like this.

Yes.

Now, all of these are good and you should trust in the Lord for all these things. But, you see, **even this is not saving faith.** We might say that when you trusted in the

Lord for your finances you had a financial-faith. You trusted in the Lord to take care of your family—you could call that family-faith. You trusted in the Lord to help you with your decisions—you might call that deciding-faith. On trips you had traveling-faith.

There is one element all these things have in common. They are temporal, aren't they? They are all the things of this life, things of this world that shall pass away. Now many people, I find, trust the Lord for all these temporal matters. But **saving faith is trusting Christ to save you**—to save you eternally.

2. WHAT IT IS—TRUSTING IN JESUS CHRIST ALONE FOR SALVATION

I never thought of it that way.

Why, neither had I. You see, I trusted the Lord for this, and that, and for the other, but to get right down to what I was trusting in for eternal salvation—I was trusting in myself. *I* tried to live a good life. *I* tried to keep the Ten Commandments. *I* tried to live by the Golden Rule. *I, I, I, I*—you see? It was "I!"

What did I ask you?— "What are you trusting in for eternal life? What are you trusting in to get into heaven?" Do you remember what you said? "I try to do the best I can. I try to live a good life according to the Golden Rule. I try to do all these things." Do you see?

Saving faith is trusting Jesus Christ *alone* for our salvation. It means resting upon Christ alone and what he has done rather than upon what I have done to get me into heaven.

This is illustrated very clearly in the life of John Wesley who started the Methodist Church. He went to Oxford Seminary for five years and then became a minister of the Church of England where he served for about ten years. Toward the end of this time he became a missionary from England to Georgia, in approximately 1735.

All of his life he had been quite a failure in his ministry though he was, as we would count men, very pious. He got up at four o'clock in the morning and prayed for two hours. He would then read the Bible for an hour before going to the jails, prisons, and hospitals to minister to all manner of people. He would teach, and pray, and help others until late at night. He did this for years. In fact, the Methodist Church gets its name from the methodical life of piety that Wesley and his friends lived.

(Wesley's experience)

On the way back from America there was a great storm at sea. The little ship in which they were sailing was about to sink. Huge waves broke over the ship deck and the wind shredded the sails. Wesley feared he was going to die that hour and he was terrified. He had no assurance of what would happen to him when he died. Despite all of his efforts to be good, death now for him was a big, black, fearful question mark.

On the other side of the ship was a group of men who were singing hymns. He asked them, "How can you sing when this very night you are going to die?" They replied, "If this ship goes down we will go up to be with the Lord forever."

Wesley went away shaking his head, thinking to himself, "How can they know that?

What more have they done than I have done?" Then he added, "I came to convert the heathen, ah, but who shall convert me?"

In the providence of God, the ship made it back to England. Wesley went to London and found his way to Aldersgate Street and a small chapel. There he heard a man reading a sermon which had been written two centuries earlier by Martin Luther, entitled "Luther's Preface to the Book of Romans." This sermon described what **real faith** was. It is **trusting Jesus Christ only for salvation—and not in our own good works.**

Wesley suddenly realized that he had been on the wrong road all his life. That night he wrote these words in his journal: "About a quarter before nine, while he was describing the change which God works in the heart through faith in Christ, I felt my heart strangely warmed. I felt I did trust in Christ, Christ alone, for salvation; and an assurance was given me that He had taken away my sins, even mine, and saved me from the law of sin and death."

There it is. That is saving faith. Repenting of his sins, he trusted in Jesus Christ alone for salvation. Now, would you say that Wesley had not believed in Jesus Christ before this night? Of course, he had. He was a biblical scholar and had studied about Christ in English, and Latin, and Greek and Hebrew. He had believed in Christ in all these languages. But he *trusted* in John Wesley for his salvation.

After this he became the greatest preacher of the eighteenth century. But it all began when he put his trust in Jesus Christ alone for his salvation.

(Resting on Christ)

Let me illustrate. You see this chair here? A lovely chair, isn't it?

Yes.

You believe that chair exists?

Yes.

Do you believe that it would hold you up?

Yes.

But, you see, it's not holding you up for a very simple reason: you're not sitting on it. That is the way I was with Christ. I believed Jesus existed. I believed he was divine. I trusted him for finances and for health, as you have done too. But, you see, saving faith is trusting in Christ for my salvation. Some people will trust the Lord for their protection when they go out at night. They wouldn't think of putting out the garbage at night without trusting the Lord to take care of them. But as far as their eternal welfare is concerned, they are trusting in their own efforts because they have never understood what the Bible teaches.

Saving faith is putting our trust in Jesus Christ alone for eternal life. Over twenty years ago I repented of my sins and transferred my trust from myself to Jesus Christ; from what I had been doing for God to what he has done for me on the cross. By a simple act of faith I transferred my trust from what I had done to what Christ had done for me. Just as I am now transferring my trust from this chair that I have been resting on (representing my good works) to this one representing Christ. Now I'm resting on only one thing: that is, Jesus Christ. No longer am I trusting what I have done; rather, I trust what he has done for me.

We've sung this in many hymns, such as, "On Christ the solid rock I stand,/ All other ground is sinking sand". . ."Nothing in my hands I bring **(good works, prayers, church-going, loving my neighbor—nothing in my hands)**, /Simply to the cross I cling." Did you ever sing this?

> Just as I am without one plea,
> **(Just as I am—a sinner, unworthy, undeserving, without one plea)**
> Except Thy blood was shed for me,
> And that Thou bidst me come to Thee,
> O Lamb of God, I come, I come.

How amazing is the love of Christ that he is willing to receive us just as we are and to cleanse us, forgive us, and give us eternal life.

(Right actions, wrong motives)

Let's say that this pen in my right hand represents eternal life. There are only two relationships you can have to it. Either you have it, as this hand does, or you haven't, as my left hand doesn't. Now if you don't have it and you believe it exists, you are going to want to get it. So you do the best you can; you love your neighbor, go to church, read the Bible, pray, give money, and then you say, "Lord, here are all the things I've done. I hope I've done enough to get into heaven."

But you see, in this case it becomes evident that everything that you've done has been for the motive of *getting* eternal life. There is this *selfish motive* underlying everything and so you couldn't possibly get it.

Furthermore, the problem is something like that old song: "Sixteen tons and what do you get;/ Another day older and deeper in debt." Sixteen conscious hours and what do we get, another day older and deeper in God's debt because every day we sin.

We could never earn eternal life. The Bible says that God came to earth and on the cross in the person of his Son he paid for eternal life—an infinite price. By his graciousness he offers it to us freely as a gift. (Move pen in right hand over to the left hand.) It is received by faith: "Faith is the hand of a beggar receiving the gift of a king." (Reach out with left hand and accept the pen from the right hand.)

This beggar reached out an unclean hand over twenty years ago and received the gift of eternal life. I didn't deserve it then and I don't deserve it now—nor will I ever deserve it. But I have it! By grace!

(The right motive for living a godly life)

Why, then, should I try to live a good life? The reason for living a godly life is gratitude. That's the motive for godly living. I'm not trying to gain something I don't have by my efforts to be good; rather, I'm saying "thank you" for the eternal life that Christ has given me.

A former president of Princeton put it this way in a book. He said that as a young man he accepted Christ and the gift of eternal life. All the rest of his life was simply a P.S. to that day, saying, "Thank You, Lord, for what you gave to me then." The motive for all is gratitude for the gift of eternal life. "The love of Christ constraineth us" (2 Corinthians 5:14).

III. THE COMMITMENT

A. The qualifying question

Rene, **does that make sense to you?**

Oh, yes, that's beautiful!

B. The commitment question

Rene, you have just heard the greatest story ever told, about the greatest offer ever made by Jesus Christ, the greatest person who ever lived. It's called the "good news," the gospel of Jesus Christ.

Now, Rene, the question God is asking you is simply this: **Do you want to receive this gift of eternal life?** This gift that the Son of God left his throne and went to die on the cross to procure for you—would you like to receive it?

Oh, yes, I would.

C. The clarification of commitment

(Transfer your trust?)

(Receive the righteousness of Christ?)

Wonderful! Let me clarify just what this involves. It means, first of all, that you are going to transfer your trust, that is, your hope of eternal life from what you have been doing to what Jesus Christ has done for you on the cross. He takes our sin and we receive his righteousness. This means that though we have failed to keep God's commandments and to live consistently by the Golden Rule, Christ perfectly obeyed all the laws of God. He has lived the perfect life. **That perfect life of Christ is imputed to us the moment we believe.** It is reckoned to our account—placed to our account—so that in the sight of God we are then accounted as perfect.

It is as though the spotless white robe of Christ's perfect character and obedience were placed upon us, and in that robe we stand faultless before God. Only in this way can we ever acquire that perfect standing that God requires of us. Do you want to **stop trusting in Rene and start trusting in Christ?**

Yes, I do.

(Receive the resurrected and living Christ?)

You receive eternal life by receiving the person of Jesus Christ. "He came unto his own and his own received him not. But as many as received him, to them gave he the power to become the sons of God" (John 1:11, 12). We can receive and know the most exciting person in the history of the world because he is alive!

We do not worship a dead Christ, but a living, glorious Savior. The most important fact in the history of mankind is that **Jesus Christ rose from the dead.** Not only is this the most important fact, beside which all others pale into insignificance, but also it is the **best-attested fact of human history.** For almost six weeks, Christ showed himself alive to hundreds of people after his passion by many infallible proofs.

For centuries men have tried to disprove the resurrection of Christ. But every effort of the skeptic has been discredited by another skeptic until the entire endeavor lies in a heap of rubble before the irrefutable fact of the empty tomb.

(Receive Jesus Christ into your life as Savior?)

Christ is alive! He says, "Behold, I stand at the door, and knock: [at the door of your life] if any one hear my voice, and open the door, I will come in to him, and will sup with him, and he with me." This means that he will have intimate communion daily in your life. He will come in to forgive you and to cleanse you and to give you eternal life. He will come into your life and make you **his child** and an **heir** of an eternal fortune **if you receive him.** Rene, **would you like to ask Jesus Christ to come into your life as your Savior today?**

Oh, yes.

(Receive Jesus Christ into your life as Lord?)

Let me say one thing. I'll say it very plainly. When Christ comes into a life as **Savior** he comes to do something for you: **to forgive you and give you eternal life.** But, also he comes as **Lord.** He comes as **Master and King.** He comes to demand something of you. He says there is a throne room in your heart and that throne is rightly his. He made you. He redeemed you. He bought you. He says that he wants to take his rightful place on the throne of your life. **Are you willing to yield your life, to surrender your life, to him, out of gratitude for the gift of eternal life?**

Yes, I would like to.

(Repent of your sins?)

He also commands us to repent of our sins. **Are you willing to repent of your sins and follow him?** That means that you will turn from what you have been doing that is not pleasing to him and follow him as he reveals his will to you in his Word. Repentance is a complete change of mind about life and death, and about God and this world. It is wrought by his Spirit working within us and it leads inevitably to a transformed life.

Rene, are you willing to repent of your sins and become a responsible member of God's forever family and follow him and serve him as a member of his body, the Church?

Yes, I am.

D. The prayer of commitment

All right, Rene. **The Lord is here right now.** We can go to him now in prayer and we can tell him that you want to **cease trusting in your own strivings** and you want to **put your trust in Christ** the Lord for your salvation and receive him as your personal Savior. Is this *truly* what you want?

Yes.

All right. May I point out to you, Rene, that the Lord is **looking at your heart more than he is listening to your lips.** He says, "Ye shall seek me and find me, when ye shall search for me with all your heart" (Jeremiah 29:13). If this is really what you mean, then the Lord will hear your prayer and grant you eternal life. Let us pray.

(Preparatory prayer)

Father, I pray that thou would grant to Rene the gift of eternal life. May thy Spirit draw her unto thyself. Grant **her faith** to believe thy promises. Grant her **repentance** to turn from her sins. **Reveal unto her Christ crucified today.**

(Prayer together)

(Heads still bowed.) Rene, the Lord has said, "Where two or three are gathered together in my name there I am in the midst of them" (Matthew 18:20). He is right here. You are not talking to me now but to him. If you really want eternal life will you say to him aloud:

Lord Jesus, I want you to come in and take over my life right now. (She repeats each phrase.) I am a sinner. I have been trusting in myself and my own good works. But now I place my trust in you. I accept you as my own personal Savior. I believe you died for me. I receive you as Lord and Master of my life. Help me to turn from my sins and to follow you. I accept the free gift of eternal life. I am not worthy of it but I thank you for it. Amen.

(Continuing in prayer with heads bowed.)

(Assurance of pardon)

Father, you have heard the prayer which Rene has prayed. And I ask that in this quiet moment thy Holy Spirit will grant unto her the assurance of life eternal; grant unto her the certainty that her sins are forgiven. Grant that she may hear in the depths of her soul thy voice saying, "Thy sins be forgiven thee. Go in peace." Grant, O Christ, that she may hear thy voice saying, "As far as the east is from the west, so far have I put thy sins from thee, never to remember them against thee anymore. He that believeth on me shall not come into condemnation. He that trusteth in me is passed from death unto life. He that believeth on me shall never perish but has everlasting life (paraphrased from Psalm 103:12; John 3:18; 5:24; 3:16). In Jesus' name, we pray. Amen.

E. The assurance of salvation

Rene, you have just prayed the most important prayer that you have ever prayed in your life. I want you to see now what Christ says about what you have just done. In

John 6:47 the Lord says something very significant. I would like you to read this. "Verily, verily, I say unto you, he that believeth on me hath everlasting life." (Have her read aloud.)

All right, Rene, in our prayer you didn't hear any angel choirs; or see any visions. However, by a simple act of faith you have placed your trust in Jesus Christ for your salvation. Is that correct?

Yes, it is.

In whom are you now trusting, Rene, for your salvation?

Jesus Christ.

He says, "he that believeth," that is, he that trusteth "in me has eternal life."—that doesn't mean an intellectual assent, for you have believed in Christ all your life in that way. This doesn't mean trusting him for temporal affairs. You've done that all your life. **Saving faith means trusting Christ alone for eternal salvation.** Is this what you have done today?

Yes.

Jesus says that the person who does that has everlasting life. Do you believe him?

Yes, I do.

Rene, if you should die in your sleep tonight, where would you wake up?

In heaven.

And if God asked why you should be in heaven, what would you say?

I am trusting Christ.

The angels are rejoicing! God said it. That settles it. Rene, if you meant in your heart what you just said with your lips, then you have the promise of Christ that he has forgiven your sins, adopted you into his family, and given you eternal life. Praise the Lord! We may rejoice in it. **Welcome, Rene, to the family of God.**

THREE
AN ANALYSIS OF THE PRESENTATION

I. BASIC CONSIDERATIONS

The essence of the evangelical faith is: "Salvation is of the Lord" (Jonah 2:9). Salvation is thus seen to be the supernatural work of the divine Trinity—of the Father who elects, of the Son who redeems, and of the Holy Spirit who applies the salvation of Christ to the hearts of men. Hence it is seen that conversion is not obtained by salesmanship, by persuasion, by rhetoric, by argumentation, or by any other human endeavor, for "salvation is of God."

I have often told my people that the lost men and women to whom they are sent with the gospel have a slight impediment. They are deaf, blind, and dead; other than that they are in fairly good shape. The modern witness for Christ should never lose sight of the statement of the Apostle Paul: "The natural man receiveth not the things of the Spirit of God: for they are foolishness unto him: *neither can he know them,* because they are spiritually discerned" (1 Corinthians 2:14).

This means that our witnessing must always be a "trilog" rather than a dialogue. It means that we are speaking not only to the lost persons before us but also to the Holy Spirit above us and within us, that he might open their eyes and enlighten their minds to understand what we are saying in order that they might be saved. The witness should be taught from the very beginning to depend not on his own persuasiveness but upon the power of the Holy Spirit, or else he is witnessing "in the flesh" and not "in the Spirit."

If "salvation is of God" then why should we witness at all, much less why should we try to do it in the best possible manner? I have often used an illustration which I think speaks to this point.

A riveter is placing rivets in the side of a steel ship. With one hand he holds up a rivet to the side of the ship; with the other he places a pneumatic gun to the rivet and drives it into the ship.

There are four elements involved in this illustration. First, the steel ship; second, the rivet; third, the riveter; and fourth, the pneumatic gun. Each plays a part. If the man could simply place the rivet to the steel ship and then push it in with his thumb, he could then say, "What a strong fellow I am!" But, of course, he cannot do this. He must rely upon the pneumatic gun.

This is analogous to the situation in witnessing. The steel ship represents the stony hearts and adamantine minds of unbelievers; the rivet represents the gospel; the riveter represents the witness; and the pneumatic gun represents the Holy Spirit—an appropriate illustration since "pneumatic" comes from the Greek word for Spirit, *"neumatikos."*

If we could by our own persuasiveness, argumentation, salesmanship, or logic press the gospel into somebody's heart and mind, then we could say, "What a wonderful evangelist I am!" but this we cannot do. Therefore, we must depend entirely upon the power of the Holy Spirit to drive the gospel home to the hearts of men.

If, however, we did not at least hold up the rivet, then the pneumatic gun would only make holes in the side of the ship. Thus God allows us the marvelous privilege of being involved in the greatest work in the world. Dr. John Gerstner put it this way: "We can save no one, but unless we proclaim to them the gospel, God *will* save no one."

II. THE LAWS OF SELLING

Having examined the divine or supernatural aspects of salvation, let us consider for a few minutes the human side of the subject. Someone has well said, "You can't sell the gospel; in fact most Christians can't even give it away." This points up two truths: One, there is something involved far beyond salesmanship, namely, the supernatural work of the Holy Spirit, and two, from the human standpoint most Christians need a better understanding of the laws of persuasion or salesmanship.

JESUS' USE OF THE "FIVE LAWS OF SELLING"

There are five great laws of selling or persuading: attention, interest, desire, conviction, and close. It does not matter whether you are selling a refrigerator or persuading men to accept a new idea or philosophy, the same basic laws of persuasion hold true. Did salesmen invent these? No, they just extracted them. They learned that is the way the human mind and heart reach conclusions and take action. This is what Jesus did, for example, with the woman at the well.

Attention. He began where she was and got her attention.

"Give me to drink."

"How is it you ask me? We have nothing to do with each other."

Interest. "If you knew who was asking you for water, you would ask me and I would give you living water." Now she was really interested.

"Where would you get living water? The well is deep and you have nothing to draw with. Are you greater than Jacob who gave us this well?"

Desire. "He that drinks of this water will thirst again, but whoever drinks of the water I give will never thirst." Now she desired ardently what Jesus offered.

"Give me this water so I will never thirst again or have to come here to draw."

Here she was: a woman of ill repute, having to go to the well at noon when no one else was there. Everyone else came in the cool of the day. She seems more interested in not going to the well to draw than in not thirsting again. "Give it to me."

Conviction (of sin or truthfulness of claims). "Go call your husband." He put his finger on her sin. Did she have to have her husband to be saved? No. That was to pinpoint her sin.

"I have no husband."

"You're right. You had five husbands and the man you live with now isn't your husband." He drove home the evidence of her sinfulness.

(DIVERSION). She tried to avoid the issue. "Our fathers worship in this mountain; you worship in that mountain. . . . When Messiah comes he will tell us about these matters."

The Close. Jesus used something from her digression to get back on the main subject and confront her with the decision she must make, "I that speak to you, am he."

Now she confronts the living Christ. She is brought to the point of decision. She must either accept or reject him.

There you see a beautiful piece of workmanship by the Master Workman, who says we should copy him in dealing with people. He made a smooth transition from where she was to where he wanted her to be.

We should familiarize ourselves with these laws of persuasion and use them to critique our presentation of the gospel to help detect places of weakness. We should ask ourselves such questions as:

> Did I fail to get their attention or to hold their interest? If so, why and what can I do to change this?
>
> How much desire was created for knowing Christ and being a part of his kingdom? How can this be increased?
>
> Was the person convicted concerning his sins and his need for forgiveness? If not, why not?
>
> Did I confront the person clearly with his need to make a decision for Christ and to commit his life to him in repentance and faith? If not, how can I do this better next time?

Such questions as these will help both trainees and trainers to better evaluate their progress in the presenting of the gospel of Christ.

III. THE PURPOSES OF THE INTRODUCTION

The introduction is of great importance and fulfills a number of significant purposes in the overall presentation of the gospel, the most important of which are the following:

1. TO PRECLUDE COMMON OBJECTIONS

The best way to handle objections is to preclude them, that is, to prevent them from coming up. Certain objections occur so frequently that steps have been taken in this presentation to preclude them. A number of such objections and the manner in which they are precluded will be seen in the following purposes of the Introduction.

2. CREATE A SMOOTH TRANSITION INTO THE GOSPEL

To grab somebody by the lapels and say, "Brother, are you saved?" is one way to begin a gospel presentation. But it will probably result in hostility on the part of many so accosted. We have found that smooth and gradual transition into the gospel is by far the more preferable method.

This means that we begin where they are, that is, their secular life and move from there gradually into the area of church, and then move easily into the spiritual realm from there. This avoids the sudden jump from the secular life where people live, to very personal questions. The objections thus precluded might be phrased in the following manner: "Get lost, buddy, I'm not interested!"

During the time of the introduction, the mood needs to be somewhat light. Often those you visit are rigid in the initial moments and not very responsive. Humor at this point can cause them to relax and change their whole attitude. Some visit as if they were "friendly undertakers" who have arrived to dispose of the body!

3. EARN THE RIGHT TO ASK PERSONAL QUESTIONS

I once heard a man walk up to a woman and say, "How are your kidneys today?" That's the truth! I actually heard the man ask that question. Her response? Did she hit him with her purse? No, she said the following: "Oh, it's much better today, thank you, doctor." I overheard those words in a hospital room. That doctor had earned the right to ask that personal question. If you doubt that, then stop the next lady you meet on the street and ask it yourself and see what happens.

All of which is to say we need to earn the right to ask personal questions. We can do this by becoming a friend, by getting to know the people, by listening to what they have to say, by showing interest, by hearing them when they talk. This is best accomplished in the section on their secular life as will be discussed at greater length below. The objections precluded by this would probably be phrased as follows: "Oh, that's too personal. I don't talk about that sort of thing with strangers."

4. FIND OUT WHERE THE PERSON IS SPIRITUALLY

Through a discussion of the person's church background or lack of it, we can form some understanding of his or her spiritual condition and of any particular spiritual problems he/she might have. We will probably see if he/she would tend to be more of a Pharisee or a Sadducee; to lean more toward legalism or license; to have some peculiar doctrinal hangup. These things will be discovered as we discuss the person's church background. If there is some peculiar bias which is discovered, the entire presentation can be slanted to help overcome the problem and thus preclude the objection.

5. FIND OUT IF HE HAS WHAT YOU ARE OFFERING TO HIM

We have come to offer him, in the name of Christ, eternal life; the privilege of knowing Christ now and everlastingly. We should ascertain whether or not the person already has this knowledge, and this may be done by the first diagnostic question: Have you come to the place in your spiritual life where you know for certain that if you died you would go to heaven? There is, of course, no point in belaboring the gospel with a person who is already saved.

6. CREATE A DESIRE TO HEAR THE GOSPEL

I have seen many people try to witness to others who quite obviously had no desire to hear what they were saying. Such a desire, however, is essential before a person will ever commit himself to Christ.

To create such a desire we should pinpoint some particular need and show the person how Christ can fulfill that need. There are many such needs: loneliness, lack of purpose, guilt, hostilities, etc. Everyone has a need for life. Christ came that we might have life and have it abundantly and eternally. This need should be strongly emphasized and its fulfillment in Christ should be demonstrated.

It has been said, "You can lead a horse to water but you can't make him drink." I think that that is errant nonsense. Place a salt tablet inside his lower lip! What I am saying is, though we can't make him drink, we can make him thirsty and he will want to drink. The Bible says that we are the salt of the earth. We ought, therefore, to be able to make people thirsty for the water of life. One way to do this is simply to tell them about the wonders of the eternal life which Christ gives and to dwell upon that for awhile. The very frequent result is to see a spiritual thirst develop in the other person.

This can be done either in a personal testimony in the introduction or after you have asked the first diagnostic question, and discovered that the person does not have eternal life. At this point you can share with him that at one time you did not but now that you do it is the most wonderful thing you have ever discovered, for the reasons which you then explain to them.

If such a desire is not created, the objections may take numerous forms, such as "I'll have to think it over," or "Thank you, but I don't think I'm ready yet to make that decision," or perhaps it will appear as some form of theological objection which is only masking the true fact that the person doesn't want what you are offering him. Therefore, it is very important to create desire by showing needs and the way that Christ can meet those needs.

7. ASK PERMISSION TO SHARE THE GOSPEL

I used to say to people, "Would you like for me to tell you how you can know this?" This, however, indicated a teacher/student relationship and showed an air of superiority on my part. This I found was definitely not right.

I then changed this question to the following: "Would you like for me to share with you how you can know this?" This worked much better but there were still a small percentage of people who would smile and say, "I don't think that will be necessary."

I finally found that by "adding a rider to the bill" I could eliminate all objections at this point. Therefore, I would suggest the following wording: *"Would you like for me to share with you how I made this discovery and how you could know it too?"*

Thus far I have never had a person say no to this question. It should be remembered, however, that this is built upon the preceding preparatory work, especially in the discussion of their secular life where I have asked questions and listened to them tell me about themselves. It would be a little bit difficult for them to say, "No, I don't want you to tell me how you made any discovery. I just want to talk about myself some more."

The obvious objection precluded by getting permission to share the gospel in this way is "I don't like people shoving religion down my throat."

8. FIND OUT WHAT THE PERSON IS NOW TRUSTING IN FOR HIS SALVATION

This is accomplished through the second diagnostic question: "Suppose that you were to die tonight and stand before God and he were to say to you, 'Why should I let you into my heaven?' what would you say?" It is vitally important to find out what they are trusting in for salvation since probably the most common objection that we run into with people who are at all church-related is, "Oh, I have always believed that."

To preclude this objection, therefore, it is vitally important to ascertain before sharing with them the gospel, what it is precisely that they are trusting in for their salvation.

9. IF THE ANSWERS TO THE DIAGNOSTIC QUESTIONS ARE WRONG, TELL THE PERSON THAT HE IS WRONG WITHOUT MAKING HIM ANGRY

The objection being precluded here is obvious but almost never explicitly stated. If it were to be stated it would be something such as this: "I don't like people telling me that I am wrong." However, it is usually not stated but appears in the form of anger and hostility, which, of course, makes a successful presentation of the gospel extraordinarily difficult.

I have found that it is possible to tell someone that he is wrong and even make him happy to hear it, if we use the vehicle of **good news** to tell him. Our response to a person's wrong answer to the second diagnostic question would be as follows: "When I heard your answer to that first question I thought that I had some good news for you. And after hearing your answer to this question I *know* that I have some good news for you. In fact, I would go so far as to say that in the next sixty seconds you're going to hear the best news that you've ever heard in your life. That's quite a claim, isn't it? Let's see if I can back it up. For years I thought the same thing that you did. If ever I were to get to heaven I had to follow all of these commandments and keep all of these rules, and do so many things, that I almost despaired of ever making it. And then I made the most wonderful discovery of my life. I discovered that according to the Scriptures, according to the historic Christian faith, eternal life—heaven itself—is absolutely a free gift. It is not earned, deserved, or worked for. It is absolutely free. Isn't that amazing?"

Telling a person that he is wrong via good news is like saying to a person who has just declared that his Aunt Sarah has died and left him $10,000, "No, you're wrong! Your Aunt Sarah did *not* leave you $10,000. I have seen the will and she left you $10 million." That's not the kind of statement that is likely to make anyone very unhappy, and yet you did tell him that he was wrong.

You will notice that the blow of telling the person that he is wrong is softened in a second way by shifting the discussion to myself and actually stating that I was wrong: "For years I thought this same thing. If ever I were to get to heaven I had to keep all of these commandments and follow all of these rules—and then I made the most wonderful discovery of my life." I am identifying myself with him in the discovery that I was wrong and also telling him that it was a wonderful discovery.

The introduction to the gospel has been designed to fulfill all of these purposes outlined above and to preclude all of the objections indicated. If the introduction is handled well the rest of the presentation is vastly easier than otherwise it would be.

BEGIN WHERE THE PROSPECTS ARE

Now let us move systematically through the presentation in order to analyze more fully and understand more clearly just what we are trying to do. As Jesus did with the woman at the well, we begin with a person where he is.

THE PRESENTATION

I. THE INTRODUCTION

A. The person's secular life. Upon entering the home the first thing with which you will deal is the person's secular life. This covers a lot of things. It will include the basic amenities of the day—questions about where the person is from and what he does. We may also talk about his family and his hobbies. At this point we will do three things:

1. Ask questions that move toward the core of his life. We will not ask merely about things on the periphery of his interest, but we will search the room for some indication of his interest. A specially placed and lighted painting; a group of portraits of children; trophies from golf, swimming, or bowling all furnish materials for saying, "Tell me something about yourself."
2. After asking this, be quiet and listen to him talk for five minutes. People usually are most interested in what they themselves have to say. By listening we earn the right to be heard and also demonstrate Christian love.
3. Then you will pay him a sincere compliment. In order to do this you will have had to listen to what he was saying.

B. His church. You are visiting from the church. It is natural for you to talk about his previous church experiences. At this point you will begin to qualify the person. Whom do you have—a "Pharisee," a "Sadducee," or a libertine? You learn more about the person, how he views the church; and what his relationship was to the church back home. *Don't criticize* his denomination, his congregation, his minister, or him as a person. You are not there as a judge or jury, but as a witness for Christ. Keep in mind that you have come to make a friendly visit and to show your interest and concern for him.

C. Our church. It is logical to move from discussing his previous church activity to his visit to your church. Find out if his impression is negative or positive, hostile or friendly. It will be helpful at this point if your service was meaningful and encouraging to him. Ask him if he noted any unique aspects of your worship and your people. Such questions as these will be helpful at this point:

"How did you happen to come to our church?"
"Do you know any of the members of our congregation?"
"How did you enjoy the service?"
"Did you notice anything different about the service or the people?"

The best preparation for an evangelistic call is *a vital worship service* for the visitors and a *friendly, helpful congregation* to greet the visitors and assist them in finding the nursery, rest rooms, etc., according to their needs.

D. Testimony. The testimony may take either of two forms. It may be a personal testimony (either your own or that of another), or it may be a church testimony. Some people prefer to use a combination of both a church and personal testimony. In the accompanying presentation, a church testimony is used in order to establish the mission of the church: i.e., to proclaim the gospel that men and women may have eternal life. (To see how a personal testimony might be used, see chapter four.)

A church testimony may be introduced in one of two ways. If the person is enthusiastic about the service that he attended and indicates that the people were unusually friendly or enthusiastic, then you could introduce the church testimony in this way: "Would you like for me to share with you why it is that I think the people at the church are so enthusiastic? It's because the people have found something in their lives which is really exciting and has given their lives a new meaning. You know, Jesus came into the world that people might have life and have it abundantly and eternally, etc." (See church testimony in longer presentation.)

If, however, the person does not seem enthusiastic over the service or did not notice anything particularly unusual about it, then you can introduce a church testimony in the following manner: (You should also work on your morning service and the friendliness and enthusiasm of the congregation.) "Since you are a visitor to our church and as yet do not know much about it, I would like to share with you some things that we're trying to do that I think you will find interesting. You know, Jesus Christ came into the world that men might have life and have it abundantly and eternally . . ." (See full church testimony in larger presentation.)

E. Two diagnostic questions. Every science has progressed to the degree that its instruments of measurement have been developed. This is true in medicine. The foundation of good medicine is sound diagnosis. Where remedies are applied without such diagnosis we say that the practitioner is a "quack." This same truth applies to the spiritual realm. Unless we can accurately diagnose the person's spiritual condition we shall very likely endeavor to apply the wrong spiritual cure, or apply the right cure in the wrong manner. Therefore, we have developed two diagnostic questions that are of invaluable assistance in determining the person's spiritual condition. In applying these we should keep in mind that whether in the realm of medicine or of the spirit, *no diagnostic tool is infallible.*

We have come to offer eternal life in Jesus Christ. The two diagnostic questions enable us to ascertain (1) whether or not they have what we have come to offer them, and (2) what they are basing their hope of eternal life upon. After ascertaining that the person does not have eternal life, it is recommended that before proceeding to the second question, permission to share with him how to have eternal life be obtained. The manner of doing this has been discussed in the seventh objective of the introduction.

It is of vital importance, not only to be able to administer diagnostic tests but also to be able to properly interpret the results of these tests. I have been told that anyone with normal intelligence could learn to give an electrocardiogram in about an hour's time, and yet it takes years of study for a doctor to be able to interpret the results. Fortunately, it will only take the average trainee a few minutes to be able to intelligently interpret the results of these two diagnostic questions, but those are minutes that are very well spent.

FOUR COMBINATIONS. There are four possible combinations of answers which may be obtained to the two diagnostic questions. These are laid out in schematized form in the accompanying illustration. The following is an interpretation of the diagnostic results of the questioning and suggested procedures for each one.

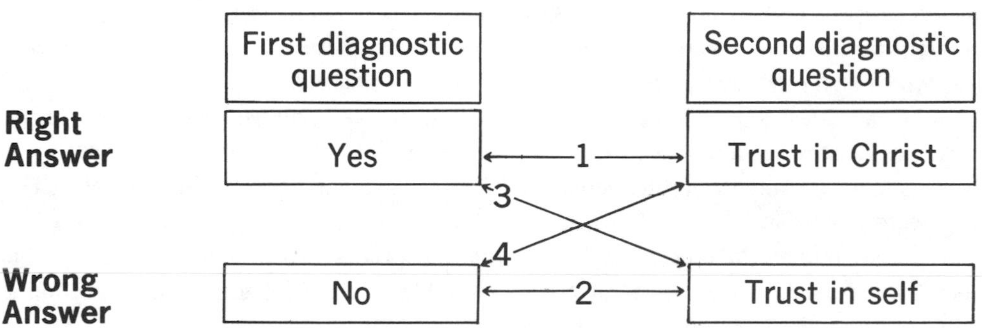

FIRST COMBINATION. **A correct answer to both questions,** that is, the person declares that he knows that he has eternal life and that he is trusting in Jesus Christ alone for his salvation.

Interpretation of diagnosis: **Apparently a Christian.** I say "apparently" because we should always remember that no diagnostic test is infallible. The person might simply be demonstrating, as happens in rare instances, that he has a head knowledge of that which he does not possess in his heart. Since we, however, are not the judge of men's hearts we will assume that he is a Christian and treat him accordingly.

Recommendation procedure:

1. Share with him other aspects of the life of your church since he is apparently a candidate for membership in your church.
2. Ask questions concerning the areas of church life in which he is most interested, so that you can further inform him of what your church is doing in those areas.
3. Share with him the nature of the evangelism program that you are involved in and what the purpose of your visit is.
4. Possibly share a brief presentation of the gospel with him or have one of your trainees do so if they have progressed far enough in their training to be able to make an effective presentation. This will challenge him in the area of witnessing and may also be used to encourage him to become a part of your church and its outreach program. Most Christians are quite impressed with another layman who can give a well organized and interesting presentation of the gospel.
5. Enlist him as a prayer partner for one person on your team.

SECOND COMBINATION. **An incorrect answer to both questions.** That is, the person declares that he does not know that he has eternal life and states that he is trusting in his own good works to get him into heaven.

Interpretation of diagnosis: **Apparently a non-Christian.** I again say "apparently" because of the small possibility that he may have misunderstood the questions and have been confused in his answers.

Recommended procedure: This is the stock answer of the non-Christian and the recommended procedure is to present the gospel as given in detail in both the smaller and larger presentations.

THIRD COMBINATION: **A correct answer to the first question and an incorrect answer to the second.** That is, they say that they know that they are going to go to heaven and the reason that God should admit them is because they have lived a good life, followed the Golden Rule, kept the commandments, etc.

Interpretation of diagnosis: This is what we call **"presumption"**—the person presumes himself to be going to heaven without any biblical foundation for that hope. These people are somewhat analogous to the Pharisees who "trusted in themselves that they were righteous."

Recommended procedure: Before you can proceed with such a person as this, his illusions must be destroyed; that is, the bubble of his false hope must be popped. This may be done in the following manner:

(Witness, commenting on prospect's answer.) Have you ever considered just how good a person would have to be to be good enough to go to heaven, or, in other words, have you ever thought just what is the passing grade?

No, I'm not really sure.

Let me tell you what the Bible says. It says, "Be ye therefore perfect even as your Father which is in heaven is perfect" and "If ye sin in one point ye are guilty of all."

You see, the passing grade is one hundred and God doesn't grade on the curve. He says that we will give an account of every idle word, and every thought, and every deed we've ever committed, and if we fail to live up to his perfect standard we fall short of the entrance requirements into heaven. After looking more carefully at what God's entrance requirements are, are you really certain how that interview would turn out? (This question should be asked in a somewhat light and jovial fashion so that the person does not feel like he's being given the third degree.)

No, I guess when I stop to think of it, I'm really not certain how that would turn out.

Well, you know, I have some good news for you. In spite of everything I've said, it is possible to know for sure that you're going to heaven, but it's in an entirely different way. Would you like for me to share that with you?

You have thus brought the prospect to realize that his confidence was misplaced and that he is not really sure at all what would happen to him and would like to know how he could be sure. Thus you have accomplished one of the basic objectives of the introduction, even with this most difficult of the four possible combinations of the answers.

FOURTH COMBINATION: **A wrong answer to the first question and a correct answer to the second.** This is, the person declares that he does not know for sure that he would go to heaven but that his only hope is that he is trusting in Jesus Christ who died for his sins.

Interpretation of diagnosis: This is most probably a **lack of assurance.** It, however, could be caused by the person having gained a head knowledge of the way of salvation but having lacked assurance because he has never really appropriated it unto himself. In either case we will deal with it as if it was simply a lack of assurance. If it was the latter problem you may find the individual a few weeks later going about telling people that he just became a Christian.

Recommended procedure: Take the prospect to some of the assurance verses in the Scripture, such as John 6:47 or 1 John 5:11,12. Using for example, John 6:47 you may proceed as follows:

Would you please read this verse for me aloud? (handing him Bible).

"Verily, verily, I say unto you, He that believeth on me hath everlasting life."

Let's look at that together for a moment. Jesus is speaking and he says, "Truthfully, truthfully, I say unto you, he that believeth or trusteth in me has everlasting life." In whom are you trusting for your hope of eternal life?

In Jesus Christ.

Then you have fulfilled the condition set forth in this verse, haven't you?

Yes.

Christ gives us here a solemn promise. He says that those who trust in him have—not will have, shall have, may have, or might have, but have as a present possession—eternal life, which of course means heaven. Do you believe that Jesus would tell you a lie?

No, I don't.

Then do you believe that he is telling you the truth in this verse?

Yes, I do.

Do you then have eternal life as Christ declares?

Well, I guess that I do.

I think that it would be helpful if we were to have a word of prayer and ask God to grant you the assurance that you need and would like to have.

All right.

Would you pray to Christ out loud the following prayer after me? Lord Jesus Christ (he repeats each phrase) I *do* trust in you for my salvation. I *do* believe that you died for me. I *do* believe your promise of eternal life. Grant unto me the assurance of my salvation. I *do* repent of my sins and desire to follow you. In thy name, Amen. You asked God to give you the assurance of eternal life. Do you now believe his promise that you have eternal life?

Yes, I do.

And if you died in your sleep tonight, where would you wake up?

In heaven.

Praise the Lord!

This prayer is similar to a prayer of commitment except for the tense of the verbs. You are not indicating that he is necessarily doing this for the first time now but merely that he does trust in Christ whenever that trust may have begun.

This approach may also prove useful in dealing with a person who gives two wrong answers but later, in spite of all that you have done, changes his story and declares that he has always trusted in Christ and cannot be moved from that opinion. Instead of arguing and angering him it might be well to point out that since he did not know for sure that if he died he would go to heaven, would he not like for you to lead in a prayer and ask God to give him that assurance. Such a prayer as this may be used to bring such a person to Christ if he really had not been trusting in him in reality.

Now we may consider a few other points relative to the use of the two diagnostic questions.

1. "Have you come to a place in your spiritual life where you know for certain that you have eternal life?"

This question brings the person to the point of saying, in effect, "I don't have eternal life." *We always want to find out if the person already has eternal life.*

Suppose you were selling an encyclopedia and you spent two hours in a home presenting a family with the wonderful advantages of owning the *Americana.* Then you would ask them what they think of it. The father turns and says, "It's marvelous. In fact, I think it's so wonderful that I bought a set last week and it's in the next room."

No encyclopedia salesman would be that stupid!

Yet many who are witnessing for Christ make this very mistake. They do not learn if the person has eternal life already. After presenting the gospel they hear these lovely words: "Oh, yes. I've always believed that."

Most people will say they are not certain that they have eternal life. This is especially true if you will emphasize the word "certain" when you ask the question: Have you come to the place in your spiritual life where you know for certain that you have eternal life and that you are going to heaven? If one says, "I know I have eternal life," you must then determine on what he is basing that hope and distinguish true assurance from presumption. The Westminster Confession of Faith points out that ". . . hypocrites, and other unregenerate men, may daily deceive themselves . . . of being in the . . . estate of salvation; which hope of theirs shall perish." Dr. McDowell Richards, president of Columbia Theological Seminary, said one day, "Assurance is having a confidence of eternal life which is rested upon the sure foundation of Jesus Christ, but presumption is presuming ourselves to have eternal life when in fact our confidence is based on nothing more than the flimsy foundation of our own self-righteousness."

PERMISSION. After ascertaining that they do not have eternal life, before we ask the second diagnostic question we should get permission from them to proceed with the gospel. The following procedure is recommended:

For years I felt the same way that you do. I certainly didn't know that I was going to heaven. In fact, I didn't know that anyone knew that or even that it was knowable. And then I made a wonderful discovery. I discovered that it was possible to know for certain that when I left this world that I was going to enter into heaven. That's the greatest thing I have ever learned in my life. I wouldn't trade it for all the tea in China. Would you like for me to share with you how I made that discovery and how you can know it too?

Yes, I would.

Wonderful! But before I get into it there is a question that I think brings the whole subject into focus, and I would be interested in your opinion on this matter. (Lead right into second diagnostic question.)

2. *Suppose you were to die tonight and stand before God, and he were to ask you, "Why should I let you into my heaven?" What would you say?*

The second question enables us to discern upon what foundation one is trusting for eternal life. Why do we ask, "Why should God let you into heaven?" rather than, "What must one do to be saved?"

The latter is a biblical question that has a biblical answer. One who has gone to Sunday school and has some acquaintance with the Scriptures will respond like a computer. Feed such a person the question in biblical language and he will push a mental button, the machine will whirl and hum and out comes the right answer: "Believe on the Lord Jesus Christ, and thou shalt be saved and thy house." This may be his sincere faith, or merely a parrot reply devoid of true understanding. You will have no way of knowing which.

In asking the question, "Why should God let you into heaven?" we feed a question that has not been programmed. There is no rote—no automatically learned—answer. Also it is a neutral question, i.e., it does not lead the person to give a rote answer.

Some have said that that question deals with "pie in the sky by and by" and that we should deal with the here and now. We have found, however, that most questions that deal with the here and now lead to vague and uncertain answers such as, "Are you following Christ in your life?" Response: "Well, more or less." Or, "Is Jesus Christ the Lord of your life?" Response: "I guess so but not as much as he should be." It is easy to see that such answers as these make it difficult to proceed in a clear fashion. We have found that the diagnostic questions selected generally get clear and unambiguous answers which facilitate the presentation of the gospel.

From the answer given, you then know what the person is truly trusting for eternal life. It's helpful at this point to rephrase the answer: "Let me see if I understand you. You would say to God . . ." and then repeat what he has just told you. This will help preclude his saying at the end, "Oh, I've always believed in Jesus Christ and trusted him alone for salvation."

HOW TO GET AN ANSWER. Often when you ask a person, "Why should God let you into heaven?" you will get an answer something like, "Well, I don't know." Is there some way to get an answer that will let you know in what he is trusting? Here are several methods we have found effective.

Change the wording. Much like a football player, you have "hit the line" and can't get through. You need to back up, gain a bit more speed, and hit it again in a different place.

Stress the significance and importance of the question. "That's really a thought-provoking question, isn't it? When I first heard it I was no theologian but I did have enough sense to realize that it's truly a significant question. I came to realize that it's the most important question in the world. If I could not give God the right answer I would miss heaven. And the other option isn't too pleasant to think about.

"I figured that was really a question I needed to know the answer to. I realized Jesus had said, 'What shall it profit a man if he gain the whole world and lose his own soul?' I know you don't have a theological dissertation prepared on the subject, but just offhand, what comes to your mind? **What do you *think* you would say if he asked you, 'Why should I let you into my heaven?' "**

Your prospect will find it harder to say again, "I don't know." You have discussed that this is really an important question—the most important question in the world according to your authority, Jesus Christ! Also, you have taken the edge off the situation by pointing out that you do not expect him to have a theological dissertation on the subject. Finally, you have changed the wording from, "What would you say?" to "What do you think you would say?"

Make the question general. In the event your prospect gives another, "I don't know," or "It's hard to say," you still want to get an answer. You will now want to change from a personal question to a general one.

"Well, I sort of felt the same way. That's a difficult question to answer. Let me change the question and take the spotlight off of you. You've been going to church all your life. I'm sure you have gathered some idea as to what the entrance requirements into heaven are. **I would be interested in what you think the entrance requirements for anyone to get into heaven are."**

If this elicits a suitable response you then may add, "Now I suppose that since we have had time to look at it, these are really the things upon which you yourself are basing your hope of getting into heaven, aren't they?"

In this case you have made it more difficult to plead ignorance. You have reminded your prospect that he's been sitting in church for years. He's not going to admit: "I'm so stupid I have not learned a thing! I just sat there sleeping!" Also the question is no longer right on him—not, "What would you say?" but "What are the entrance requirements?" (in general for anyone). On only very rare instances will you ever have to go beyond this to get an answer to the question.

Tell what your answer was. However, what if he still is evasive and doesn't know? You might do this, but only as a last resort. **"Well, here's what I thought.** You have to keep the Golden Rule and live by the Ten Commandments, be a good citizen and neighbor, and not hurt anyone intentionally. Are these the ideas that have been going around in your mind?"

Here you are on the dangerous ground of putting out words for him to claim as his own. This tends to be leading. The only reason for using this approach is that by this time your prospect has given good evidence that he is not trusting Christ and probably is trusting some form of good works but has not been able to verbalize it.

Agree that he doesn't know. If there is still no answer, or if again he acknowledges that he does not know what he would say, you can now nail it down with, **"Then you just really don't know how to get into heaven, do you?**

"You're sort of like the man in Jesus' story. The king came to him and said, 'Friend, how camest thou in hither?' Do you know what he said? He said the same thing you said! He was speechless! He really didn't know what to say. Do you know what happened to him? The servants bound him and cast him into outer darkness. Now, we don't want that to happen to you, do we?

"Do you remember the '$64,000 Question' that used to be on TV? If a contestant gave the wrong answer he would be told, 'Step down.' And you know, the same thing happened if he gave no answer. There are some situations like that in life where a wrong answer and no answer produce the same result. It's a long way to step down from God. And we don't want you to have to do that. Would you like me to share with you what the biblical answer to that question is?"

How to deal with their wrong answer. Usually you will not have to go through most of the above, for you will get an answer to your question on the first or second attempt. The problem then arises as to how to deal with the wrong answer that they have given you. Let me share a word of my own experience over the years in dealing with this problem in the hope that you may avoid some of the mistakes I have made.

I began by answering the question directly: "No, that is not correct, Mr. Jones. The answer the Bible gives is quite different from your answer." The problem I ran into here should be obvious. Someone has said that the most pleasant words in the English language are "You are right," which would seem to indicate that some of the most unpleasant words are "You are wrong." These words tended to raise the hackles on my prospect's neck and I often found myself engaged in an argument right at the outset. I won a number of arguments and lost a great many people.

Finally I decided to try a different tack. Instead of telling them from the onset that their answer was wrong, I said that their answer was interesting but that it raised a number of questions. And then I went into the gospel and waited until the end of the gospel presentation to tell them that they had been wrong. However, I now discovered a new problem. Since some time had elapsed since they had given their answer I found that many people would now try to wiggle out of their answer or else deny they had ever said it. So I found myself right back where I started.

After a good many years of struggling with this problem, I was led by the Lord to a solution. I had thought that there must be a way to tell them from the onset that they were wrong and yet make them happy to hear it. I am delighted to say there is a way that this can be done. We now respond to their wrong answer something like this: "You know, Mr. Jones, when you answered that first question ('Do you know for sure you have eternal life?') I thought I had some good news for you. But after hearing your answer to this second question ('Why should God let you into heaven?') I *know* that I have some good news for you. In fact, I would go so far as to say that in the next sixty seconds you are going to hear the greatest good news that you have ever heard in your entire life! That's quite a statement, isn't it? Well, let's see if I can back it up. All my life I thought just what you said* —if ever I were to get to heaven I would have to earn, deserve, or merit it. And then I discovered the most wonderful

* If this is not your experience and you can't make this statement then you can say, "Multitudes of people have thought just what you said."

thing in the world—that according to the Bible, heaven—eternal life—is absolutely a *free gift!* Isn't that amazing?"

This should be said with great enthusiasm and exuberance. I have found that usually it will produce an enthusiastic and open response on the part of the listener. This is due to a number of factors: (1) it is such tremendous good news; (2) it is almost universally unknown by the unregenerate person; (3) the shock effect of hearing the most unexpected news right at the beginning; (4) and very importantly, the enthusiastic and exuberant manner in which the Good News is told precludes a hostile reaction.

BRIEF REVIEW

By this time you have come far from the front door. As the door opened you were strangers. Now your prospect knows you as one interested in him, his background, and his opinions. He also knows you are knowledgeable in the spiritual realm. You know a great deal about him. You know his interest in the church, his attitude toward our church, his view of himself, and most important, his eternal destiny as of this moment. If he is lost, you hope by God's grace that his destiny will change within the next hour or two. You are now ready to present the facts of the gospel.

II. THE GOSPEL ITSELF

In the Introduction you have found out what the person is trusting for salvation. Equally important, he has found out. Until you helped him clarify it, he probably wasn't aware of what he was trusting for eternal life. We begin now to tear down this foundation which is inadequate. Now we are about to show the product and show the prospect that he needs it. Remember, you put the value on your product by the way you speak about it. It will seem as valuable to your prospect as it does to you. Think about what you are saying. Talk about God's Good News in a manner befitting the greatest story ever told! The expression on your face may be far more important than the words on your lips. Start thinking about heaven before talking about it!

Beware of your attitude at this point lest you convey: "Would you like ME (wise guy) to tell YOU (stupid) how you can get smart (like I am)?" In other words, avoid talking down to people. People who have been going to Sunday school classes and worship services know a lot of facts that form a spiritual jigsaw puzzle. Each Sunday they get another piece or two to put in the box. This week they got a sermon about the Good Samaritan. That was nice. Into the box it goes. Occasionally they shake all the pieces around but they don't seem to fall together. Christianity seems to be just a large number of pieces floating through the air—Noah, David and Goliath, the Tower of Babel, Jesus healing a blind man, and a little man up in a tree—isolated stories without much meaning and with no interrelationship. A few pieces are missing. These we supply as we present the gospel. These key pieces enable everything else to fall into place.

The things in this presentation that most people don't know are:

1. Man cannot save himself
2. God is holy and just and must punish sin
3. Christ is God
4. His death on the cross was for our sins

5. He offers heaven as a gift
6. The meaning of grace
7. The meaning of faith.

These are the points we must emphasize. To verbally underscore them you must stop and say these key points deliberately. You dare not go through the whole gospel at the same pace and in the same tone of voice, or finally your host will say, "that's very interesting. It's time to go to bed. I can hardly keep my eyes open." Charles Spurgeon says if you gently rock the cradle you will put them to sleep, but if you give the cradle a good jerk the babies will wake up!

Man cannot save himself. Most people know that they are sinners even though they may not realize the seriousness of that accusation. Many times they have heard, "All have sinned." So they conclude that sin is something everyone is doing, therefore it cannot be so bad. "Oh, yes, I'm a sinner. But not so bad a sinner that I can't go to heaven by being reasonably good."

They don't know that because they are sinners and God's standard is perfection they cannot qualify for heaven.

Here we must clear the deck. The Scripture says to tear down and to build up. We have to tear away, clear away, the old foundation on which they have built their hope of eternal life before we can build a new one. In telling a man that he is a sinner and cannot save himself you simply show him that what he has told you will not work. By showing him what the standard is and that he has fallen short of the standard, you convey the idea that he needs to hear more of what you are offering him.

It is good at the end of "I. Grace" to show that what he is trusting is inadequate—that no one could get to heaven on that basis. You might say, "You understand now that because God's standard is perfection, and none of us have come up to it, it is impossible for anyone to get to heaven by doing enough good things?" His reply would be, "Yes, I do."

Now your prospect has reaffirmed that you not only understood him correctly and knew what he meant when he answered the question as to why God should let him into heaven, but now he sees that what he meant is an impossibility.

The reason this is a good place to do this is that you have not given him anything to substitute for it yet. After you have given him the right answer he might say, "Oh, no! I didn't mean that! I meant this—what you just said." But by the end of point one you haven't given the right answer. All you have done is taken away what he was trusting in formerly.

Occasionally one will disagree with you and say, "No, that's not what I meant." He realizes that he may have shown what he's trusting in is wrong. He may not want to admit this. Your reply in such a situation is, "Wonderful! I'm glad that I found this out now for I thought that's what you meant. Tell me, what did you mean?" Thus you can get another commitment from him at this point. All he is going to do is point to some other part of himself—that is, to something else in himself that he is trusting in. Then you can continue with the gospel.

God is just, and must punish sin. The nature of God is an element left out of many presentations of the gospel. To leave it out, especially in the present day, deprives the gospel of much of its meaning. Perhaps 200 years ago most people had valid conceptions of God. This is not true today. Ultimately most theological heresy is caused by a misconception of the nature of God. When we fail to understand his nature we cannot understand his gospel. Many church people hold a Christian Science concept of God as merely love. If this is a person's view of God, he will fit all you say as you present the gospel into that mold and it will be meaningless to him. God is love—so what if man is a sinner? God is love—so what if Christ died? God is love—so why worry whether everyone believes in him if everyone will be saved anyway?

A good argument could be made that the second commandment is the one most frequently broken today: "Thou shalt not make unto thee any graven images." You may have heard the story of two servicemen who returned to base on Saturday night after a week's leave. They had lived it up wildly during the week and had done everything a serviceman could do on leave. On Sunday morning they went to chapel to find the chaplain preaching on the Ten Commandments. As they were slinking out the door after service, one was heard to say to the other, "Well, at least I ain't made no graven images lately!" But the problem with all he had done, basically, was involved with the fact that he started with a graven image—not made of wood or stone but conjured in the factory of his mind! Men create gods in their own image.

One time I was reading to a lady what God said he would do to the guilty. She said, "Oh, my God would never do that!" After much effort to persuade her otherwise I finally said, "Madam, you are right. Your god would never do that. The problem is, your god doesn't exist except in your own mind. You have created a god in your own image, according to your own liking, and now you have fallen down and worshiped him. This is idolatry."

This is one of the most prevalent sins of our day. How often have you heard it said, "God would never do that!" What God wouldn't do it? The God of the Bible? He says a thousand times exactly what he will do. If one says God wouldn't do these things, he is speaking of the god he has made up: a false god.

Therefore, in a time when this heresy is so prevalent, we need to stress the true nature of God—that he is not only loving and kind and merciful, but that he is also holy and cannot condone sin. He is also righteous and has promised to punish sin and visit our iniquity with stripes. It is the nature of God that makes the whole concept of Christ's person and work meaningful.

We have found that we can avoid many arguments on the justice and righteousness of God if we will first deal clearly with the great biblical truth that God is love. And after expounding on his mercy, grace, and love we can then introduce the subject of his justice in the following way: "But the same Bible that tells us that God is merciful and loving also tells us that the same God is just and righteous and must deal with sin."

Christ is God. In our society people know many facts about Jesus of Nazareth, but many do not know he is divine. When they hear "Jesus is the Son of God" they have some faulty understanding. Perhaps they believe he is only different in degree from every human being. "Are we not all the sons of God?" they ask. They do not see anything unique about Jesus except he was more successful than we in keeping God's Law and he was a brilliant teacher. For others, the claim that Jesus was the Son of God means that he was more than a man, but they believe he was less than God. In other words, he was God and man mingled in one nature so he is seen as a superhuman being but not as a fully divine being. We must underscore the truth that the Babe of Bethlehem's manger was none other than the Word of creation, the mighty God who created and sustains heaven and earth and all things.

His death on the cross was for our sins. Nearly everyone we meet knows that Jesus died on the cross of Calvary. Relatively few are aware of the significance of that death according to the teaching of the Scriptures. The death of Christ has no meaning for a man until the concept of imputation grasps his soul as it did Luther's. One must see that his sins were laid to Christ. He must realize that Christ assumed his guilt. As Paul put it, God made Christ to be sin for us that we might be made the righteousness of God in him. The cross has meaning for a man when he knows that his guilt was imputed to the Son by the Father; and when he knows, further, that the Father laid upon the Son the hell that every sinner deserves. Let a man see his sin laid on Christ on the cross and then that cross has meaning for him.

A word about visual illustrations will be in order here. It is very helpful if we can enable the person to whom we are speaking not only to hear the gospel but also to see it as well. This may be accomplished by the use of illustrations, that is, the employment of concrete objects in action situations. Examples of such illustrations are the following:

1. The transference of the "book of our sins" from the hand representing self to the hand representing Christ and the subsequent falling of the wrath of God upon that sin. This is used to illustrate what Christ has done for us.
2. The chair illustration in which you illustrate the transference of our trust from what we have done, indicated by the chair in which we are then sitting, to what Christ has done for us, visualized by another chair in the room, to which we transfer our weight. This is an illustration of saving faith.
3. The motive for living a godly life. In this illustration a pen or small vase or other object from the person's table may be used to represent the gift of eternal life. This illustrates that one's efforts to do good works are done out of gratitude for the gift received rather than in an effort to obtain it. This illustration is placed at the very end of the presentation in order to fit good works into their proper place since everyone knows that good works have something to do with Christianity. It is important that we put them in their proper place or else the person will put them in an improper place.

In using an all-visual illustration it is important for the witness to fix his own eyes on the object which he is using rather than to look at the person to whom he is speaking. This will call the listener's attention to the illustration and enable him to properly understand it.

He offers heaven as a gift. Making this statement just once does not deal with the point. Every religion in the world teaches that man must earn the favor of God by doing something. He must qualify himself. He must make himself worthy of God's gifts. In contrast, Christianity proclaims that God's favor, his blessings, and heaven itself can be had only as free gifts. You cannot obliterate the non-Christian concept of making yourself worthy of God's favor by saying the contrary statement only once. Say it numerous times in different ways! "Heaven is free! Eternal life is God's gift to you. His favor is given graciously. You do not—you cannot—earn your way to heaven. Never can you deserve to dwell with the holy, sin-hating One." After all this, *maybe* he will understand—maybe he won't. Pray that God graciously will open the ears of your prospect and give him understanding!

The meaning of grace. Everyone seemingly has heard of "grace." Perhaps it is the most frequently used concept in Christian circles. Tragically, however, few can tell you what grace means. The non-Christian adage, "God helps those who help themselves," is deeply embedded in the American mind. Because our ancestors dug and clawed a nation out of the wilderness, the American traditionally wants to stand on his own two feet. He feels he must carry his share of the load, all of which is commendable. However, if this spirit carries over into an understanding of grace it can be eternally fatal.

God has revealed himself as "the Help of the helpless." So long as a person thinks he must contribute his own efforts to the work of God, he does not understand his true condition or the work of Christ. He does not realize that sin has incapacitated him so that he cannot do anything meritorious in God's sight. Neither does he know the sufficiency of Christ's sacrifice. By adding his supposed goodness to the work of our Lord he says he believes Christ's work to be insufficient.

Paul's teaching in Romans 11:6 is that grace and works are mutually exclusive. "If by grace, then is it no more of works: otherwise grace is not more grace. But if it be of works, then is it no more grace: otherwise work is no more work." This must be communicated to your prospect if he is to make a good profession. For salvation your prospect may be trusting wholly in Christ, wholly in self, or partially in Christ and partially in self. Many unsaved who are related to the church fall into the latter category. However, that position is essentially the same as trusting fully in self. "Assuming that Christ has done his part sufficiently, if I am to be saved I must do my part acceptably. If, on the other hand, I am lost, it must be because I did not do enough to win God's favor." Thus is the logic of partial trust in Christ and partial trust in self. As one has said, "Grace is not the thread of gold decorating the garment, rather, like the ancient mercy seat, it is gold, pure gold through and through."

The meaning of faith. This, too, is crucial, for this is the point of personal appropriation of eternal life. John Calvin said that the Roman Catholic church taught him the deity of Christ, the Trinity, the atonement; but the one thing the church did not teach him was how to appropriate the atonement for himself. Even today there are those who know all of the doctrines of the faith but they don't know how to get eternal life for themselves. Their problem: an inadequate or false concept of saving faith.

Theologians have rightly pointed out that there are three elements to saving faith: knowledge, assent, and trust. We may know about something without giving assent to it. For example, one cult teaches that Christ is incarnate today in a man in India. I know about this but I do not assent to it. Similarly, one may have a knowledge that the Bible teaches that man is a sinner who cannot save himself, without assenting to the truth of this statement. Thus to knowledge must be added assent to the facts of our historic faith. However, one can know about, and assent to, many historical facts without trusting them. We know about Alexander the Great and assent to the historical record concerning his conquests. Further, we assent to the fact that he was a military genius. However, I hope no one is trusting Alexander to do anything for him! That would be rather ludicrous. Added to knowledge and assent is what Luther termed *"fiducia"*: trust.

As you present the gospel, keeping the note of "What are you trusting in for salvation?" you can effectively illustrate the meaning of saving faith with the use of an empty chair. Let that chair represent the Lord Jesus. Your prospect knows it is a chair. He believes (assents) that the chair will hold him off the floor, provide comfort to his body, and relax his weary spirit. But it's not doing any of these things for one obvious reason: he's not sitting in it. Neither is that chair of any benefit to you for the same reason. Now the chair in which you are sitting can represent all you once trusted for eternal life. Point out that this is inadequate to your needs and when God shakes the world in the final judgment it will drop you into hell.

By actually moving from the "chair of your own good works" to the "chair of Jesus Christ" you visually and verbally illustrate the meaning of trusting Christ alone for salvation. Just as you no longer are in "the chair of your good works" but in "the chair of Jesus Christ," so you have transferred your trust for eternal life from yourself to the Lord.

A more subtle substitute for saving faith is trusting the Lord for temporal well-being while trusting self for eternal life. Some have difficulty making this distinction, but the distinction is necessary. It spells the difference between weal and woe eternally.

Let us consider Luther. Before his conversion he was not an agnostic, skeptic, or atheist. He believed in God. While in the monastery he undoubtedly trusted God for many things. When he made the pilgrimage to Rome, did he not trust the Lord for safety, lodging and meals, and health? Certainly! Similarly, John Wesley trusted the Lord to take him safely from England to his mission post in the New World. All the while these men were trusting themselves for a successful journey from earth to heaven! They knew about, and trusted in, "transportation by faith" long before they knew and trusted "justification by faith."

You can use "the chair of Jesus Christ" to illustrate the concept of trusting him for *temporal matters.* As you restate your prospect was trusting God for health, you can place glasses or a pen on "the chair of Jesus Christ." Trusting him for travel mercies can be represented by a key ring. A billfold will indicate trust in God for financial needs. All the while the prospect himself is still sitting in "the chair of his own good works." He is still trusting himself for the eternal well-being of his soul.

III. THE COMMITMENT

A. The qualifying question: "Does this make sense to you?" Many people are afraid to ask for a commitment when they finish presenting the gospel because they do not know whether they have brought the person with them or have lost him somewhere along the way. The qualifying question which is "Does this make sense to you?" will elicit a response which is either positive or negative. A positive response will be something of this sort: "Oh, yes, that is wonderful! Why didn't I hear it before?" etc. A negative response will be something like: "Well, that is very complicated. I will have to give this a lot of thought. I'm not sure . . ."

What to do: If the response is positive you know that the person is with you and you are ready to ask the commitment question. If the response is uncertain then go back to the beginning and quickly review the main points of the gospel, asking as you go, "Do you understand this point, 'Man is a sinner'?" etc.

B. The commitment question: "Would you like to receive the gift of eternal life which Christ is offering to you?" It is important to know exactly how you are going to ask for the commitment and even what words you are going to use. For the inexperienced, this is a tense moment and the commitment question should be thoroughly learned. This will help the novice through his anxiety.

This question is chosen for two reasons:

1. By it you are coming out of the gospel at the same place that you went in. That is, you began your presentation by asking the person if he would like for you to share with him how he could have eternal life. Having done that, and having ascertained that he has understood, you are now asking him if he would like to receive this eternal life.

2. You are asking for your initial commitment at the most positive point possible. "Would you like to receive the free gift of eternal life?" This is obviously a better place to begin than some such question as, "Would you like to crucify your old nature?"

C. The clarification of the commitment. One danger at the point of closing is that the novice fears to ask for a commitment. Therefore, to overcome that hesitancy to close, we have endeavored to make this as simple and as pleasant as possible.

However, another danger at the point of closing is a premature commitment—a commitment which is not based on a thorough understanding of what is involved in accepting Christ as Savior and Lord. Therefore, at this point we recommend clarification. This would involve essentially the questions found in the commitment section of the presentation. These questions involve an elaboration of the meaning of faith.

The emphasis to be given at this point will depend upon the attitude of the person to whom you are speaking. If he is evidently repentant and moved, perhaps even to tears (as occasionally has been the case), then this need not be belabored. If, however, the person seems to be thinking that he just might get in on a good deal without its affecting his life, then the aspect of repentance and the lordship of Christ should be heavily emphasized.

REPENTANCE AND CHURCH PARTICIPATION. In the paragraph about repentance they are asked if they are willing now to become a responsible member of God's forever family, the Church. This is inserted to help bridge the gap between the witnessing situation and active participation in the body of Christ. The person should be made to understand that repentance involves a new way of life and it involves following and serving Christ in his Church.

D. The prayer of commitment. Many have been lost at this point because of the way in which they were asked to pray. It is especially true of adults and older people who have perhaps been in church for many years and should know how to pray, but have never prayed audibly in their lives. They are horrified at the thought of having to pray spontaneously in front of a stranger. Therefore, in asking them to pray, I have found the wording very helpful (note especially the pronouns):

Well, Rene, if this is really what *you* want, *we* can go to the Lord in prayer right where we are. *I* can lead *us* in prayer and *we* will tell him what you have told me just now—that you want Christ to come into your heart to be your Savior and Lord and you want to repent of your sins and receive the gift of eternal life. Is this really what you want, Rene?

Yes, it is.

All right, then, let us bow our heads in prayer.

In the prayer itself I recommend three parts which are helpful:

1. Pray for him: that God would give him faith and repentance.
2. Pray with him: in the actual commitment almost any statement from the gospel outline is appropriate here, allowing him to repeat it after you.
3. Pray for him: that the Holy Spirit will grant him assurance. Give the Spirit of God some time to seal these things to his heart (an example of such prayer is at the end of the longer presentation).

E. The assurance of salvation. At this point it is important to point him to the promises of God and to help him take hold of them by faith. A very simple and forthright promise which we almost always use is John 6:47. After the prayer the witness might say something like this:

Rene, that was the most important prayer that you ever prayed and the most important decision that you have ever made. I would like to show you what Christ has to say about what you have just done. (Open your New Testament and let her read aloud John 6:47. After she reads it, say:)

Hold that place for a moment and let us analyze that carefully. It is Christ the Son of God, the King of the Kingdom, who is speaking. He says, "Truthfully, truthfully, I say unto you, he that believeth on me"—and we have shown that this is not merely an intellectual assent (you have had that all your life)—but "he that trusteth in me alone for salvation, he that resteth upon me for eternal life, hath" (that is Old English for "has")—"a present possession—eternal life." By the way, eternal life in the Bible always means "in heaven." (Some people think that eternal life merely means a continued existence somewhere, somehow.)

Now, Rene, you just told Christ in your prayer that you trust him alone for your salvation. As best you know your heart, Rene, did you really mean that?

Yes.

Well, Rene, do you believe that Jesus Christ meant what he said in this promise you just read?

I do.

Then let me ask you this question: If you died tonight in your sleep—and you just might!—where would you wake up?

In heaven.

Who said so?

Jesus Christ.

(Reaching over and shaking her hand . . .) If you really meant in your heart what you just said in that prayer, then you have the promise of Jesus Christ that your sins are forgiven, he has adopted you into his family, and has given you eternal life. (The "if" clause is inserted here in order not to give a person a false assurance. We are saved by *trusting* in Jesus Christ, not by *saying* that we trust in Jesus Christ.) Let me welcome you, Rene, to the family of God.

FOUR THE PROPER USE OF TESTIMONY

A TOOL FOR EVANGELISM

If a Christian is to be an effective witness for his Savior, the first tool he needs is a clear, forceful personal testimony. If you have met God in Jesus Christ in your own life, you have found God working according to his promises. Your experience of God's faithfulness is the substance of your testimony. As you prepare your testimony, realize you are fashioning an evangelistic tool so you will be a more proficient witness.

Some Christians give admirable testimonies—testimonies with zip and life—testimonies devoid of rough spots and trite platitudes. However, others stumble and bumble in a disorganized, uninteresting, ineffectual manner. We must sharpen our tools and learn to use them effectively.

Scripture says, "This is the record, that God has given us eternal life and this life is in his Son. He that hath the Son hath life" (1 John 5:11, 12). Eternal life is received by trusting Jesus Christ. We are dealing now with the proper use of personal testimony as an evangelistic tool. Throughout this section we use the phrase "eternal life" as equivalent to "trusting Christ" or "becoming a Christian." If you use the name of Christ repeatedly in your testimony you will find that often it programs your prospect so that his answer to the second diagnostic question does not truly reflect his own relationship to Christ. The word "Christian" is such a highly connotative word that using it in the testimony can also generate difficulties.

Giving a personal testimony is the first aspect of witnessing—simply telling what eternal life has meant to you. When Jesus healed the demoniac in Gadara, he said, "Go home to thy friends, and tell them how great things the Lord hath done for thee, and hath had compassion on thee." Now, if you cannot tell someone that Christ has saved you, you are not an evangelist; you are an evangelistic field and you need an evangelist to lead you to conversion.

This is not to say that you must know when you were converted. However, you must know if you have been converted. Many people don't know when they became Christians. One of the great preachers of our generation, Dr. Peter Eldersveld, said that he could remember clearly when he was three years old, and he knew that at that time he trusted in the blood of Jesus Christ alone for his salvation. He was well taught by his parents, and came to a very early faith and could remember nothing else.

In order to witness for Christ you must have the assurance that you have eternal life and that Christ Jesus is your Savior.

Three times in the Book of Acts, Paul gives his personal testimony. If we study these accounts we will discover that the three essential elements are:

1. What I was before I received eternal life.
2. How I received eternal life.
3. What eternal life has meant to me.

A. A POSITIVE EMPHASIS

EMPHASIZE THE POSITIVE

One of the common errors in giving a testimony is to belabor the first point and minimize the third. Just the opposite should be our method. You do not help the people by giving them a tedious life history. They have no particular interest in where you attended school, where your parents live, or when you moved from here to there. Rather, do as Jesus commanded the demoniac: "Go . . . and tell how great things the Lord hath done for thee." Emphasize the positive benefits.

I remember one Christian who accompanied me on an evangelistic call. In response to my request that he give a testimony, he said, "When I accepted Christ, I lost all my friends. They wouldn't have anything to do with me. Then I lost my job. You know, all the people who do worldly things (and he mentioned half a dozen things that evidently thrilled the people we were visiting) give you up when you give up these worldly practices." It was as if he had given a five-minute discourse on why one should not become a Christian! Suppose you saw a cigarette ad that showed an emaciated man, his countenance manifesting excruciating pain, and he said to you, "Smoke my brand of cigarettes. It will help you develop cancer more quickly. You can have less wind if you join us. And your hair will smell worse!" Such an ad would not convince you to buy that brand! It seems that many Christians are about that effective when they tell why a person ought to become a Christian. Emphasize the positive benefits of having eternal life.

Let us now consider the parts of a testimony and see how each can be made meaningful to others.

WHAT I WAS BEFORE

Here you either encourage people to "tune you out" or sit up and listen carefully to what you are saying. At this point you are making an effort to identify with your prospect, and have him identify with you. As has been said earlier, the use of personal testimony helps to preclude the objection raised when the prospect is asked questions about his spiritual life that are "personal."

IDENTIFY WITH YOUR PROSPECT

In the conversation concerning his secular life and church background, you have gained enough insight to determine whether your prospect is self-righteous, a libertine, an agnostic, indifferent, etc. In telling him what you were before Christ, select truthful statements about yourself that will enable him to see himself in your life. For example, you discover your prospect to be a self-righteous intellectual who is caring for his elderly parents. You would make a fatal mistake by saying, "My parents did not do right by me. They did not give me any religious instruction, and their reprobate lives led me to become a wretched character. I embezzled my employer's funds and was unfaithful to my wife. Then I met Christ." Your prospect would think, "Good, you needed him, but I don't!" And he would start watching his silverware in case you had a spiritual relapse.

How much better to say to your pharisaical philosopher: "I never gave any thought to the reason I was here in the world until one day such and such happened. Oh, I knew there was a heaven, but I never gave much thought about how I could get there." It does no good to tell a very righteous person what a great criminal you were; instead, tell him just the aspects of your life that were similar to the life of your prospect. You thereby let him know that you were the same as he is. Then when you tell him you found something very vital that was missing from your life, he will sense something is lacking in his life. If we give a strong statement of our certainty of eternal life and the fantastic value of that assurance, this will act as a logical stepping stone into the first diagnostic question.

DO NOT GIVE ANSWERS BEFORE YOU ASK THE QUESTIONS

As we present the gospel, it should have certain elements of mystery. You confront the prospect with a problem in a manner that identifies him with the problem. As you let him see and feel the problem, the suspense mounts and he gets into the problem; then you solve the problem by presenting Christ in the gospel. However, you do not want to give any answers to questions you will ask later.

Suppose you were witnessing to John, and Barbara is your companion on the visit. Before you establish what John is trusting for his salvation, you ask Barbara to give her testimony. She says, "The pastor came to see me and asked me why I thought I should go to heaven. I didn't know I needed to trust only in Christ, so I told him I hoped I was good enough to get in. I went to church every Sunday, and helped needy people at Christmas, and never intentionally hurt anyone. But the pastor told me I could never get to heaven that way because I was a sinner and needed the cleansing blood of Jesus Christ. So I stopped trusting what I was doing, and started trusting Christ's work on the cross for me."

Now you turn to John and ask, "John, what are you trusting for eternal life?" His certain reply will be, "I am trusting in the blood of Christ." He may not have the slightest idea about why Christ's blood avails for anything, or what is involved in the act of trusting him for salvation. He is just parroting the "right answer" he heard Barbara give in her testimony.

If the testimony is used during the "introduction of the gospel" (see outline), speak in general terms as you tell how you received eternal life. That is, tell what your life was like before and then say something like this: "And then I received eternal life and everything was changed." Then go on to tell of the changes in your life. It will be noted that you have not told them anything about how you received eternal life or that it was a gift received by faith.

If, however, the testimony is all you have time for, you must make especially clear just how you passed from death unto life.

CAN'T REMEMBER WHEN OR HOW

There are some Christians who have no recollection of when or how they became Christians. They received Christ at such an early age that they do not remember ever not being a Christian. How shall these people give a testimony?

Whether they remember it or not, we know how they became Christians. They came to understand that they were sinners in the sight of God. They came to realize that God loved them and Christ died for their sins. They came to trust in him for their salvation and to receive him as Lord and Master of their lives. How do we know that that is the way that they became Christians? Because that is the only way that anyone becomes a Christian. Whether this happens in an emotionally packed hour in an evangelistic crusade, or whether it happens gradually when the person is two, three, four, or five years old, every Christian has come to understand those things and to trust in Jesus Christ.

The important things, however, to emphasize for anyone, are the benefits that eternal life has brought to us. This is especially important for the person who was reared in a Christian home and church and whose life-style has not drastically changed. However, his internal feelings, purposes, and motives have been changed by Christ, and these things should be emphasized in his testimony.

A Christian who has backslidden drastically and then returned to a closer fellowship with Christ need not include this in a testimony of this type, since the introduction of this whole new area will only serve to confuse the person to whom you are speaking.

Sometimes laymen like to use the testimony of their pastor to get into the gospel. This can be helpful if the prospect has come to the church and heard him preach. It might be introduced with such words as, "Did you ever happen to hear how our pastor got into the ministry?"

"Yes" testimony. A trainer gives his or her testimony before presenting the gospel. The concluding line is something like, "And I am very certain that if I died tonight in my sleep I would awaken in heaven." Then the trainer turns to the trainees on the team and asks, "John and Mary, do you know for certain if you died tonight you would go to heaven?" The trainees smile and enthusiastically say, "Yes!" This is what we call a "Yes" testimony.

There are two specific benefits to the "Yes" testimony. (1) It helps shy, reluctant trainees to break the sound barrier. (2) It reinforces the testimony of the trainer and thus increases the credibility of what he has said and what he will say in presenting the gospel.

The "Yes" testimony is especially helpful early in the training semester.

Lower resistance. You should always personalize your presentation of the gospel, but this is especially important if you sense the prospect is becoming resistant or hostile. People will argue doctrine till the blood runs. But they cannot argue your personal experience.

To encourage commitment. Sometimes it is especially helpful to bring a positive word of personal testimony into the presentation prior to the qualifying question. If the prospect appears timid or fearful, this may encourage him to give a positive response.

B. MOTIVES FOR RECEIVING ETERNAL LIFE

WHAT ETERNAL LIFE HAS MEANT TO ME

Here you must not generalize or you will lose your audience. To be effective, you must be specific. You can say, "It is wonderful!" What exactly is wonderful? Or you may say, "I have peace." Exactly what do you mean? In what way do you have peace? Be specific—make your testimony concrete.

BE SPECIFIC

"It is wonderful to know when I lay my head on my pillow tonight that if I do not awaken in bed in the morning, I will awaken in paradise with God."

"I had a Christian son killed in Vietnam, yet my heart is filled with peace because I know he has eternal life. Even though he was killed by an enemy mortar, he has a home now in heaven, and one day we'll be reunited there."

People remember specifics. They forget generalities. What are some points we might make in sharing what eternal life means to us?

FELLOWSHIP

He provides us with Christian fellowship and friends. Why do unsaved people attend church? The answer: friendliness. Friendliness is significant to people because they are lonely. A basic human need is that of friendship. When people hear that God creates a fellowship, they find this meaningful.

LOVE

He fills us with his love. Our homes in America have every luxury conceivable. However, many lack the essential ingredient of love. Strife and jealousy lurk in gadget-filled rooms, and many marriages are little better than an armed truce. People long to be loved. A testimony to the love that God brings into a life and a home may awaken your prospect to a need that has not been met for years.

FORGIVENESS

He forgives us and relieves us of our sense of guilt. A major problem with which people are unable to cope is guilt. Guilt fills our psychiatric hospitals, for it fractures the human personality. It causes anxiety and depression. It creates havoc in the human heart. The greatest picture of relief from guilt is in Bunyan's allegory. As Christian kneels at the cross, the burden of guilt falls off and rolls into the empty tomb, never to be seen again. The burden of guilt is lifted at Calvary.

A FRIEND IN MY TROUBLE

Christ is himself a Friend to lean upon in trouble. He imparts strength to the discouraged, the worn down, and the defeated. It has been charged that Christ is a crutch. How do you answer that? "That's fine. I'm a cripple. I need a crutch."

ADOPTION

He adopts us into his family. "He sets the solitary in families." God becomes our Father and we become brothers and sisters in Christ. Frequently we can say to a person who has just accepted Christ, "Welcome into the family of God. I have just discovered something. We are related. You and I are brothers and sisters, and we are members of the greatest family on earth: God's family."

NEW PERSPECTIVES

He gives a whole new perspective on life. One of the most devastating questions you can ask anybody is "What are you living for?" Most people have no idea. When one becomes a Christian, all this is changed. We are given a clarity and perspective unknowable by the non-Christian. The enigmas of the universe, the questions that perplex people begin to fall into place, and we begin to see the puzzle of life more clearly.

FREEDOM FROM FEAR

He delivers from the fears of living and dying. Many people are fearful. Some will say they are not afraid of hell. But they are afraid to take the garbage out at night.

C. WRITE IT OUT FIRST

In the light of the preceding discussion, you will find it profitable to write out your own testimony. As you prepare your testimony bear the following in mind:

1. Avoid clichés that are meaningless to the non-Christian.

These jangle unbelieving ears. For example: "Receive Christ and you'll receive a blessing." This is so common to us, but the non-Christian will cringe at the thought of receiving a blessing. What is it to receive a blessing? How does it come? by mail? or does it fall from the sky? We must always distinguish the *connotation* from the *denotation* of a word. The denotation is what the word actually means according to Webster or a theological dictionary. For example, the word "evangelism" is undoubtedly, by derivation, one of the most beautiful words in our language. It comes from the word "evangel"; in turn it comes from "good angel," and it is the glad tidings. Nothing could be more beautiful.

However, what does evangelism *connote* to some people? It stirs up images of Elmer Gantry and people on the street corners beating drums and shouting, and doing all sorts of unpleasant things. The connotations of the word are the barnacles it picks up as it sails the sea of life.

2. Avoid giving a travelogue dealing with externals and missing the spiritual matters.
3. Avoid vague generalities that are meaningless.
4. Avoid answering questions you intend to ask later. Don't give away the mystery.
5. Avoid a frivolous attitude toward the gospel.
6. Use humor constructively. If the situation becomes tense, you can relieve the prospect's rage by saying something funny.
7. Identify with your prospect.
8. Use direct and indirect quotations to arouse interest.
9. Speak pictorially. "I was in bed, and the gospel came on the clock radio. Fortunately it was out of my reach, so I couldn't just roll over and turn it off. I got out of bed and just about the time I got to the radio . . ." Here is a situation that people can visualize. If they are not seeing in their minds the thing you are talking about, they are probably seeing something that they are thinking about, rather than listening to you.

SHARPEN YOUR TOOLS

Now you can shape, sharpen, smooth, and perfect your personal testimony, and fulfill the admonition of the Apostle Peter: *"Be ready always to give an answer to every man that asketh you a reason of the hope that is in you"* (1 Peter 3:15). Go over your testimony and get rid of the rough spots. Eliminate the trite saying. Get zip and life into it, and then ask God to help you use it. In three minutes you should be able to effectively tell what you were before receiving eternal life, how you receive it, and what it has meant in your life.

FIVE
HANDLING OBJECTIONS

When you present the gospel, the arch foe will have his workmen doing their best to block your presentation. Fears and doubts will arise in your own heart and your prospect will raise objections. Earlier we have discussed how we handle our fears. In this chapter we will discuss what we do when an objection is raised.

A. BASIC ATTITUDES IN HANDLING OBJECTIONS

1. AVOID ARGUMENT

Our natural tendency is either to meet an objection head-on and beat it down, or to run. This tendency must be overcome for the sake of your prospect's eternal welfare. Negatively, we say: never argue.

Often it has been said that the only way to win an argument is to avoid it, and the best way to avoid it is to preclude it. That is, anticipate it and lead your prospect to agree with the Scriptures before he can raise the objection. Any skillful debater can easily win a point in an argument, but by doing so you can arouse hostilities in the prospect that will cause you to lose your "fish."

2. SHOW POSITIVE ATTITUDE

On the positive side you may meet every objection with: "I'm glad you said that!" You ought to be glad that your prospect has enough freedom to express his inner feelings to you. As you deal with his objections, you clear away the props which have deluded him into a presumptuous sense of security. You are glad when he shows he is listening and assimilating what you are presenting.

3. USE SINCERE COMPLIMENT

If the person to whom you are speaking begins to become hostile or irritated, a sincere compliment can be very effective in reducing tensions. The following is an example: "You know, John, you are an intelligent person and obviously well read, and it's a real pleasure to discuss these things with someone as interested in spiritual matters as you are." Such a comment will end many arguments before they get started.

B. BASIC METHODS OF HANDLING OBJECTIONS

1. PRECLUDE OBJECTIONS

We have already seen in our previous discussion of the introduction and gospel that the skillful handling of material can preclude many common objections. This skill combined with a gracious and loving attitude can do much to prevent a presentation from degenerating into an argument.

2. POSTPONE

If an objection is raised you must decide whether it is essential to answer it before you can continue, or whether this objection is extraneous to the gospel and can be dealt with later, or not at all.

For example, if you ask him if he knows that he is going to heaven, and he replies that he does not believe in heaven, you obviously cannot continue without dealing with his objection. On the other hand, if he raises the question of the heathen in Africa, this is obviously a matter which can be put off in the following way: "That's an interesting question, and I would love to discuss it with you. If you don't mind, would you hold it in abeyance until we finish what we're talking about, and if you will bring it up then, we can take a look at it together."

In this way you do not have to spend a lot of time answering extraneous objections; you also discourage his bringing up other nonessential matters, and since you have left the responsibility of bringing it up again with him, if he does not do so you need not answer it at all.

3. ANSWER QUICKLY

If his objection deals with an essential aspect of the gospel and you would not be able to continue without responding to it, then answer it as quickly as possible and return to your presentation.

Outline: servant, not master. However, you need not be a slave to the outline. You may show wisdom if you take up the matter "out of place." Often what is out of place in the printed presentation can be "in place" in the living situation.

Most often, however, your prospect will introduce matters on which you have not planned to talk. Suppose you are in the middle of the story of John Wesley's conversion and your prospect says, "I don't see why there have to be so many divisions in the church. Wesley started the Methodist Church which broke off from the Anglicans. And you're not a Methodist. Why can't you all get together?"

Don't panic. First, don't panic! Obviously this matter is extraneous; neither a discussion of church history and denominational origins, nor a discourse on the modern ecumenical movement would be of any value at this point. It is also obvious that you have lost your prospect's interest. Now you need to do two things. First, you need to get back on the track, and then you need to recapitulate so that your prospect may pick up your train of thought which he had lost. One approach might be:

Avoidance. "I'm glad you asked that, for I can see it is something that would hinder your understanding of just what saving faith really is. I don't want to mislead you as to what the key is that opens heaven's door. Now we've seen that neither intellectual assent nor temporal faith will open that door. You must trust the living Lord to do something for you. Just as Wesley had a certain kind of faith, he recognized that it was not saving faith. He wrote in his journal . . ." (continue presentation).

In this manner you turn the conversation away from the extraneous matter and refresh his memory of what you were talking about before his mind wanders from your point. Pascal, the famous French mathematician, philosopher, and theologian stated an important principle which I have tried to apply in my life. He said, "In essentials, unity; in nonessentials, liberty; and in all things, charity or love."

Return the conversation to the presentation at the point where you left it. "I suppose just because we're human we will always have differences of opinion. It's interesting, though, that I can quote the founders of other denominations in presenting the gospel to you. The mainstream of the Christian church has been united for 2,000 years on the matters we've been discussing, such as man's sinfulness, God's holiness, and Christ's deity. We don't want nonessentials to cause you to reach heaven's door without the right key to open it, do we? For years Wesley thought he had the key to heaven. But it wasn't until after he worshiped in Aldersgate Street Chapel that he could write . . ."

4. RESEARCH AND RETURN

Many Christians are very concerned that their witness will be completely ineffective if the person asks them any question which they cannot answer. This is, of course, not true. If the witness does not know the answer to a question he can simply say: "That's a very interesting question and I would like to know the answer to it myself. If you really want to know, I'll find out and get back to you with the answer. In the meantime, let's get back to the point which we were discussing . . ."

At this point it is important that the Christian realize exactly what he is and is not called to be. He is not called to be the judge or the jury and pass sentence upon the person whom he is visiting. He is not called to be the prosecuting attorney or even the defense lawyer. God is the judge and jury, Satan is the prosecuting attorney, and the Lord Jesus Christ is the advocate. He is not even called upon to be an expert witness. A minister would qualify as such, but not a layman. He is called simply to be a witness. That means that he has seen or experienced something about which he has firsthand knowledge, and his character demonstrates that these experiences are credible or believable.

If a person witnessed a shooting on a street corner, the fact that he knew little about guns, about their manufacture, caliber, velocity, or range would in no way impair his testimony that he saw someone shoot and kill another person. If however, a ballistics expert who would qualify as a technical witness demonstrated the same ignorance about the caliber, range, and muzzle velocity of the weapon, he would not only ruin his testimony, he would probably lose his job. You remember the man in the Scriptures who was born blind and healed by Christ. The Pharisees tried to make him into an expert witness. He refused by saying, "I don't know about that, but this one thing I know, whereas I was blind, now I see" (John 9:25).

C. ANSWERS TO COMMON OBJECTIONS

THE HEATHEN

Another extraneous matter that is commonly introduced is the question of the heathen. If your prospect becomes uncomfortable as you talk about "the heathen" in his living room, he will likely try to start you talking about the heathen in India, Africa, or New Guinea. Needless to say, such a tactic should never divert the evangelist from his objective. The woman at the well tried to change the subject when Jesus got close to her personal needs. He brought her back quickly by saying in effect, "What we are doing here now is of much greater urgency than settling a theological debate." This is "Pandora's Box." We dare not open it or we may never be able to share the gospel.

In handling this matter you need to focus your concern on the individual you are witnessing to. "Bob," you might say, "that's a good question, but I believe we can safely leave the heathen in Africa in the hands of a God who is infinitely just and infinitely merciful. Tonight I want *you* to know for certain that *you* have eternal life. The Bible says you can know that you have eternal life, and you have told me that you aren't sure what would happen if you died tonight. Let's confine our discussion to what God has said about you and your eternal welfare. Perhaps later we can see all he has said about those who never hear the gospel."

I have found that this almost always satisfies the person who raises this objection and precludes a very difficult theological discussion which is going to be very unsatisfying to the unregenerate mind.

If, however, after making a profession he still raises the question of the heathen, you might want to answer it in the following way, perhaps drawing for him the following diagram to help him in his understanding. The problem revolves around the question: "Would God send the heathen to hell for simply not believing in a Christ that they never heard of?"

The answer to the question *stated in this form* is, "No." This is not to say that they will not go to hell, but it is to say that this is *not the reason.* They are indeed lost and on their way to eternal perdition, which of course, is a basic motive for the entire Christian missionary enterprise.

The *argumentum ad absurdum* (argument to absurdity) is applicable here. If every one who did not hear of Christ went to heaven, then I have a far more effective plan for world evangelization than any heretofore devised. Simply close all the churches, fire all the ministers, burn all the Bibles, and all other religious literature, and in a few generations no one will have heard of Christ and everyone will go to heaven! Obviously this is absurd.

Instead of moving into the future, the same argument can be used about the past.

And if we go back to the day before Christ died, practically no one had heard of him, and therefore everyone was on his way to heaven, and therefore Jesus came into the world and succeeded in getting a great many millions of people lost. This, too, is an absurdity. Christ did not come to condemn, but to save those who were already condemned. Men are condemned for only one thing—their sins. To hear of Christ and to reject him is indeed the most heinous sin a man can commit but it is, nevertheless, but one of thousands of sins which he has committed.

The fallacy of the argument rests in this: that no one is truly ignorant of God or of his will for his life. The Scripture declares that God has revealed himself to all men in at least one of the following three ways (see accompanying illustration):

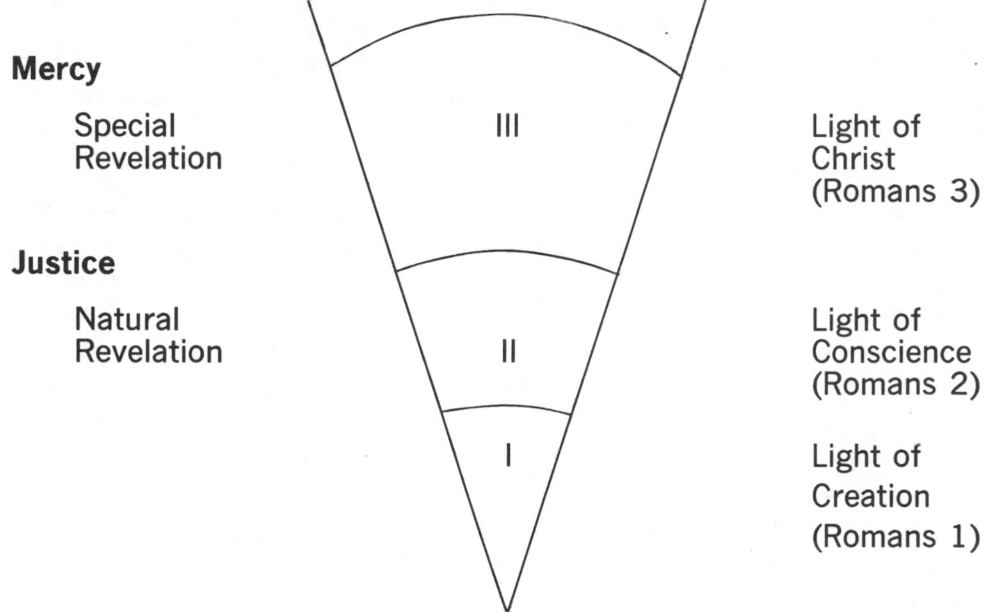

All men receive either justice or mercy. If they receive Christ they receive mercy. If not, they receive justice. Justice means that men get precisely what they deserve in light of what they have done, based on what they know. God will be unjust with no one.

1. The light of creation. God has revealed himself to all mankind in the light of his creation. The psalmist said, "The heavens declare the glory of God; and the firmament sheweth his handiwork. Day unto day uttereth speech, and night unto night sheweth knowledge. There is no speech nor language where their voice is not heard" (Psalm 19:1–3). The Apostle Paul said, "Because that which may be known of God is manifest in them; for God hath shewed it unto them. For the invisible things of him from the creation of the world are clearly seen, being understood by the things that are made, even his eternal power and Godhead; so that they are without excuse" (Romans 1:19, 20). Thus we see that the creation of the cosmos bears eloquent testimony to the existence of a Creator, as can be seen by the fact that everywhere, even among the most primitive of tribes, there is found a belief in a god. The only exception to this being in modern times where by sophisticated and ungodly evolutionary arguments men have been taught to pervert the truth and their eyes are blinded to the obvious. "They suppress the truth in unrighteousness."

2. The light of conscience. God has placed within each one of us a "moral monitor" which continually passes judgment upon the rightness or wrongness of our deeds, words, and thoughts. The Apostle Paul describes this thusly: "Which shew the work of the law written in their hearts, their conscience also bearing witness, and their thoughts the mean while accusing or else excusing one another; in the day when God shall judge the secrets of men by Jesus Christ according to my gospel" (Romans 2:15,16).

By repeatedly ignoring the still small voice of conscience, a man's heart may be hardened in sin and his conscience seared as with a hot iron, but he is nevertheless guilty for each of these acts of sin that brought him into that condition.

That man has such a conscience and is not altogether devoid of a sense of right and wrong, and thus cannot plead ignorance at the Judgment, is witnessed by two obvious facts:

a. Everywhere throughout the world men condemn one another for doing wrong and thus remove any possibility of saying at the Judgment, "I did not know that it was wrong." The Apostle Paul speaks eloquently of this: "Therefore, thou art inexcusable, O man, whosoever thou art that judgest: for wherein thou judgest another, thou condemnest thyself; for thou that judgest doest the same things. But we are sure that the judgment of God is according to truth against them which commit such things. And thinkest thou this, O man, that judgest them which do such things, and doest the same, that thou shalt escape the judgment of God?" (Romans 2:1–3).

b. Everywhere men commit sins under the cover of darkness. They may be so hardened as to commit cannibalism at lunch, but they steal chickens at night.

3. The light of Christ (see Revelation, page 84.) What are some other common objections that arise? What are some ways in which we handle them?

THE MOST COMMON OBJECTION

Quite often we will get to the point of explaining what saving faith truly is and the prospect will say something like, "That's what I said I was trusting in when you asked me." Obviously, you can't grab him by the lapels and cry, "Liar!"

This objection comes up so often that we must take special care to get an answer to the question: "Suppose that you were to die tonight and stand before God and he were to say to you, 'Why should I let you into my heaven?' what would you say?" Not only must we get an answer, we must also understand the answer and get our prospect to agree that we understand what he is saying. There is no harm, after getting the answer to the question, in saying, "Now let me see if I understand you. You're saying . . ." Then rephrase what he has just said. He will either acknowledge or deny that your understanding is correct.

This is particularly important when the prospect has been quite religious but has not understood the gospel. This type of person is the type most likely to deny that he had given the wrong answer.

If you have sufficiently clarified the answer to "the question," your prospect is unlikely to reverse himself at the end and say, "Oh, I've always trusted in Christ for salvation!"

Grant what he has believed. If, in spite of all your efforts, you come to the end of the presentation and he still says, "Oh, I have always believed that," the following answer is recommended:

"I know that you have always believed in God and in Christ as his divine Son—that he was born of a virgin and died on the cross and rose again from the dead—and I'm sure that you have even trusted in him for many temporal needs in your life, such as sickness, travel, etc. But when it came right down to what you were trusting in for your hope of eternal life, like myself and so many people, you were trusting in your own efforts to try to be good enough.

"Do you remember what you told me? You said, 'I try to follow the Golden Rule and keep the Ten Commandments and do the best I can.' Don't you think that it would be a good idea to place your trust for eternal salvation in this One in whom you have always intellectually believed and also trusted for many temporal things?"

What you have done in this answer is to give him credit for everything that he has believed: for his intellectual assent to the historic facts of the gospel, and for his temporal faith. The reason that this is important is because he may think that you are denying that he has ever believed in God or believed in Christ, even intellectually, or that he has ever trusted in him for anything. And this confusion will lead to hostility on his part if he thinks you are denying that he believes these things. Therefore, you give him credit for everything which he has believed, but point out that the one crucial thing which is needful for his salvation he has not done, namely, to place his trust in Christ for his eternal salvation.

GOD ISN'T LIKE THAT

Another frequent objection is raised at the point of God's holiness and justice. "God isn't like that! He would never punish anyone." We need to realize that the biblical teaching of the just God "who will by no means clear the guilty" is unpopular even in many so-called Christian circles today.

To deal effectively with this or any other open denial of biblical truth, you must *appeal to authority*. No help comes from saying, "I think you're wrong!" The matters under discussion are beyond what you think or what your prospect thinks. Assuming that he is a rational being of sound intelligence, what he thinks could be as valid as what you think. An external authority must be called upon to settle the matter.

Rationalism. You could proceed by saying, "I'm glad you said that, because you have raised a very important question. It is what is known as the epistemological question. Epistemology is that branch of philosophy which deals with the question: How do we know? How do we know what God is like? or, How do we know what he will do? How can we come to know the truth about God? There are two ways.

"One way is called *rationalism*. We simply sit down like Rodin's Thinker and meditate about God and reach some conclusions about what he is like. The problem with this method is that we do not have sufficient data to form valid conclusions about God. This approach of rationalism has led mankind down some strange and bizarre religious paths.

"We can say, 'I think God is all love and will send no one to hell.' Or, 'I think God is a demon and will send everyone to hell.' Someone else may sit and think about God and conclude, 'I believe God is the sum total of human experience.'

"We could in a similar way reason about the color of eyes that people on Mars may have. You think they're all red eyed. I might conclude they have polka-dot eyes. Your opinion is as good as mine because we have no data on which to base our conclusions. However, if somebody goes to Mars and returns and tells us that they have red, white and blue-striped eyes, then we have good reason for placing our confidence in this person who has been there. His conclusion is based upon facts."

Revelation. "There is another way in which we can come to the knowledge of God. He has come from where he is to where we are, and he has condescended to give us knowledge of himself, his purposes, and his will for us. This method is known as *'revelation.'* For reasons I'll not go into now, the Christian church has held that God did reveal himself through the Scriptures and preeminently in his Son. So now the question is not what either of us thinks; rather, the question is, 'What has God said in the Bible and through his Son Jesus Christ?' "

I DON'T BELIEVE THE BIBLE

Often as you begin presenting the gospel, your prospect will say, "I don't believe the Bible. You'll have to convince me some other way than referring to the Scriptures." Many laymen are devastated by this objection, and their attempt at presenting the gospel fizzles. This need not be the case. Such an objection can be the springboard into the gospel itself. The Apostle Paul, as he preached in the Greek cities, appealed to the Scriptures even though the people listening to him did not believe in the Scriptures. He did not try to convince his audience of the veracity and the authority of the Scriptures. Rather, he proclaimed them, and the Holy Spirit worked and used the proclamation to save some who then came to believe the Bible to be true. In witnessing, our primary function is proclamation, not defense.

The judo technique. This is actually a rather easy objection to deal with. When it comes at the beginning of a presentation of the gospel I would suggest that a person not use the approach of a boxer who would meet the blow head-on and try to overwhelm his opponent with counter punches, but rather that he use the technique of the judo expert wherein the force of his opponent's blow is used to throw him.

The individual who uses this objection is usually a person who has had at least some college education and exposure to some course on the Bible, biblical criticism, or something of this sort. And there is usually an accompanying intellectual pride which says something like this: "I used to believe those fairy tales when I was in kindergarten, but now I am an educated man and am far above believing such things." It is this intellectual pride which can be used to turn this objection into an opportunity for presenting the gospel, somewhat as in the following illustration:

"You don't believe the Bible, John? That's very interesting and it certainly is your privilege not to believe it, and I would fight for that right on your part. However, if the Bible is true then obviously you must accept the consequences. But I would like to ask you a question. The main message of the Bible, which has been unquestionably the most important literary work in human history, is how a person may have eternal life. So what I would like to know is, what do you understand that the Bible teaches about how a person may have eternal life and go to heaven?"

He may reply that he does not believe in eternal life, to which you may respond, "I'm not asking you what you believe, but I am asking you what you *understand.* It would be a rather unintellectual approach to reject the world's most important book without understanding even its main message, would it not? What do you *understand* that the Bible teaches as to how a person may have eternal life? What is your *understanding* about what the Bible teaches on this subject?"

In about 98 percent of the cases he will respond by saying that it is by keeping the Ten Commandments or following the Golden Rule or imitating the example of Christ, etc. You may then respond, "That is just what I was afraid of, John. You have rejected the Bible without even understanding its main message, for your answer is not only incorrect, but it is diametrically opposite to what the Bible teaches. Now, don't you think that the more intellectual approach would be to let me share with you what the Scriptures teach on this subject and then you can make an intelligent decision whether to reject or accept it?"

Now the tables have been completely turned. Instead of being superior to the Scriptures and above even listening to them, he now finds himself ignorant of even their basic message and he must decide whether to listen to the message of the Scriptures or be found to be not only ignorant but also an obscurantist who desires to remain in his ignorance. This is the last thing in the world that his intellectual pride will allow him to be; therefore, he will almost invariably give you permission to tell him the gospel. At this point you pray mightily that the Holy Spirit will take the gospel which is the power of God unto salvation and use it to quicken him from the deadness of his sin.

Apologetic method. If this objection is raised toward the end of the presentation, then your answer will have to be quite different. We have found that the apologetic method of presenting the classical evidences of Christianity can be helpful at this point.

One of the most important classical evidences for the inspiration of the Scriptures is prophecy. The Bible says, "Despise not prophesyings. Prove all things; hold fast to that which is good" (1 Thessalonians 5:20, 21). How do we know that the prophets of the Bible have been sent by God and speak for him?

God presents us with that same question: "How will you know that a prophet is sent from me? By this ye shall know that he shall tell the future and if what he prophesies does not come to pass then I have not sent him" (Deuteronomy 18:22). The gift of prophecy is one of the methods by which the Bible authenticates itself as the Word of God.

Now, some people would again not appreciate the significance of this because they do not realize that this also is something which is strikingly absent from all other religious writings. For example, the writings of Buddha are totally lacking in any sort of specific predictive prophecy about the things of the future. In the writings of Confucius, there is absolutely nothing of any predictive prophecies. In the case of the Koran, the scriptures of the Muslims, we find only the prophecy of Mohammed that he would return to Mecca, a "self-fulfilling prophecy," which he himself, of course, fulfilled. This is quite different from the prophecy of Christ, who said that he would rise from the dead. And that is just one of several thousands of prophecies that occur in the Scriptures and which are of the most *specific, concrete, and definite* nature.*

If the person says, "The Bible is just a book written by men," you might read to him some of the Old Testament prophecies concerning Jesus Christ without telling him what you are reading. And then ask him "About whom have I been reading?" and he will probably respond, as one man did to me, by saying, "You have been reading about the lineage, birth, ministry, suffering, death, and resurrection of Christ." To which I responded, "That is correct, but all of the verses that I read to you are found in the Old Testament which was completed almost four hundred years before Christ was born, and no skeptic or atheist alive claims that even one of the verses which I read was written after the birth of Jesus. If the Bible were just a book written by men, then how did the writers know these things?"

The following are a few of the key Old Testament prophecies concerning Christ and their New Testament fulfillment.

OLD TESTAMENT PROPHECY	**NEW TESTAMENT FULFILLMENT**
SEED OF THE WOMAN **Genesis 3: 15—B.C. 4004.** And I will put enmity between thee and the woman, and between thy seed and her SEED: it shall bruise thy head, and thou shalt bruise his heel.	**Galatians 4: 4—B.C. 5.** But when the fulness of the time was come, God sent forth his Son, made of a woman, made under the law. **1 John 3: 8—A.D. 90.** For this purpose the Son of God was manifested, that he might destroy the works of the devil.
THROUGH ABRAHAM **Genesis 22: 18—B.C. 1872.** And in thy SEED shall ALL THE NATIONS of the earth be blessed; because thou hast obeyed my voice.	**John 11: 51, 52—A.D. 33.** And this spake he not of himself: but being high priest that same year, he prophesied that Jesus should die for that nation; And NOT FOR THAT NATION ONLY, but that also he should gather together in one the children of God that were scattered abroad.
MOCKED **Psalm 22: 7, 8.** All they that see me laugh me to scorn, they shoot out the lip, they shake the head, saying, He trusted on the Lord that he would deliver him, let him deliver him, seeing he delighted in him.	**Matthew 27: 39–44—A.D. 33.** They that passed by reviled him, wagging their heads. . . . Likewise also the chief priests mocking him with the scribes and elders, said, . . . he trusted in God: let him deliver him.
GALL AND VINEGAR GIVEN HIM TO DRINK **Psalm 69: 21.** They gave me also GALL for my meat; and in my thirst they gave me VINEGAR to drink.	**Matthew 27: 34—A.D. 33.** They gave him VINEGAR to drink mingled with GALL.
INTENSITY OF HIS SUFFERING **Psalm 22: 14, 15.** I am poured out like water, and all my bones are out of joint: my heart is like wax: it is melted in the midst of my bowels. My strength is dried up like a potsherd: and my tongue cleaveth to my jaws; and thou hast brought me into the dust of death.	**Luke 22: 42, 44—A.D. 33.** Father, if thou be willing remove this cup from me . . . And being in an agony, he prayed more earnestly and his sweat was as it were great drops of blood falling down to the ground.

* D. James Kennedy, *Truths That Transform* (Old Tappan, New Jersey: Fleming H. Revell Company, 1974), p. 138.

OLD TESTAMENT PROPHECY	**NEW TESTAMENT FULFILLMENT**
HIS SUFFERINGS BEING FOR OTHERS **Isaiah 53: 4–6, 12—B.C. 712.** Surely he hath borne *our* griefs and carried *our* sorrows . . . He was wounded for *our* transgressions. He was bruised for *our* iniquities. The Lord hath laid on him the iniquity of *us all.*	**Matthew 20: 28—A.D. 33.** The Son of man came to give his life a ransom for *many.*
PRECEDED BY JOHN THE BAPTIST **Malachi 3: 1—B.C. 397.** Behold, I will send my messenger; he shall prepare the way.	**Luke 1: 17—B.C. 7.** He shall go before him to make ready a people for the Lord.
HIS MINISTRY COMMENCING IN GALILEE **Isaiah 9: 1, 2—B.C. 740.** In GALILEE of the nations. The people that walked in darkness have seen a great light; they that dwell in the land of the shadow of death, upon them hath the light shined.	**Matthew 4: 12, 16, 23—A.D. 27.** Jesus departed into GALILEE . . . The people which sat in darkness saw great light; and to them which sat in the region and shadow of death light is sprung up. . . . And Jesus went about all GALILEE teaching in their synagogues.
ENTERING PUBLICLY INTO JERUSALEM **Zechariah 9: 9—B.C. 487.** Rejoice greatly, O daughter of Zion: shout, O daughter of Jerusalem: Behold, thy King cometh unto thee: . . . having salvation.	**Matthew 21: 5—A.D. 33.** Tell ye the daughter of Zion, Behold, thy King cometh unto thee.
WORKING MIRACLES **Isaiah 35: 5, 6—B.C. 713.** Then the eyes of the blind shall be opened and the ears of the deaf shall be unstopped. Then shall the lame man leap as an hart, and the tongue of the dumb sing. . . .	**Matthew 11: 4–6—A.D. 31.** Jesus answered and said . . . The blind receive their sight and the lame walk, the lepers are cleansed, and the deaf hear, the dead are raised up, and the poor have the gospel preached to them.
REJECTED BY HIS BRETHREN **Psalm 69: 8.** I am become a stranger unto my brethren, and an alien unto my mother's children. **Isaiah 63: 3—B.C. 698.** I have trodden the winepress alone.	**John 1: 11—A.D. 30.** He came unto his own and his own received him not. **John 7: 3, 5—A.D. 32.** His brethren therefore said unto him, Depart hence . . . For neither did his brethren believe in him.
JEWS AND GENTILES COMBINE AGAINST HIM **Psalm 2: 1, 2.** Why do the heathen rage, and the people imagine a vain thing? The kings of the earth set themselves, and the rulers take counsel together, against the Lord and his anointed.	**Acts 4: 27—A.D. 33.** For of a truth against thy holy child Jesus, whom thou hast anointed, both Herod and Pontius Pilate, with the Gentiles, and the people of Israel were gathered together.
BETRAYED BY A FRIEND **Psalm 41: 9.** Yea, mine own familiar friend, in whom I trusted, who did eat of my bread, hath lifted up his heel against me.	**John 13: 18–21—A.D. 33.** I speak not of you all; but that the scriptures may be fulfilled. He that eateth bread with me hath lifted up his heel against me. . . . Verily, verily, I say unto you, that one of you shall betray me.
SOLD FOR THIRTY PIECES OF SILVER **Zechariah 11: 12—B.C. 487.** If ye think good, give me my price; so they weighed for my price THIRTY pieces of silver.	**Matthew 26: 15—A.D. 33.** What will ye give me, and I will deliver him unto you? And they covenanted with him for THIRTY pieces of silver.
HIS PRICE GIVEN FOR THE POTTER'S FIELD **Zechariah 11: 13—B.C. 487.** Cast it unto the potter: a goodly price that I was prized at of them. And I took the thirty pieces of silver, and cast them to the POTTER in the house of the Lord.	**Matthew 27: 3, 7—A.D. 33.** Judas brought again the thirty pieces of silver to the chief priests and elders . . . and they brought with them the POTTERS field to bury strangers in.
SPIT UPON AND SCOURGED **Isaiah 50: 6—B.C. 712.** I gave my back to the smiters, and my cheeks to them that plucked off the hair: I hid not my face from shame and SPITTING.	**Mark 14: 65—A.D. 33.** And some began to SPIT on him, and to cover his face, and to buffet him. **John 19: 1—A.D. 33.** Pilate took Jesus and scourged him.
NAILED TO THE CROSS **Psalm 22: 16.** They pierced my hands and my feet.	**John 19: 18—A.D. 33.** They crucified him. **John 20: 25—A.D. 33.** . . . in his hand the print of the nails.
FORSAKEN BY GOD **Psalm 22: 1.** My God, my God, why hast thou FORSAKEN me?	**Matthew 27: 46—A.D. 33.** Jesus cried, My God, my God, why hast thou FORSAKEN me?

OLD TESTAMENT PROPHECY	NEW TESTAMENT FULFILLMENT
PATIENCE AND SILENCE UNDER SUFFERING **Isaiah 53: 7—B.C. 710.** Yet he opened not his mouth . . . As a sheep before her shearers is dumb, so he openeth not his mouth.	**Matthew 26: 63—A.D. 33.** Jesus held his peace. **Matthew 27: 12, 14—A.D. 33.** When he was accused of the chief priests and elders, he answered nothing. . . .
HIS GARMENTS PARTED AND LOTS CAST FOR HIS VESTURE **Psalm 22: 18.** They part my GARMENTS among them, and cast lots upon my vesture.	**Matthew 27: 35—A.D. 33.** And they crucified him and parted his GARMENTS, casting lots: that it might be fulfilled which was spoken by the prophet.
NUMBERED WITH THE TRANSGRESSORS **Isaiah 53: 12—B.C. 712.** He was numbered with the TRANSGRESSORS.	**Mark 15: 27, 28—A.D. 33.** And with him they crucify two thieves. And the scripture was fulfilled which saith, And he was numbered with the TRANSGRESSORS.
INTERCESSION FOR HIS MURDERERS **Isaiah 53: 12—B.C. 712.** And made intercession for the transgressors.	**Luke 23: 34—A.D. 33.** Then said Jesus, Father, forgive them; for they know not what they do.
HIS DEATH **Isaiah 53: 12—B.C. 712.** He hath poured out his soul unto death.	**Matthew 27: 50—A.D. 33.** Jesus yielded up the ghost.
NOT A BONE OF HIM BROKEN **Exodus 12: 46—B.C. 1491.** Neither shall ye break a BONE thereof. **Psalm 34: 20.** He keepeth all his bones: not one of them is broken.	**John 19: 33, 36—A.D. 33.** When they came to Jesus and saw that he was dead already, they brake not his legs. For these things were done that the scripture should be fulfilled . . . A BONE of him shall not be broken.
PIERCED **Zechariah 12: 10—B.C. 487.** They shall look upon me whom they have PIERCED.	**John 19: 34, 37—A.D. 33.** One of the soldiers with a spear PIERCED his side. . . . And again another scripture saith, They shall look upon him whom they pierced.
BURIED WITH THE RICH **Isaiah 53: 9—B.C. 712.** He made his grave . . . with the RICH in his death.	**Matthew 27: 57–60—A.D. 33.** There came a RICH man named Joseph . . . who went to Pilate, and begged the body of Jesus . . . and laid it in his own tomb.
HIS RESURRECTION **Psalm 16: 10.** Neither wilt thou suffer thine Holy One to see corruption.	**Luke 24: 6, 31, 34—A.D. 33.** He is not here, but is risen. . . . And their eyes were opened, and they knew him; and he vanished out of their sight. . . . The Lord is risen indeed.
HIS ASCENSION **Psalm 68: 18.** Thou hast ascended on high. Thou hast led captivity captive: thou hast received gifts for men: yea, for the rebellious also, that the Lord God might dwell among them.	**Luke 24: 51—A.D. 33.** While he blessed them, he was parted from them, and carried up into heaven.
SITTING ON THE RIGHT HAND OF GOD **Psalm 110: 1.** The Lord said unto my Lord, SIT thou at my right hand.	**Hebrews 1: 3—A.D. 60.** When he had purged our sins . . . SAT down on the right hand of the Majesty on high.
THE CONVERSION OF THE GENTILES TO HIM **Isaiah 11: 10—B.C. 713.** There shall be a root of Jesse, to it shall the Gentiles seek; and his rest shall be glorious. **Isaiah 42: 1—B.C. 712.** Behold my servant, He shall bring forth judgment to the GENTILES.	**Acts 10: 45—A.D. 41.** And they of the circumcision which believed were astonished, as many as came with Peter, because that on the Gentiles also was poured out the gift of the Holy Ghost.

MODERN PROPHETS. There are over 2,000 specific prophecies in the Bible which have already been fulfilled. This is particularly astounding when we recall that there are no such prophecies in the "scriptures" of any other religion, and when we consider some of the modern efforts to duplicate this feat. Probably the most notable of modern so-called prophets is Jeane Dixon. We are often told of the prophecies which she has made which have come to pass, but we are not often told about her mistakes.

Take the decade of the fifties, for example. In that decade she prophesied who each of the presidential candidates of each of the major political parties would be. And she prophesied the winner of each of three presidential elections: in 1952, in 1956, and 1960. How well did she do? She missed every winner of every presidential election and she missed every candidate in every party for each of these elections.

Several years ago the *National Enquirer* magazine listed sixty-one prophecies by the ten leading seers in the world, reporting events that were supposed to transpire in the last six months of that year. Compared to the prophecies of Scripture it should be relatively easy to predict those things which lie so close at hand. How well did they do? Believe it or not, they missed all sixty-one prophecies! Some of their remarkable forecasts were that Pope Paul would retire in that year and the Roman Catholic Church would be taken over by a committee of laymen; that George Foreman would retain his heavyweight crown in his bout with Mohammed Ali in Africa; and that Ted Kennedy would get his campaign for President into high gear. The only difference between the prophecies of these modern prophets and those of the Bible is that our modern seers were unfailingly wrong and the biblical prophets were unfailingly right. A significant difference, to say the least.

BIBLICAL PROPHECIES. These biblical prophecies deal with almost every nation and scores of cities with which Israel had some dealings. It cannot be said that these prophecies were written after the events for many of the events took place hundreds or even thousands of years after the prophecy was made. Nor can it be said that they are vague and obscure, because they are highly specific in their details. Nor can it be said that they are merely lucky guesses because there are over 2,000 of them which have infallibly come to pass. Nor can it be said that these were things which were likely to take place because they were indeed extremely unlikely events. It would repay the individual who wants to be a good witness for Christ and who wants to be able to defend his belief in the Scriptures, to familiarize himself with some of the details of several of these prophecies. I am including here some of the prophecies about two countries. They are quite different and they are astounding to relate. I have taken these from my book *Truths That Transform,** where a great many other such prophecies are also described for the student who would like to do further research in this area. But let us consider the kingdoms of Babylonia and Egypt and what God had to say about them and the great cities that had been built in them.

BABYLONIA.** Consider the magnificent kingdom of Babylonia. Babylon was probably the greatest city that was ever built. Here was the magnificent temple of Belus; and here were the world famous Hanging Gardens.

She drew her stores from no foreign country. She invented an alphabet; worked out problems of arithmetic; invented implements for measuring time; conceived the plan of building enormous structures with the poorest of all materials—clay; discovered the

---

* D. James Kennedy, *Truths That Transform* (Old Tappan, New Jersey: Fleming H. Revell Company, 1974), p. 138.

** [Condensed from *Truths That Transform,* D. J. Kennedy (Old Tappan, New Jersey: Fleming H. Revell Company, 1974), pp. 146–153.]

art of polishing, boring, and engraving gems; studied successfully the motions of the heavenly bodies; conceived of grammar as a science; elaborated a system of law; saw the value of exact chronology. In almost every branch of science, she made a beginning. Much of the art and learning of Greece came from Babylon. But of this majestic kingdom, this Babylon the Golden, God said, ". . . Babylon, the glory of kingdoms, the beauty of the Chaldees' excellency, shall be as when God overthrew Sodom and Gomorrah" (Isaiah 13:19). This is but one of over one hundred specific prophecies that were made concerning Babylon alone. The specificity of these prophecies is so great that they cannot possibly be said to be obscure as are the Delphic Oracles. Nor can they be said to have been written after the event, because many of the details of the prophecy were not fulfilled until centuries after the Septuagint translation of the Hebrew Old Testament into Greek in 150 B.C. It is not possible to give a later date for these prophecies. Nor can it be said that they have not been fulfilled, for any school boy with a good encyclopedia can ascertain that they have been minutely fulfilled. In these prophecies concerning the future of great cities and kingdoms, God has stamped his *imprimatur* on the Scriptures, confirming them as divine revelations in such bold letters that "He that runneth may read" (Psalm 147:15). Nor can it be said that they are simply lucky guesses, because there are thousands of such prophecies in the Scriptures which have been minutely fulfilled. Nor yet can it be said that they concern events which were likely to take place. Indeed, many of the events were totally without precedence in the history of the world and were so incredible and unbelievable in their very nature, that even though history has fully confirmed them to be true, we still stagger at the audacity of the prophets who made such bold statements.

WALLS DESTROYED. Consider the great walls of Babylon. Herodotus tells us that these walls had towers which extended above the two-hundred-foot walls to a height of three hundred feet. The walls were a hundred-eighty-seven feet thick at the base and were fourteen miles square, according to one ancient authority. The triple walls of Babylon were the mightiest walls that were ever built around any city. Concerning these walls God says, in Jeremiah 51:58, "The broad walls of Babylon shall be utterly broken . . ." Also, "And they shall not take of thee a stone for a corner, nor a stone for foundations; but thou shalt be desolate for ever" (Jeremiah 51:26). Consider these astounding facts. (1) The wall is to be broken down, (2) it is to be broken down completely, (3) it is to be broken down permanently. It cannot possibly be said that these prophecies did not come to pass. Even the skeptics attest their fulfillment. "Where are the walls of Babylon?" asks Constantin Volney in his *Ruins.* Major Keppel said in his *Narrative* that in common with other travelers, he totally failed in discovering any trace of the city walls.

Nor can anyone say that the prophecy was made after the event, for the walls were not suddenly destroyed. The city was taken by stealth by the Medes and Persians and the destruction of her walls was a slow process that took centuries. The walls were still in existence in the time of Alexander the Great. They still jutted into the sky at the time of Christ. In the fourth century A.D., some remains of the walls were still there, a stark reminder that the prophecy had not yet been completely fulfilled. Then the most astounding event took place. Julian the Apostate, Emperor of Rome, determined to rid the Roman Empire of Christianity and reestablish paganism, was doing all in his power to destroy the belief in the Scriptures. However, God had said that even "the wrath of man shall praise [him]" (Psalm 76:10). While engaged in a war with the Persians near the remains of Babylon (although he had no idea of the prophecy that he was fulfilling), Julian completely destroyed the remains of the wall of Babylon lest it afford any protection in the future for the Persian army. And thus the prophecy was brought to fulfillment by one of the greatest antagonists of Scripture of all time.

One cannot say it was inevitable that the wall would be destroyed. The Great Wall of China is not nearly as large or as strong, and yet, though it is older, it still stands today. The walls of Jerusalem and many other ancient cities, though destroyed many times in part, have been rebuilt and still remain to our time. I have personally walked atop the great walls of Jerusalem, which God said would be destroyed, but also he said that they would be built again in troublous times. In the case of the Babylonian wall and the Jerusalem wall, exactly what God said has come to pass. (Jeremiah 39:8; Daniel 9:25; Micah 7:11; Isaiah 33:20.)

When Babylon was the mistress of the world, containing within its mighty walls one hundred ninety-six square miles of the most magnificently developed city of all time, with beautiful parks, lakes, aqueducts, and hanging gardens, the prophet Jeremiah made this astounding prophecy: "Because of the wrath of the Lord it shall not be inhabited, but it shall be wholly desolate" (Jeremiah 50:13). Even more astonishing is the further prophecy of Jeremiah: ". . . and it shall be no more inhabited for ever; neither shall it be dwelt in from generation to generation" (Jeremiah 50:39). This was an astonishing prophecy, for it was virtually without precedent. Many ancient cities in the Near East had been destroyed, but always they had been built again on the ruins of the previous cities. There is evidence of sometimes twenty or thirty cities being built on the very same site. Babylon was most excellently situated on the Euphrates. It had fine possibilities of commerce. It was militarily almost invincible. Its fields were so fertile that Herodotus, having visited there, was afraid to describe what he saw lest he be thought insane.

Have these astonishing prophecies been fulfilled? Babylon was described as the tenantless and desolate metropolis (*Mignan's Travels,* p. 234), a barren desert in which the ruins were nearly the only indication that it had been inhabited. Regarding Babylon, Isaiah said, "Nor dwelt in from generation to generation" (Isaiah 13:20). In the sixteenth century, there was not a house to be seen at Babylon (*Ray's Collection of Travels,* Rawolf, p. 174). In the nineteenth century, it was still desolate and tenantless (Mignan, p. 284). In the twentieth century, ruins are all that remain of the once magnificent city where King Belshazzar saw the handwriting on the wall (John Elder, *Prophets and Diggers,* p. 106). "It shall never be inhabited," prophesied Isaiah (Isaiah 13:20). Ruins composed like those of Babylon of heaps of rubbish impregnated with niter cannot be cultivated (*Rich's Memoirs,* p. 16). The decomposing materials of a Babylonian structure doom the earth on which they perish to a lasting sterility (*Sir R. K. Porter's Travels,* vol. 2, p. 391). Thus God guaranteed the fulfillment of his prophecies. ". . . thou [Babylon] shalt be desolate for ever. Babylon shall become heaps, a dwellingplace for dragons, an astonishment, and an hissing, without an inhabitant" (Jeremiah 51:26, 37).

NO TENTS. There are other amazingly specific details in this prophecy. Consider this detail: ". . . neither shall the Arabian pitch tent there." Has this come true? Captain Mignan said that he saw the sun sink behind the Mujelibah, and obeyed with infinite regret the summons of his guides who were completely armed. He could not persuade them to remain longer. Due to apprehension of evil spirits it is impossible to eradicate this idea from the minds of these people (*Mignan's Travels,* pp. 2, 198, 201). Continues Isaiah: "Neither shall the shepherds make their fold there" (Isaiah 13:20). All the people of the country assert that it is extremely dangerous to approach this mound after nightfall on account of the multitude of evil spirits by which it is haunted. By this superstitious belief they are prevented from pitching a tent by night or making a fold (*Rich's Memoirs,* p. 27).

WAVES IN THE WILDERNESS. Consider these two specific but apparently contradictory prophecies. "The sea is come up upon Babylon: she is covered with the multitude of the waves thereof" (Jeremiah 51:42). And, ". . . a desolation, a dry land and a wilderness" (Jeremiah 51:43). Now note the amazing fulfillment: For the space of two months throughout the year the ruins of Babylon are inundated by the annual overflowing of the Euphrates so as to render many parts of them inaccessible by converting the valleys into morasses (*Rich's Memoirs,* p. 13). After the subsiding of the waters, even the low heaps become again sunburnt ruins and the sight of Babylon like that of the other cities of Chaldea is a dry waste, a parched and burning plain (*Buckingham's Travels,* vol. 2, pp. 302–305).

In spite of the unimaginable fertility of the plains around Babylon, God had said, "Cut off the sower from Babylon, and him that handleth the sickle in the time of harvest . . ." (Jeremiah 50:16). On this part of the plain both where traces of buildings were left and where none had stood, all seemed equally naked of vegetation (*Porter's Travels,* vol. 2, p. 392). "And Babylon shall become heaps" (Jeremiah 51:37). And again, ". . . cast her up as heaps, and destroy her utterly: let nothing of her be left" (Jeremiah 50:26). Babylon has become a vast succession of mounds; a great mass of ruined heaps. Vast heaps constitute all that now remains of ancient Babylon (*Keppel's Narrative,* vol. 1, p. 196).

These prophecies are presented here as examples of the over one-hundred specific prophecies relating to the city of Babylon (Isaiah 48:14; Jeremiah 51:29). The wrath of the Lord was poured out upon Babylon. God said, "The Lord . . . will do his pleasure on Babylon . . . for every purpose of the Lord shall be performed against Babylon. And I will bring upon that land all my words which I have pronounced against it, even all that is written in this book . . ." (Jeremiah 25:13). Let us close this discussion of Babylon with the words of one who looked with his own eyes upon the fulfillment of these prophecies. "I cannot portray," says Captain Mignan, "the overpowering sensation of reverential awe that possessed my mind while contemplating the extent and magnitude of ruin and devastation on every side" (*Mignan's Travels,* p. 117).

REBUILD BABYLON. Thus God threw down the gauntlet to all unbelievers. Do you want to disprove the Scriptures? It is very easy! Simply rebuild Babylon! God said it shall never be inhabited; it shall never be rebuilt, but it would always remain a desolation. There was a man who set out to rebuild it. I should tell you about him. He had all of the wealth of the whole world at his command. His name was Alexander the Great. After conquering the world, he decided to have a trade route by sea from Babylon to Egypt, and he decided to make Babylon his central headquarters for his worldwide empire. He issued six hundred thousand rations to his soldiers to rebuild the city of Babylon. Alexander the Great, the ruler of the world, said, "Rebuild Babylon!" and God struck him dead! He was immediately taken with a fever and within a few days he was dead. The ruins of Babylon still stand in mute testimony. "I, the Lord, have spoken it! It shall never be inhabited again!" (Jeremiah 50:39).

EGYPT—BASEST OF THE KINGDOMS. Compare these prophecies of destruction with what the Bible says about Egypt. God said that Nineveh, Assyria, and Babylonia would be completely destroyed and not be rebuilt. What if he had said that about Egypt? Ah, how the skeptics would laugh. But he didn't. ". . . they shall be there a base kingdom. It shall be the basest of the kingdoms; neither shall it exalt itself any more above the nations: for I will diminish them, that they shall no more rule over the nations (Ezekiel 29:14,15). . . . the pride of her power shall come down. . . . And they shall be desolate in the midst of the countries that are desolate, and her cities shall be in the midst of the cities that are wasted (Ezekiel 30:6,7). And I will make the land of Egypt desolate (Ezekiel 29:12). . . . and the country shall be destitute of that whereof it was full (Ezekiel 32:15). And I will . . . sell the land into the hand of the wicked: and I will make the land waste, and all that is therein, by the hand of strangers: I the Lord have spoken it (Ezekiel 30:12). . . . and there shall be no more a prince of the land of Egypt" (Ezekiel 30:13).

Let us note that the fate of Egypt is not, as in the case of Nineveh and Babylon, to be utter extinction, but rather, "they shall be there." Egypt was to continue to exist as a nation but "a base nation." "The basest of nations" (Ezekiel 29:14,15). It is to be diminished and emptied of that whereof it was full. Have these prophecies been fulfilled? After the defeat of Antony, Augustus found such great wealth in Egypt that he paid out of it all the arrears of his army and all of the debts that he had incurred during the war. Still he feared that the wealth of Egypt would present to him a rival. For six hundred more years Alexandria continued to be the first city in the Roman Empire in rank, commerce, and prosperity. A hundred years later the Muslim hordes attacked Egypt and conquered it. They were overwhelmed by the sight of the city's magnificence and wealth. Future invaders were equally astonished at the wealth of Egypt, until the nation was reduced to a state of abject poverty, finally being brought to the place of international bankruptcy which brought about the Anglo-French dominion of Egypt.

NO PRINCE. One of the most astonishing parts of the prophecy is the statement, "There shall be no more a prince of the land of Egypt" (Ezekiel 30:13). This prophecy is particularly striking when we note that for approximately two thousand years before the prophecy was made, Egypt had had Egyptian princes sitting upon its throne 98% of the time. It seemed as if this would continue forever. But God declares that there shall no more be a prince of the land of Egypt. What a startling declaration! There has been ample time for the testing of the prophecy, for there continued to be a prince on the throne of Egypt until the last several decades when a democratic form of government was accepted. But were any of these princes Egyptians? Let us have that question answered by the pens of skeptics and infidels. Constantin Volney said: "deprived two thousand three hundred years ago of her natural proprietors, Egypt has seen her fertile fields successively prey to the Persians, the Macedonians, the Romans, the Greeks, the Arabs, the Georgians, and at length the race of Tartars, distinguished by the name of Ottoman Turks, the Mamelukes soon usurped the power and elected a leader" (*Volney's Travels,* vol. 1, pp. 74, 103, 110, 193). After Volney's time, Mohammed Ali established the princedom again in Egypt but he, himself, was not an Egyptian. Rather he was born at Kavala, a small seaport on the frontier of Thrace and Macedonia. His father was an Albanian aga. After this, Egypt was ruled by the French and the English. The skeptic Edward Gibbon confirms this testimony where he states: "a more unjust and absurd constitution cannot be devised than that which condemns the natives of a country to perpetual servitude under the arbitrary dominion of strangers and slaves" (Gibbon, *The Decline and Fall of the Roman Empire,* chapter 59).

Today, Egypt, which has for over two millennia suffered under the despotic hand of strangers, has been reduced to one of the basest of nations. My guide to the Holy Land a few years ago said that he had been to Egypt thirty or forty times, but he was never going back again because it was so foul, so vile smelling, so poverty ridden that he couldn't stand another trip. His stomach couldn't take the cities of Egypt any more. "I will make thee the basest of nations" (Ezekiel 29:14,15).

These are but a few of the thousands of prophecies with which the Scripture abounds, which are found in no other religious writings of the world, and which are clear evidence that the Scripture has been written by the hand of God.

How firm a foundation, ye saints of the Lord,
Is laid for your faith in his excellent Word!
What more can he say than to you He hath said?

"I am God and there is none like me, Declaring the end from the beginning, and from ancient times the things that are not yet done" (Isaiah 46:9,10). "Hereby ye will know the prophet is come from me because he will tell the future" (see Deuteronomy 18:22) as the Bible and no other book, unfailingly and infallibly, does. The Scriptures are the Word of God. "Sanctify them through thy truth," said Christ, *"thy word is truth"* (John 17:17).

"The Scriptures cannot be broken!"

RELIGION IS A CRUTCH

Another objection that is often raised is that religion is a crutch for the weak, for those who are afraid to face life as it really is. They say that man, being afraid of the lightning and thunder and the storms that sometimes beat upon us, has invented a god to whom he can flee for refuge. Is this really the case? Dr. R. C. Sproul in *The Psychology of Atheism** has answered this objection very effectively. I paraphrased his answer recently in talking to an unbeliever who raised this objection.

* Dr. R. C. Sproul, *The Psychology of Atheism* (Minneapolis: Bethany Fellowship, Inc., 1974), pp. 42ff.

I said: "Do you really believe that? Do you really believe that I am afraid of the lightning and thunder and storms?" The truth is that I have been through a number of hurricanes and actually enjoyed them! There is very little about the world in which we live today that really frightens modern man. The devil is a great liar, but I will tell you what the truth about this matter really is.

"Though there are many wonderfully appealing aspects to the Christian God, his love, his compassion, his mercy, his longsuffering, etc., there are also threatening aspects to the Christian God which make any earthly terror pale by comparison. There is his justice and the judgment to come. There is his anger against sin and the wrath which he has promised to pour out upon it. And there is the prospect of everlasting punishment in hell. Rightly, the Scripture concludes, 'It is a fearful thing to fall into the hands of the living God' (Hebrews 10:31). And Jesus declares that we should not fear him who is able to kill the body and after that there is nothing more that he can do, but rather that we should fear him (God) who is able to plunge both body and soul into hell. Yea, says Christ, I say unto you, fear him. The truth of the matter then is that rather than the believer creating an imaginary God to whom he may flee, the unbeliever has created an imaginary world in which God does not exist in order to flee from a just God who is infinitely angry with him because of his sins. This is the truth of the matter, as every unbeliever knows deep down in his soul."

I DON'T BELIEVE IN HEAVEN

This is an objection that you might receive as soon as you ask the first diagnostic question. I would suggest that you respond somewhat as follows:

"I assume then that you don't believe in the Bible, for the Bible obviously teaches that there is a heaven. It is, of course, your privilege not to believe in the Bible, but I would like to ask you a question." At this point you would use the "judo approach" answer to the objection, "I don't believe in the Bible." Thus you are using that answer as a funnel into which several objections can be poured.

GOD WOULDN'T ASK THAT

This is an objection that is sometimes raised to the second diagnostic question. I would recommend a response something like the following:

> "Well, I'm certain that God doesn't need me to write his script for him. That's why I used the word 'suppose.' *Suppose* that you were to die and God were to say unto you. . . . I think that question brings the whole matter into focus and is helpful for our thinking. Suppose he were to ask you that, what do you think you would say?"

If this answer does not suffice, then you might also say the following:

> "I am sure that I do not know exactly what questions God will ask us, but Jesus indicates in Matthew 7:22 some answers that people will be giving to a question asked them at the final Judgment. He says, 'Many will say to me in that day, Lord, Lord, have we not prophesied in thy name? and in thy name

have cast out devils? and in thy name done many wonderful works?' Though the question which they are answering is not explicitly stated, it certainly is implied that it is something like 'Why should you be admitted?' "

WHAT ABOUT REINCARNATION?

This is a question which is more often raised today with the increasing interest in oriental religions. I would respond as follows:

"The Bible says, 'It is appointed unto men *once* to die, but after this the judgment' (Hebrews 9:27). Thus the Bible teaches that man dies only once and after this there comes the Judgment. And the Scriptures make it very plain that after the Judgment there comes either heaven or hell. I wonder if you understand why people believe in reincarnation? It is, of course, a belief of Hinduism and Buddhism but not of Christianity. It is an incorrect conclusion drawn from two correct understandings. These people realize, first, that to dwell with God one must be perfect and, second, that man is at present sinful. Therefore, they postulate a series of thousands of reincarnations during which time man gradually becomes better and better until finally he arrives at perfection. This same basic idea is seen in the concept of purgatory, that man must be made perfect before he can enter paradise. In this case, however, it is not by reincarnation but through a stay in some fiery place of purgation. A common garden variety of this concept held by many Americans is, 'I'm not good enough now to live with God, but if I just work a little harder, I'm sure that one day I will arrive by loving my neighbor and doing the best I can.'

"All three of these views ignore the atonement of Jesus Christ and his perfect righteousness. By his death he once and for all takes away all of our sin, and by his perfect obedience in this life he clothes us with his righteousness so that we are instantly made perfect to stand in the presence of God, clothed in the righteousness of Christ alone."

WE HAVE OUR HELL RIGHT HERE ON EARTH

This is an objection which is not infrequently heard. A recommended response is the following:

"You know, you're right! At least in part. That's just what the Bible says. We do have an 'earnest' of our inheritance right here in this world. I'm sure you know what 'an earnest' is. Earnest money paid down on a house is a pledge that more is to come. The word is even more interesting in Greek. The Greek term translated 'earnest' is *arabòne.* It was used in Greek for a swatch of material. For instance, a woman who was planning to recover her couch would bring home a swatch to hold up to the wall and curtains and chairs. Of course, the swatch would be meaningless and her action would be ridiculous unless there was a roll of material back at the shop with which to cover the couch. That, of course, is precisely the lie that the devil would like us to believe. He keeps saying to us, 'Oh, that swatch of hell is all there is.'

But God is saying, 'The whole roll is waiting for you when you die.' Well, I would like to tell you something exciting. The Bible also makes plain that it's possible to have a little bit of heaven right here on earth. Wouldn't that be vastly better than a taste of hell? Let me tell you how."

If a person does not believe in God's justice and hell, you may proceed to show that the prophets Isaiah (57:21) and Ezekiel (33:11), the apostles Peter (2 Peter 2:4, 6, 9) and Paul (Romans 2:4, 5) and the Lord Jesus himself (Mark 16:16; Luke 13:3; John 3:18, 36) taught that God will assuredly punish sin.

HELL ISN'T REAL

In dealing with the denial of the reality of hell, sometimes we find it helpful to say, "You know, it is a fact of psychology that we deny most passionately those things we fear most desperately. I wonder if the reason you don't believe in hell is that deep down in your soul you fear that if there is such a place you might go there?" Often the reply is, "I guess you're right!"

You must go on then and assure your prospect, "I don't want you to believe in hell so that you can live your life in mortal terror of going there. You can know for sure that you're not going to hell. That's what the gospel is all about. I believe in hell, but I know that I'm not going there because of God's promise. This is much better than saying, 'I know I'm not going to hell because I don't think there is such a place.' "

I'LL DO IT LATER, NOT NOW

I once talked to a young man of about twenty-two who told me that. He said he believed in God and in Christ intellectually and believed that the Bible was true and some day planned to accept Christ as his Savior. But first, he said, "I've got a lot of living to do." I remonstrated with him for some time but finally when I saw that I could not persuade him, I let him go, reminding him that the Bible says that he who, being often reproved, hardeneth his neck, shall suddenly be cut off and that without remedy. A week later I heard that he was driving down the highway about seventy miles an hour when a truck stopped in front of him with a tailgate down. He was instantly decapitated. I remembered the words that I had spoken unto him. "He that hardeneth his neck shall suddenly be cut off and that without remedy."

I'LL HAVE TO THINK ABOUT IT

There are some situations in life in which we face two options. But while we're considering which of these options to take, we're already in one of them. For example: your car stalls on the railroad track; the train is coming. You have two options: to try to start the car and save both yourself and the car, or to get out and run and at least save your life. While you are considering these two options, however, you are already in one of them. You are in the car and the train is getting closer. So it is with God. You have two options: to accept Jesus Christ as your Savior, or not to accept him. While you are making up your mind about that issue, you are already in one of the options. You have not accepted him and the moment of your death, which is uncertain, draws nearer, and eternity looms before you.

I BELIEVE WE ARE SAVED BY BOTH FAITH AND WORKS

It might help if we remember that ultimately there are only three possible religions: First, there is that religion wherein it is taught that a man will become acceptable to God by his own works, his own doings, keeping commandments, following certain rules of morality, piety, benevolence, etc. Second, there is that religion that teaches simply that man will be saved by faith in Christ. Third, there is that religion which teaches that a man will be saved by a combination of the two—both by faith and by works.

We might do well to identify those groups which hold to these various concepts. Most pagan religions believe that man will be saved by his works, by keeping some set of rules, whether it be the eightfold path of Buddha, the teachings of the Koran or any of the others. Christianity teaches that man is saved by grace alone through faith. It is the teaching of most of the cults (such as Jehovah's Witnesses, Mormonism, etc.) that man is saved by faith and works.

Does James contradict Paul? It is interesting that the great literary man, Ruskin, said that there was only one book in the world that made it clear concerning faith alone and works and that was the Bible. Some people have said that the Bible contradicts itself at this point. They have specifically said that James contradicts Paul, for Paul is one of the major teachers of the concept of grace by faith, though it is taught throughout the New Testament. On the surface these passages appear to contradict themselves. The apparent contradiction in James 2:14 states, "What doth it profit, my brethren, though a man say he hath faith, and have not works? can faith save him?" Further in verse 20, "But wilt thou know, O vain man, that faith without works is dead?" In verse 21: "Was not Abraham our father justified by works, when he had offered Isaac his son upon the altar?" And in verse 24, "Ye see then how that by works a man is justified, and not by faith only." Now listen to Paul in Romans 3:28 where he gives this great conclusion of his fullest presentation of the Christian gospel: "Therefore, we conclude that a man is justified by faith without the deeds of the law." In Ephesians 2:8,9 is stated, "For by grace are ye saved through faith; and that not of yourselves: it is the gift of God: Not of works, lest any man should boast." In fact in Galatians 2, he says the same thing six different times: "Knowing that a man is not justified by the works of the law, but by the faith of Jesus Christ, even we have believed in Jesus Christ, that we might be justified by the faith of Christ, and not by the works of the law: for by the works of the law shall no flesh be justified." Both negatively and positively he asserts this truth six different times. So there is no question about the fact that there apparently is some contradiction! But is there in reality? In seminary, my Greek professor stated that he thought there was a contradiction between James and Paul. However, after learning the Greek language and studying the passage in James in the original text, he found that the supposed contradiction evaporated.

Same truth defended. Let us see if there is indeed a contradiction or if Ruskin is right and the Bible is indeed the only book that is absolutely clear on the subject of faith plus works. Are Paul and James defending two different truths? I believe that a careful examination of the text and context will reveal that they are both defending the same truth against different errors or against a different set of antagonists.

An illustration might be of a seventeenth or eighteenth century damsel dressed in a white gown who is being attacked by two different bands of cutthroats. She is being defended by two heroes who have drawn their swords. Approaching from the north is one group of brigands and cutthroats who have set their hearts upon destroying this fair damsel, and one hero is fighting them while another hero has taken his stand at her other side and is fighting another group of cutthroats who are coming from the south. Though they are both defending the same truth they are, in fact, fighting in opposite directions. And so are Paul and James.

Different errors fought. Let us look first at the people to whom they are speaking. Paul is addressing the Pharisees or the heathen who would attempt to justify themselves by their own efforts. He is dealing with the legalist who is saying that by keeping some set of rules, whether it be the Ten Commandments of the Old Testament or whether it be the laws of some heathen religion, he will obtain the favor of God. It is against this legalist that Paul is so adroitly fighting. James, on the other hand, is addressing the members of the Christian church—a particular portion of the members of the Christian church—the hypocrites therein. You have heard it said that there are too many hypocrites in the church. That is not a recent saying. James is saying the very same thing right here, for he is talking to the professing members of the church. These are the people who think they will be saved by professing the right faith in Jesus Christ and they have come to the place where they say, "We see that a man is not saved by his good works. What we must do is profess our faith in Christ and hold to the right doctrines and be a part of a church which is sound in the faith." Yet there is absolutely nothing in their lives that would evidence the fact that a real faith exists.

Once a lady became very distraught with me after I had told her the gospel of Christ, of the free grace of God, and the proffered gift of eternal life to those who would trust or believe in Jesus Christ. She sat up indignantly in her chair and said, "Do you mean to tell me that all I have to do is sit here and say I believe in Jesus Christ and I will go to heaven?" My answer was, "No ma'am, that's not what I said." She asked, "Well, what did you say?" And I replied, "If you will believe or trust in Jesus Christ you will have eternal life as a free gift." She said, "You said it again! All I have to do is say that I believe or trust in Jesus Christ and I'll go to heaven." Again I answered, "No, ma'am, that's not what I said. I didn't say it now, I have never said it in the past under any circumstances, to any one, anywhere, at any time. I have never made such a statement and never will because it is absolutely false." She asked, "Well, what did you say?" I said, "I did not say that you would be saved by *saying* that you believed in Christ, but rather by *believing* in him." James says here: "What doth it profit, my brethren, though a man have faith and have not works? Will faith save him?" Is that what James said? It is not! He said: "What doth it profit, my brethren, though a man *say* he hath faith, and have not works? can faith save him?"

Unfortunately the King James Version does not deal too accurately with the last part of that verse. If you examine the Greek text, the phrase is *hay pistis.* It uses the definite article and should be translated, "What doth it profit, my brethren, though a man *say* that he hath not works, can that faith save him?" In order to understand what James is saying you have to know that throughout this whole chapter, when James talks about faith he is talking about a "said" faith, a profession of faith. He never means "What shall it profit if a man have faith and not have works." Because it is not possible that a man truly have real faith and not have works.

Three key words. There are three key words in this passage in James. The first one we have just mentioned. It is the word "say." "Though a man *say* he hath faith" (verse 16); "Yea, a man may *say,* Thou hast faith, and I have works" (verse 18).

The second word is "show." It is found in verse 18. "Shew me thy faith without thy works, and I will shew thee my faith by my works."

The third word is the word "see" which is found in verses 22 and 24. "Seest thou how faith wrought with his works . . ." and "Ye see then how that by works a man is justified."

Self-righteous or barren orthodox. Faith is invisible. A man may *say* that he has faith but you cannot see it, nor can you show it apart from works. There is absolutely no way that anyone can know that you have faith apart from your works. That is precisely why, at the Judgment, people are judged by their works. By their works they demonstrate the reality of their faith though they are saved by faith. But the genuineness of that faith is shown to the world, and they see that that faith is real by the works which the people have done. So we see that Paul is dealing with the self-righteous and James, on the other hand, is dealing with the barren orthodox—those who believe that by the correctness of their creed they will be saved, those who may be expert on the confession, may argue it with great eloquence, believe it in all of its details, may confess the Apostles' Creed, the Westminster Confession; yet they have no fruit, no joy, no love, no peace, no works, no service for Jesus Christ.

Paul is talking about those who would deny faith in the cross of Christ for salvation, and James is talking about those who would demean that faith and reduce it and diminish it down to nothing other than a bare naked mental assent. For Paul, faith is an act of the entire, the whole interior being of man. It is an act of the mind which accepts the deity of Christ and his atoning act in his resurrection as true. It is the act of the affections which respond to the love of God and in turn love God with all of the heart and mind, strength and soul. It is an act of the will which bows to the sovereignty of God and determines to follow Jesus Christ. Paul says that we are saved by faith, but he says it is a faith which worketh by love. Even in Ephesians 2:8,9 in which it says that we are saved by faith apart from works, it goes on in the next verse to say that we are created in Christ Jesus *unto* good works which God has prepared for us.

We also see that James and Paul are using the concept of works in a different sense. Paul is talking about those people who would do works in order to be saved, works which would lead to salvation. James is telling people that they need those works which flow out of salvation and result in salvation. True faith reaches up to connect us to the dynamo of the universe, to the Holy Spirit of God, and it always results in a transformation of life, by the surging of the power of God into our lives. A man may say that he has faith, but if he does not demonstrate that transformation of life, then his faith is spurious.

The importance of trusting in Christ alone for our salvation may be further explained in the following way:

Faith and works boats

"Imagine that you are out in the middle of a lake and there are two rowboats and you are standing with one foot in each boat. One boat, however, is filled with holes and is sinking fast. It is obvious that unless you do something you will soon be in the lake. The boat with the holes represents ourselves with all of the leaks caused by sin. The boat without holes represents Christ. It should be obvious that with one foot in each boat we shall end up in the same place that we would have ended up if we had had both feet in the boat marked 'self.' The only safe place to be is to have both feet firmly planted in the boat marked Christ.

Rope or thread?

"Or to change the picture, suppose that you were trying to cross from one cliff to another one which is a hundred feet away. It is five thousand feet down to the rocks below. You have, however, a one-inch-thick piece of rope which is capable of holding up several tons. There is a difficulty though, for you have only fifty feet of rope. I say, 'Do not worry! I have fifty feet of thread. We can tie my thread to your rope and then tie that to trees on either cliff and then you can go across.' You decline my offer and I respond, 'What is the matter? Do you not trust the rope?' 'Yes,' you say, 'I trust the rope but I do not trust the thread.' Then let's change the story and make it ninety feet of rope and only ten feet of thread. You're still not comfortable. Then suppose we make it ninety-nine feet of rope and only one foot of thread. One inch of thread? You see, if you have one inch of thread, you will be just as dead on the rocks below as if you tried to cross on a hundred feet of thread. The rope obviously represents what Christ has done and the thread represents what we have done. We must trust in Christ alone. As Charles Spurgeon put it, 'If we have to put one stitch into the garment of our salvation, we shall ruin the whole thing.' "

I DON'T BELIEVE IN THE RESURRECTION OF CHRIST

The resurrection of Christ is the best established fact of antiquity. I have never met a person who has read so much as one book on the evidences for the resurrection of Christ who did not believe it. I have met many people who did not believe it, but they have never examined the evidence. A nineteen-year-old young man once said to me, "Well, it's just your opinion. There's no evidence to support it." How foolish is that statement, and yet it represents the opinion of many people. The Christian faith is the only evidential and historical religion in the world. The Bible never calls us to blind faith, but it calls us to faith in evidence. Blind faith is faith without evidence. The Bible calls us to believe in "many infallible proofs." Are these proofs able to stand up to the light of criticism?

Dr. Simon Greenleaf was more qualified to examine such evidence than any man who ever lived. He was the Royall Professor of Law at Harvard University and was declared by the Chief Justice of the Supreme Court of the United States to be the greatest authority on legal evidences that had ever lived. He was the highest authority on evidence that could be quoted in any English-speaking courtroom in the world. After writing voluminously on the laws of legal evidences he decided to turn the searchlight of his knowledge of evidence and his ability to sift the true from the false toward the evidence for the resurrection of Christ.

He minutely examined each thread of evidence concerning the resurrection of Christ and concluded that in any unbiased courtroom in the world, if the evidence for the resurrection of Christ were presented it would be adjudged to be an absolute historical fact. This was the opinion of the greatest authority on evidence that the world has ever known—Dr. Simon Greenleaf of Harvard.

I DON'T BELIEVE IN LIFE AFTER DEATH

The fundamental reasons for our believing in life after death are the resurrection of Jesus Christ from the dead and the unambiguous declarations of Scripture that man has been made for eternity and will live forever, either in heaven or in hell. Many scientists have been quite skeptical over the possibility of life beyond the grave. However, it is worthy of note that recently several scientists have caused a stir in the scientific world by announcing that the conclusions of their investigations have led them to believe that life goes on beyond the grave. These conclusions have been reached from careful interviews with hundreds of people who have been pronounced "clinically dead" and have later been revived and have told of the experiences that they have had in the interval. I have personally talked with people who have experienced in this world a foretaste of either heaven or hell. Since there is no consensus either in medicine or in law as to just when death takes place, these experiences leave some questions to be answered. But they do provide interesting modern testimony to the fact that people live on beyond death, either in joy or in torment.

I have found these testimonies to have a very sobering effect upon some skeptical individuals. The following information, therefore, may be used with discretion in answering the objection, "I don't believe in life after death":

"The evidence is now conclusive: There *is* life after death." This is not the statement of an overenthusiastic preacher or of some recondite theologian in his ivory tower, but the somber pronouncement of a scientist made to a large group of other scientists. The statement: "The evidence is now conclusive: There *is* life after death." The speaker: Dr. Elizabeth Kubler-Ross, psychiatrist. The occasion: a national conference on "death, dying and beyond," in which a thousand scholars, medical experts, and professionals in the care of the dying participated.

Dr. Kubler-Ross was apparently not a Christian nor even a particularly religious person, but that was her sober conclusion from the examination of hundreds upon hundreds of cases of terminally ill patients. In her testimony she declares that she has carefully scrutinized the statements of hundreds of people who have had the experience of being pronounced clinically dead (legally dead), who have been resuscitated and have told of what happened during that interval.

You have said in the past, "Oh, well, when somebody goes there and comes back, then I will listen." Well, friend, start listening, because someone has been there and has been back—not merely someone, but four or five hundred different someones. Their statements have been carefully analyzed and compiled by scientists, by not only Dr. Kubler-Ross but others as well, including Dr. Raymond Moody of the University of Virginia. By the way, where did this national conference take place and where was this startling declaration made? The University of California at Berkeley! Right out of the center of the counter-culture comes new proof of life beyond death. Dr. Kubler-Ross says that hundreds of cases of individuals who have died and have had out-of-body experiences have been scientifically verified. "We've just been afraid to admit it," she said.

Would you like to know what happens when you die—what the experience of dying is like? Five hundred people have testified to that experience, and the amazing thing is the unanimity of their testimonies. They have been collected from a wide variety of people, from all sorts of backgrounds, by a number of different scientific investigators. Dr. Moody of the University of Virginia sums up all of his findings in this way: "There is a buzz or a ring at the moment of death, followed by rapid progression through an enclosure or tunnel toward light. [*I am the light of the world.*] There is surprise at being outside the body. Next comes a panoramic review of one's life." And note this: People who were paraplegics, who have been paralyzed for years, have legs they could move; they have a body, a spiritual body, albeit, with legs that they could move and limbs that they could use. And astounding as it is to report, those who had been blind for many years finally had eyes through which they could see. In fact, in every case they reported on the people that came into the resuscitation room—people who were blind reported on who was there, what they did, and what they said.

They all reported floating up out of their body and looking down on all of the people in the resuscitation room, and described accurately the details of what they had seen. These were not just a few, but over five hundred separate cases taken from all over the world. And then, note this: Every one of these people reported seeing, usually at a distance, a person whom they described as a religious "figure." This was even true for atheists. The Bible says that there is one with whom we have to do, and that One is Jesus Christ! Even atheists will have to appear before him. There is no escape! Many were quite irritated at being brought back into their limited and often crippled physical bodies.

Dr. Kubler-Ross said, in conclusion, to her colleagues, "We now have factual support, replicated again and again, in hundreds of cases by different people. For me, there's no longer a shadow of a doubt. I used to say, 'I believe in life after death.' Now I *know.*" One thousand medical professionals and scholars stood to give this psychiatrist a standing ovation when she concluded.

UNIVERSALISM

Occasionally you will meet a universalist who will object, "Everyone will be saved." This is the same objection "hell isn't real," only in a little different dress. Some Scripture that is useful in putting the lie to universalism is, "Then shall he say also unto them on the left hand, Depart from me, ye cursed, into everlasting fire, prepared for the devil and his angels . . . these shall go away into everlasting punishment: but the righteous into life eternal" (Matthew 25:41, 46).

NOT NOW

Often one will hear the gospel and agree to its truthfulness but will not want to receive Christ at the moment. Of course, such an attitude is presumptive. The prospect assumes that he will have another opportunity to respond to God's gracious invitation. Probably he will; possibly he will not. The evangelist has a responsibility to press the urgency of the matter and persuade the prospect. Jesus warned of the fool who said, "Soul, thou hast much goods laid up for many years; take thine ease, eat, drink, and be merry," only to hear the frightful words, "Thou fool, this night thy soul shall be required of thee." Paul echoed the same thought: "In the day of salvation have I succoured thee: behold, now is the accepted time; behold, now is the day of salvation" (2 Corinthians 6:2).

Device of Satan. Regardless of the form of the objection, recognize it as a device of Satan to prevent your proclaiming the gospel. Recognize, further, that you are not calling on your prospect in order to defeat him in a debate. By precluding objections and by dealing with those that arise in a matter-of-fact manner, you can succeed in presenting your prospect with enough information to make a decision.

SIX
ILLUSTRATIONS

Following are a number of illustrations that we have found effective in illuminating the gospel. The illustrations available for this purpose are limitless. Perhaps you will have good experience with some other illustrations. Since all of life is an illustration of spiritual truth, every sermon, book, or even the commonplace occurrences of everyday life provide abundant illustrations of spiritual truth. It should be noted that most illustrations are designed to point out one significant truth.

GOD'S HOLINESS—OUT-OF-TUNE INSTRUMENT

Imagine an orchestra playing in concert and one instrument is out of tune. The conductor would not eliminate the entire orchestra; however, he would have to cast out the bad instrument. Spiritually, we are out of tune with God. He is righteous; we are unrighteous. He is perfect; we are imperfect. God is sinless; we are sinful. Just as it was necessary to cast out the discordant instrument for the orchestra to remain an orchestra, it was necessary for the One in perfect harmony with himself to cast man out. God cannot exist with sin. He can have nothing to do with that which is other than he is, and he is absolutely perfect, holy, and righteous.

GOD'S HOLINESS—MISCARRIAGE

You can liken our relationship to God to that of a mother who has carried her baby almost full term and then has a miscarriage. The mother has grown to love the child; she anticipates the fellowship and presence of the child. However, the child has something in his biological makeup that actually acts in opposition to the mother's own biological makeup. This is the way it is spiritually. Man is actually a creature of God. However, man worked against God and introduced discord. Now God must cast away his creature. He still loves man, but if man remained in union with God it would destroy the perfection of God, and God would no longer be God.

GOD'S JUSTICE—BANK ROBBER

Suppose I were to rob a bank of $5,000. A hidden camera takes movies of me doing it and the teller and the other eye witnesses identify me as the culprit. When I am brought before the judge he asks, "How do you plead?" I am guilty and the evidence is undeniable and so I respond, "I am guilty, your Honor." He then sentences me to five years in prison for armed bank robbery. Suppose I were to say to him, "Judge, I am very sorry that I robbed the bank. You have the money back and no one was hurt. I promise you I will never rob another bank if you will just let me go." Would the judge be just if he let me go? He has a standard of justice that must be satisfied. If judges let bank robbers off simply because they said they were sorry and promised not to rob any more banks, there is not a bank in the land that would be safe. God is much more just than any human judge. And he cannot simply excuse our sin.

MAN'S INABILITY—BROAD JUMP

Let the sofa and the coffee table represent the two sides of an incredibly deep canyon. Say the width is one hundred feet. Now we can imagine all the men, women, and children that have ever lived or ever will be born on earth lined up on one side. They have to get to the other side, let's say, to save their lives from an impending danger. They will be lost if they don't make it. They have to jump. Now do you have any idea what the broad jump record is? Between twenty-eight and thirty feet! How many people from the whole human race can jump the one-hundred-foot-wide canyon? None! That's exactly right! No one would make it, although some would do better than others. Some would jump way out—twenty feet or more. Some would only make it a few feet. Some cripples would just stumble over the edge. But none would make it all the way! All would fall short of the mark. All would fall to their death.

This is the way it is spiritually. There is a gap between man and the kingdom of God. We try as hard as we can to jump the gap. We go to church, keep God's commandments, don't intentionally hurt anyone, and jump out here as far as possible. That's the way I was in my own life—jumping hard! I had comfort from the fact that I was jumping farther than many. I figured God would accept those who jump the farthest. I knew no one was perfect so I figured he would accept those who did the best. I thought that God would lower his standard. But this would mean that God grades on the curve. He does not! I learned this was wrong. He has only one standard: perfection. Jesus said, "Be ye perfect even as your Father in heaven is perfect." I am not perfect. Suddenly I recognized that those people I looked down on who were not doing as well as I in being good were no worse off than I. I knew we were all going to the same death. Regardless of how good we were, none was good enough to get across the canyon. We are all doomed to the same eternal death. We will all go to hell if we have to make ourselves good enough for heaven. There must be another way across, or there is no way at all.

MAN'S INABILITY—LEMON TREE

The reason we cannot keep God's commandments is that we do not have the nature to act according to his will. We have no inner ability to keep them. Imagine that you have a lemon tree in your yard. All it can produce is sour lemons. Now if you want to grow oranges, you may decide to pull off all the lemons from your tree and then stick sweet, juicy oranges in their place. In a few minutes your tree could be covered with the sweetest oranges in town. Everyone looks and sees your "orange" tree—but in reality all you have is a lemon tree with dead oranges on it. You haven't changed the nature of the tree.

Our human nature is sour. Often we don't like it and we resolve to do better. We try to throw away the fruits of our sour nature. We get rid of the bottle, clean up our language, and try to better family and business relationships. All we are really doing is picking off lemons and sticking on oranges. We get rid of bad habits and acquire good ones. However, this does not change the source of the stream of life. Our nature is untouched by our resolutions and reformations. We are as powerless to make our hearts good as we are to make a lemon tree into an orange tree. We need a new nature. The Bible says, "If any man be in Christ he is a new creation."

MAN'S INABILITY—CHINESE NATURE

If the Central Intelligence Agency wanted you to be an agent behind the bamboo curtain in China, you would be trained to talk, act, look, and think Chinese. You would go to school and learn the Chinese language so that you could speak it fluently without a trace of accent. After studying the mores of China and watching films of Chinese physical characteristics, you could duplicate their mannerisms. Perhaps you would undergo plastic surgery and have your face changed so that you would look Chinese. Then you could enter Communist China and be welcomed as one of them. You then would do everything in the Chinese manner. No difference would be noticeable. As far as anyone in China is concerned you are Chinese. Now let me ask you—would you be Chinese? No, not if you did not have Chinese parents. Nothing you can do will change your race.

Actually, it's the same way spiritually. You may talk and dress like a Christian. You may join Christian organizations and sing Christian songs, and in all ways act like a Christian. However, none of these things will make you a Christian. You were born a sinful man and you have the nature of a sinful race. Nothing you can do outwardly can change this fact. Just as you would have to have been born of Chinese parents to be Chinese, so you need a new birth spiritually to be a Christian. It's impossible for you to become a Chinese. However, with God all things are possible, and you can be born anew spiritually and become a child of God. Those who have been born again put their trust for eternal life in Jesus Christ alone.

CHRIST'S WORK—HUMAN PREDICAMENT EQUATION

You can take the human predicament and make an equation out of it. Man's sinfulness plus God's justice can equal only one thing: eternal hell for man. That is what we deserve. However, there is another factor in the equation. If we add to man's sinfulness and God's justice the factor of God's love, again one answer is possible: the cross of Christ. Because God loved his people with an everlasting love, it was necessary that Christ provide redemption through the blood of his cross.

GOD'S JUSTICE—AREOPAGITE

It is said that none ever could claim he was dealt with unjustly by the Areopagite in Athens. His sentence always proved to be upright. How much more is this true of the righteous judgment of God who must be justified.

GOD'S MERCY—DYING THOMAS HOOKER

When Thomas Hooker lay dying, a friend said, "Brother, you are going to receive the reward of your labors." He humbly replied, "Brother, I am going to receive mercy." We need nothing but mercy, but mercy we must have or we are lost. Justice would give us what we deserve—hell. God in his infinite mercy and grace gives heaven.

A huge crowd of people were watching the famous tightrope walker, Blondin, cross Niagara Falls one day in 1860. Blondin crossed the rope numerous times—a 1,000-foot trip, 160 feet above the raging water. The story is told that he spoke to the crowd, asking if they believed he could take one of them across. Of course, they all gave their assent. Then he approached a man and asked him to get on his back and go with him. The man who was invited refused to go. It is like that with Jesus Christ. Mental assent, or even verbal assent, is not enough. There must be trust—not strength—but trust in Christ alone.

FAITH—OBJECT DETERMINES VALUE

Have you ever considered what makes faith valuable? Some seem to think that faith has an intrinsic value and they say, "Have faith!" I submit that faith must be in a valuable object if the faith itself is to be valuable. Faith in the wrong object is not valuable—it is disastrous. You may have all the faith you can muster in the brakes of your car; however, if the fluid line is broken your brakes will not stop the car and neither will your faith. If you awaken in the night with a headache and stumble into the dark bathroom, and in faith take a tablet which you think to be aspirin but mistakenly take a roach tablet, they may inscribe on your tombstone, "He died in faith," but your faith was in an object not worthy of your confidence. Many pregnant women took the mysterious drug thalidomide in the faith that it would make their pregnancy easier. Their faith did not prevent their bearing deformed children. Faith, to have any value, must be in a valuable object. When it comes to your eternal welfare, only Jesus Christ is worthy of your confidence and trust. To have faith in anyone else or in anything else is disastrous.

GOOD WORKS—FRIEND'S GIFT

Good works cannot add to the gift of salvation. Suppose your best friend (or wife, husband, mother, etc.) were to surprise you with a beautiful gift, and let's suppose your response would be that of immediately digging into your purse or wallet for a couple of bills to help pay the expense. What an insult it would be! Suppose the gift was an expensive coat, and you offered back five dollars. This would result in wounding the giver. Well, what about offering one dollar—or say, twenty-five cents, or a nickel, or even a penny! No, the smaller the gift, the greater the insult. You must accept gifts freely. If you pay even a penny, it is not a gift. It is that way with salvation. Even a small attempt to pay for our salvation forfeits our receiving it. We will never be able to say one day in heaven, "Look what Christ and I did!" It will be all him—none of me. As God says in his Word, "For by grace are ye saved through faith, and that not of yourself; it is the gift of God, not of works, lest any man should boast."

GOOD WORKS—PRICELESS CABINET

A famed cabinet maker is very fond of you. He wants to surprise you with the greatest gift you'll ever receive. Unknown to you, he gathers all the money he has. He takes all his life's savings, and though he has to deny his own son the privileges that others have, he sells all that he has, cashes in stocks and bonds, and hunts the world over to find the best wood that money can buy. The priceless unfinished wood is brought into his shop. Day and night he works to produce the most perfect, the most beautiful table the world has ever known. He goes without food, without sleep, and his health is neglected. Finally, the butting, the sawing, the gluing, the fitting, and the sanding are all done. He finishes this masterpiece by hours and hours of hand polishing. Finally, the last stroke is made with the cloth. The next day he comes to your door with his men holding the table draped in cloth. You welcome him in and he unveils the priceless gift. What will be your response? Let's say you run and grab a piece of sandpaper and make a move toward the table. This expert craftsman stops you short and exclaims, "It's finished!" It is like this with salvation. God paid a priceless sum in giving Jesus on the cross for us, who himself cried out, "It is finished!" We can add nothing—not one thing! We have only to receive—undeserving as we are. To change anything about that gift of God is to refuse it. Where then are good works? They are in the honoring of the giver. Just as that table will be placed in the open for all to see, and just as all who see it will be told all about the glory and mercy of the man who made it, so we will by the nature of our acceptance lift up God in our lives and proclaim what he has done for us. And this will be evidenced in all that we do and say.

GOD'S ONLY FORGOTTEN SON

This is a powerful illustration which can be used at the end of a presentation if the person is hesitating about his willingness to place his trust in Christ.

> "Suppose that the police were to break into this room right now with guns drawn and take me away handcuffed to prison. You, of course, would be startled, and when you read in the newspaper that I was being tried for multiple murders and bank robberies you would be even more surprised. After you heard that I had been convicted and sentenced to die in the electric chair you would no doubt be amazed indeed. Since, however, you know me and you are supposed to 'love your neighbor' even as you love yourself, you decide to try to do something to help me.
>
> "You go down and speak to the judge and say, 'What can I do to help?

I'll do anything at all. I will even be willing to give my life for him,' to which the judge replies, 'That would not be a sufficient sacrifice for this man has killed many people. However, we would accept the life of your child. That would be an adequate sacrifice.' You go home and agonize. You have but one child—a lovely young daughter. You pray; you wrestle with your decision; and finally you decide that if you really are going to love me, even as yourself, that you must do this. And so you bring your child down to the prison where you are told, 'You must do it. *You* shave her head; *you* put her in the chair; and *you* pull the switch.' And so, as your child looks pleadingly at you and says, 'Mommie, why have you forsaken me?' you cover her head and watch her writhe and die as you pull the switch. The guards inform me of what has been done by you in my behalf and that because of that I am free to go home.

"A few days later you are sitting in a booth in a restaurant having dinner. I come in behind you with a friend and sit down, not seeing you. You overhear my friend say to me, 'According to the newspapers you had been condemned and were to die in the electric chair. What happened? How is it that you're free?' And then to your astonishment you hear my reply, 'Oh, it was all a big mistake. When they looked at the record of my life they saw that I was really a pretty nice fellow. There were a great many people that I had not killed and numerous banks that I had not robbed. Why, I had even put money in some banks! And helped several old ladies across the street in years gone by. After weighing my whole life, they decided to let me go and therefore I am free.'

"As you listen to these incredible words there flashes into your mind a picture of your daughter writhing in the electric chair. And you know in your heart that the *only* reason that I am walking around alive is because on the other side of town there's a new grave with your daughter's name on the marker. How do you feel about me now? I think that is the way that God might feel about you if you had come before him today and told him all about your good works without even a word about his Son who died on the cross. A little boy in the first grade in Sunday school was reciting John 3:16, but he got it slightly mixed up and I think that he is a picture of many of us. He said, 'For God so loved the world that he gave his only *forgotten* Son.'"

SEVEN
DOS AND DON'TS

After several years of "hitting our heads against stone walls" and finding that in many cases the same stone walls bruise our heads in the same way, we have searched for ways of avoiding the collision. Following is a list of some practical do's and don'ts that contribute to the success of our lay evangelism program.

Don't carry a large Bible on your visit! A New Testament **in your pocket or purse** will furnish all the Scripture you will need. A large Bible in your lap can have the same effect as a .45 revolver. Your prospect will wonder, "What's he going to do with that?" Never show your "weapon" until you are ready to use it. At the right time you can "draw and shoot him alive!"

Don't give the reference when you quote Scripture. You need to know the reference, but giving the location of each verse that you use can interrupt your prospect's train of thought.

Do quote just the relevant portion of the verse. For example, we use 1 John 5:13 when we affirm that the Bible was written that men might know they have eternal life. We quote only: "These things are written that ye . . . may know that ye have eternal life." The rest of the verse would introduce matters not germane to the discussion at that point. People do not get all the meaning in a long verse. They can be easily lost. Concentrate on the portion of the verse that bears on the discussion at the moment.

Do anticipate objections and preclude them, if possible. When an objection arises, deal with it in a manner that indicates that you are not threatened by it. Handle objections in a straightforward, matter-of-fact manner and return to the main course of the discussion.

Do stress the positive benefits of the gospel. Some indicate by their manner of presentation that coming to Christ is one of the greatest disasters of life. Certainly this is not the case.

Don't use leading questions. If you know just a little psychology you can get your prospect to say yes to anything. However, you cannot manipulate a person into the kingdom of God.

Don't use misleading questions. For example, "Tell me, Mr. Jones, what do you think you have to do to earn your way to heaven?" Such a question misleads your prospect. He may be trusting in Christ but you come with a voice of authority implying that he can do something to save himself. You have misled him. He may give you information that he does not truly believe, and the rest of your conversation would be in vain.

Do start where the person is. Do not assume that mid-twentieth century people know very much about the contents of the Bible.

Do dangle your bait in front of the prospect. Do not shove the hook down his throat.

Do ask permission to ask questions. It is wise also, occasionally, to ask your prospect's permission to continue discussing the matters at hand, particularly if you sense some reticence on his part to continue. His simple "Yes" to "Would you like me to share with you what I learned about how to get to heaven?" will preclude his seething with rage as you proceed.

Do ask your prospect's opinion. He will feel more kindly to you if you indicate that you are an intelligent man who values his opinion.

Do listen to your prospect talk so that you can intelligently refer to statements he has made as you make your presentation.

Do be conservative in your estimation of what happens on your visit. You may see a profession of faith. Only time will tell if your prospect was born again, accepted the Lord, and was converted.

Don't feel you have to secure a profession regardless of what you might have to do to get it. High-pressure tactics are to be abhorred.

Do be overly modest as you talk about your church. Do not convey the idea that yours is the only church that presents the gospel.

Do avoid critical comments about other congregations, ministers, and denominations. It is true that many are unfaithful to the Lord. But you will lose your prospect's confidence if he feels you try to build your flock by tearing down others.

Do smile, especially as you ask the two commitment questions. If you are too intense, your prospect may feel he is being pinned down, and resent it.

Do make your exit sweet—even if the gospel is rejected. Remember: it is the gospel—not you—that has been rejected. The harvest is not until the end of the world—the prospect may yet be drawn to Christ.

Do watch your grooming and manner of dress. Sloppy shoes and unpressed suits do not speak well of the King you represent. Skirts that are too short can be distracting. Neatness is most important. A good rule: Dress in a way that will not draw attention away from your message.

Do ask a friend if you have bad breath, and encourage an honest answer. If you have it, do something to get rid of it or your prospect will be thinking of ways to get rid of you!

Don't sit in the car at the prospect's house and pray before you go to the prospect's door. Pray before you get to your prospect's residence.

EIGHT
FOLLOW-UP

The Great Commission commands us to make disciples, not merely get decisions. To go with the gospel is only the beginning. A disciple is a functionally mature, responsible reproducing member of a local church.

PREREQUISITES

There are a number of prerequisites to produce disciples of this nature.

1. a healthy church
2. effective evangelism
3. heart
4. perspective
5. work
6. intelligent procedure

1. A HEALTHY CHURCH

A healthy, functionally mature local church is where discipleship begins. New Christians are not orphans to be institutionalized, nor do they merely join the "Christian country club." They are born into the family of God. The local church is the microcosm of that universal family. The church may have a number of task groups within it, but no single task group *is* the church. Where the Word of God is properly preached and taught, baptism and the Lord's Supper properly administered, and discipline properly exercised—there is the church.

The church is a family—the forever family of God! It is composed of the young and the old, the mature and the not-so-mature.

Functional maturity. For the local church to be functionally mature it must have a significant percentage of its members who are functionally mature. First Corinthians 13 provides a model of perfect maturity. This certainly is a goal worthy of aspiration.

We are to be motivated by love in all that we do. As we are motivated by love we best reflect the God who is love. Thus motivated we will seek to discover the gifts the Spirit bestows upon us. Then we will use these gifts within the local body where he places us.

No believer can be functionally mature apart from a vital relation in the local church. The recognized leaders of the local church must be models of functional maturity. Then those who are less mature will see the truth of God's Word in their lives and more easily duplicate their dedication.

Balance of Word and Spirit. Functional maturity requires acceptance of Scripture as God's Word and reliance upon the Holy Spirit to enable you to be all you were meant to be. You will never be more filled with the Spirit than you are filled with God's Word.

Do not seek to be saturated with Scripture and ignore the Spirit of love. You will become an argumentative Pharisee, harsh and abrasive. On the other hand don't totally concentrate on the Spirit of love without the objective truth of God's Word. You will become an emotional, unstable, ignorant fanatic. God wants us to walk in obedience. He wants you to give as much of yourself as you can to as much of Christ as you know, on a daily basis.

Proper priorities. This balance of the Word and the Spirit will enable you to have proper priorities. Proper priorities will enable you to effectively use your time and become what God intended you to be. In general terms proper priorities are:

1. God
2. God's people
3. the world

PRIORITY ONE—GOD. Priority one is God. Jesus said, "Love the Lord your God with all your heart, with all your soul and with all your mind" (Matthew 22:37, NIV). To Moses, God said, "You shall have no other gods before Me" (Exodus 20:3, NAS). We are urged to "seek first the kingdom of God and his righteousness" (Matthew 6:33, NIV).

PRIORITY TWO—GOD'S PEOPLE. Priority two is God's people—the church. When you are in proper relationship with God it will show itself by being in proper relation with his people. This means visible identification with them. You worship in the celebrating assembly. You participate in group Bible studies. There you discover your gifts and use them. You find a soul-friend and grow together toward maturity. You partake of the vital life in the small cell groups and your life is transformed.

PRIORITY THREE—THE WORLD. God leaves us here for the primary purpose of bearing witness to the world. Our relation to him and his people will be perfect in heaven. We were eligible to enter heaven the moment we trusted Christ. Therefore, we must be still here to be channels through which he can reach those who are yet to believe.

2. EFFECTIVE EVANGELISM

Out of the healthy functionally mature local church grows effective evangelism. The gospel must be proclaimed without compromise. But persons must be respected and communicated to in a way that enables them to intelligently accept or reject the gospel. Our Lord indicates in the parable of the sower that those who reproduce 30, 60, and 100 percent are the ones who heard the gospel with understanding (Matthew 13:23). It is impossible to properly disciple or follow up on someone that has not been effectively evangelized. A spiritually stillborn person has no life to live to develop.

3. HEART

Paul said to his spiritual children in Thessalonica, ". . . we were gentle among you, like a mother caring for her little children. We loved you so much that we were delighted to share with you not only the gospel of God but our lives as well . . ." (1 Thessalonians 2:7, 8, NIV). To be a parent requires a God-like love.

It requires a special kind of love for parents to properly care for helpless infants. When they are hungry or thirsty, when their diaper is dirty, they cry out for attention—regardless of the time. Unless parents care for the child with a God-like unselfish love, it will not become what it was meant to be.

Likewise, rearing spiritual children to become functionally mature disciples requires a special God-like love—giving, unconditional, sleepless! Scripture says, "We love because he first loved us" (1 John 4:19). The more you open yourself to God's love, the more it can flow through you to those who need it.

4. PERSPECTIVE

To properly disciple another requires a vision of what the grace of God can do with a sinner. The Apostle John said to his spiritual offspring, "I have no greater joy than to hear that my children are living according to the truth" (3 John 4, NIV). Those who are satisfied with merely proclaiming the gospel and receiving professions are like immoral seducers. The seducer is satisfied merely to exploit and then tell of his exploits rather than to enter into a meaningful marriage commitment. Do not judge the effectiveness of your evangelism-discipleship by what you see in the person you have evangelized. Measure your effectiveness by your spiritual grandchildren. If those you evangelize and disciple produce good disciples who can disciple others, then you have done your job well.

Ask God to give you the eternal heavenly perspective on life. Endure as seeing him who is invisible (Hebrews 11:27). Move toward the city whose builder and maker is God (Hebrews 11:10). With eternity's values in view, we are much more willing to let God's grace mold our lives and make us into models for discipling others.

5. WORK!

There is more glamour and adventure in evangelism than there is in developing functionally mature disciples. To the Colossians Paul said, "We proclaim him, counseling and teaching everyone with all wisdom, so that we may present everyone perfect in Christ. To this end I *labor, struggling with all the energy he so powerfully works in me*" (Colossians 1:29, NIV). Disciple-making requires expenditure of energy. It is laborious, hard work, but rewarding. Paul urged, "Therefore, my dear brothers, stand firm. Let nothing move you. Always give yourselves fully to the work of the Lord, because you know that your labor in the Lord is not in vain." (I Corinthians 15:58, NIV).

6. INTELLIGENT PROCEDURE

It is not enough to do a job right. The right job must be done in the right way.

Prayer. Intelligent procedure begins and ends with prayer. Paul said, "Night and day we pray most earnestly that we may see you again and supply what is lacking in your faith" (1 Thessalonians 3:10, NIV). "With this in mind, we constantly pray for you, that our God may count you worthy of his calling, and that by his power he may fulfill every good purpose of yours and every act prompted by your faith" (2 Thessalonians 1:11, NIV).

By prayer you may pursue every person you have opportunity to share the gospel with. God will move in response to your petitions and work through the circumstances surrounding them.

Correspondence. Intelligent procedure also utilizes written correspondence. Most of the New Testament epistles are follow-up letters. Correspondence can be used to reinforce personal contact or to maintain contact with individuals that are too far away to personally disciple.

Personal involvement. Intelligent procedure includes personal involvement with the people hearing the gospel. This begins with your own relationship to the Lord. Christ has made you a new creature (2 Corinthians 5:17). You are acceptable to God the Father in him (Ephesians 1:6). If God, the Son—the righteous Judge of the universe—accepts you, who can condemn you? (Romans 8:31-35). As you accept his acceptance of you in Christ, you are free to grow.

As you walk with Christ you should be a model of dedication for those you are seeking to disciple. This is not an empty egotism but the authentic demonstration of redeemed humanity. There is, what Luther called, an alien dignity that God gives to his people. Paul, writing to the Thessalonians said, "We did this, not because we do not have the right to such help, but in order to make ourselves a **model** for you to follow" (2 Thessalonians 3:9, NIV). To the Philippians he said, "Brethren, join in imitating me . . ." (Philippians 3:17, RSV). To the Corinthians he declared, "Follow my example, as I follow the example of Christ" (1 Corinthians 11:1, NIV). Whether you like it or not, you are going to "multiply after your kind." Therefore be sure you are the kind that should be multiplied.

You are responsible to personally do what you can do as a spiritual parent. Then you are responsible to use the resources of the whole local family of God to provide all that is needful to properly disciple your spiritual children. Individually you will be able to do many things face-to-face and on the telephone. Some of your discipling activity will be with the cell units of your church, such as the witnessing team. You should also use the sub-congregation (choir, Bible study group, etc.) within your local assembly.

The importance of the whole local assembly gathered to celebrate and worship is impossible to overestimate. All of these dimensions: individual, cell, congregation, assembly, are personal avenues for discipleship.

The specific suggestions for procedure in the following pages are only a few of the things that can be done in discipling a new believer. These suggestions are provided as those most directly related to the Evangelism Explosion ministry in the local church. The Holy Spirit gives guidance in each local situation.

IMMEDIATE FOLLOW-UP (SAME DAY AS PROFESSION)—SAMPLE CONVERSATION*

Welcome to the family of God and Happy Birthday!

Today is very important for you. Did you think when you got up this morning that it might be your spiritual birthday? It's good for that decision to be registered in writing. This card entitled "My Decision for Christ" is something I want to give to you as a reminder that you prayed to receive eternal life today. Let's read it together:

> "My decision for Christ.
> Knowing that I have sinned and that I need the Lord Jesus Christ as my Savior, I now repent and trust him to pardon and deliver me from sin's guilt and power.
> I give him control of my life.
> As he gives me strength I shall seek to be a responsible growing member in his forever family."

Is this the decision that you have just made?

> Yes.

Then let's put today's date on this line and, since this is your decision, you put your name on the line marked for signature.

(Let him sign the card.)

I'm putting my name and phone number on the card also. That's so you can contact me anytime I can be of assistance to you. Keep this card in your wallet. You can call it your spiritual birth certificate. It will help you remember that today you prayed to receive new life—eternal life.

This *Welcome to the Forever Family* booklet is a present I would like to give you. We have talked quite a lot today. You will not remember everything that has been said. I would like just a few more minutes to point out some very important thoughts contained in this booklet. After we are gone, you should read it very carefully.

If you read it aloud it would take only ten minutes. Understanding what is in this

* Quotations in indented paragraphs are taken directly from the booklet, *Welcome to the Forever Family* When you see *** it means the *Welcome* booklet has more to say on the point that is not quoted in this sample conversation.

booklet can add a great deal of meaning to your life. Will you read it for me—for yourself?

Yes, you make it sound important.

Believe me, it is. Let's look at it together now.

"Birth brings life, then life should grow. God tells us that we should 'grow in the grace and knowledge of our Lord and Savior Jesus Christ.' Each day we are to grow more like Jesus. God wants us to be 'conformed to the image of his Son.'

Eternal life is a free gift received by faith alone. But as long as God leaves us in this world, there will be need for growth. The growth and development of eternal life is a costly process. It requires faith and loving obedience.

Growth comes by proper use of the means provided by God. He wants you to enjoy a full and healthy spiritual life and has provided for this.

"A word of caution: No one has eternal life simply because he **says** that he trusts Christ. Only the person who **truly trusts** Christ has eternal life. The person who has eternal life will hunger for God's Word. He will read it regularly and want to study it with others. He will want to worship with God's people. He will want his life to be clean and pleasing to God. Anyone who does not demonstrate the desire to grow in his spiritual life by using the means that God has provided should not deceive himself into thinking that he has eternal life.

The five means of growth provided by God are:

1. The Bible
2. Prayer
3. Worship
4. Fellowship
5. Witness"

Let's look at what God says about these five means of growth.

THE BIBLE

First, the Bible is God's Word.

***

"God has given us the Bible to feed our souls. Jesus said, 'Man shall not live by bread alone, but by every word that proceeds out of the mouth of God.'

"The Gospel of John is a good place to start reading. 'Gospel' means 'good news.' John wrote his book so that we might know the good news about who Jesus is and what eternal life is. John was Jesus' closest friend. He was an eyewitness to most of the events he records. In a court of law today his testimony would be considered very significant."

I would like to give you this copy of the Gospel of John. It's small so that you can carry it with you. I would like to challenge you to . . . read at least a chapter a day. The chapters are so short that this won't take more than ten minutes a day. Do you think you could do that?

I'm sure I could.

When a verse really stands out and God impresses its truth on you, underscore it with a pencil or pen. This will help you find it when you need it again. When you have any questions about what a verse means, put a question mark by it in the margin.

Seven-day call back appointment. By this time next week then, you will have read at least seven chapters. It would be of value to you for us to get together and talk about any questions you might have. Is this same time and day next week all right for you, or would there be a better time?

(Establish your seven-day call back appointment at this time. Then continue with the *Welcome to the Forever Family* booklet. If it is necessary to abbreviate the immediate follow-up, you may do so *after* you have established the seven-day call back appointment.)

PRAYER

The second means for spiritual growth is prayer.

"Prayer is the way you communicate with God.

"Prayer is your lifeline to God. He keeps no office hours. He is available anytime. There is no need for a special 'holy vocabulary' when you talk to him. You can talk with complete freedom of speech. There is nothing too little or too large for you to tell God."

***

WORSHIP

The third means for spiritual growth is worship.

God wants you to worship him.

***

"To worship God means giving him the number one place in your life and showing it to the whole world by gathering with his forever family on the Lord's Day."

***

"Related to worship are **baptism** and **the Lord's Supper.**"

"Jesus commanded those who trust in him to be baptized in the name of the Father and of the Son and of the Holy Spirit. Water baptism in the local church is a visible indication to all that the person being baptized is a vital member of God's forever family—the church.

"If you feel you are in the church where God wants you to be, then be faithful to him there.

***

"If you are not actively involved in a local church family you should ask God to guide you to the place where he wants you to be. We would be delighted if he wants you to be in our church."

"Jesus also commanded us to observe what is called the Lord's Supper.

***

"God in a special way strengthens you as you share in these with his people around his table."

FELLOWSHIP

"Fellowship with other believers grows out of your relationship with God. Fellowship means sharing your life with others and them sharing their lives with you.

***

"Each member of God's family is important and valuable to God. Christ died for each one. All must seek to grow together. After all, we will be together for all eternity."

***

WITNESS

The last means of growth is witness.

"Those who have eternal life are responsible to share the good news with others.

***

"If we truly have fellowship with the Father and Jesus Christ we will seek to share it with others. Anyone who is content to go to heaven alone, probably is not really headed that way.

***

SATAN

"Satan will seek to stop this growth in your life.

***

"Satan is a supernatural, powerful person, but God the Holy Spirit is always able to overcome him. The Apostle John, after many years in God's forever family, encouraged some new believers with these words, 'You are from God, little children, and have overcome them; because greater is he who is in you (the Holy Spirit) than he who is in the world (the devil).'

"What God starts, he always finishes.

***

"Satan will try to cast doubts in your mind about the reality of what God has done for you. When Jesus was tested by the devil, he quoted Scripture and overcame the testing."

I'd like to ask you to learn by heart this promise from God's Word. "God so loved the world, that he gave his only begotten Son, that whoever believes in him should not perish, but have eternal life."

This is God's promise of salvation to all who believe. It's found in John, chapter three, verse sixteen. If you are trusting in Christ, you can personalize this verse by writing your name in the blanks.

God so loved____________________, that he gave his only begotten Son, that if ____________________ believes in him, ____________________ will not perish (pay the penalty for sin), but ____________________ will have eternal life.

Do you think you could learn this promise by heart by this time next week?

***

I am sure I can.

Good. We will say it together next week.

Bible study group. You can find good fellowship and added understanding of the Word of God by enrolling in a Bible study group. We have a group that lasts only three weeks. You would enjoy it. It meets at 9:15 at the church. Would you be able to go with me next Sunday? I can pick you up or we can meet at the church a few minutes before the group begins.

I could meet you at the church about five minutes before the group starts, if that's OK.

Cassette Tapes. Another way that I get a lot of help in learning the Word of God is with the use of cassette tapes. I've got one that has been very helpful to me. I'd like to share it with you. Would it be all right if I dropped by with it tomorrow about this same time? It would only take a few minutes for me to drop it off.

That sounds interesting but I don't have a tape player.

That's OK, I have a player I will loan you. This last paragraph in your *Welcome* booklet is what I would like to leave you with.

Not even death can destroy this relationship!
Eternal life is even better after death. The Apostle John said, "I saw a new heaven and a new earth; for the first heaven and the first earth passed away.

> . . . I heard a loud voice from the throne, saying, 'Behold the tabernacle of God is among men, and he shall dwell among them, and they shall be his people, and God himself shall be among them, and he shall wipe away every tear from their eyes; and there shall no longer be any mourning, or crying, or pain: the first things have passed away.' And he who sits on the throne said, 'Behold I am making all things new. . . . He who overcomes shall inherit these things, and I will be his God and he will be my son.' " This gives something great to look forward to! But in the meantime, if you want power and purpose in your life, use the means God has provided and—keep growing!

CHURCH NEXT SUNDAY

We must go now. By the way, since you will be at the Bible study group at 9:15, I guess you will want to stay and go to the 11:00 worship service. Would it be all right with you if we attend together? I'd like to introduce you to some of my friends after the service.

That would be fine.

In the front of the *Welcome* booklet there is a list telling you how to grow in God's forever family. Check off each thing as you do it. We will bring another booklet on *Prayer in the Forever Family* next Wednesday.

Once again, welcome to the family of God. I'll drop by this same time tomorrow with the tape and the player and see you at church Sunday about ten minutes after nine, and next Wednesday we will see how you are doing with your Bible reading.

ANALYSIS OF IMMEDIATE FOLLOW-UP

WELCOME TO THE FOREVER FAMILY BOOKLET

Throughout the printed immediate follow-up conversation, there are quotations from the *Welcome to the Forever Family* booklet. These are indented so you can easily identify them. You can read the paragraphs from the booklet with the new profession. This keeps you from having to learn a large quantity of material. Leave the booklet with the new convert so that he has something in printed form to guide him. Be sure to emphasize that "understanding the things in the booklet can add a great deal of meaning to his life," and that it can be read in less than ten minutes. Then get a commitment from him to read it.

HAPPY BIRTHDAY

The last sentence in the gospel presentation is "Welcome to the family of God." The immediate follow-up begins with, "Happy Birthday!" The birth of a child is an experience that is familiar to all. Physical birth and spiritual birth are comparable experiences. This helps the new profession understand a little bit of what is happening in his life. Also the concept of birthday reinforces the idea that a person is born into a family—the family of God. It is important that the reality of this decision be registered in permanent form on the "My Decision for Christ" card.

MY DECISION FOR CHRIST CARD

Using the "Decision" card provides the new convert with a tangible indication that he has prayed to receive the gift of eternal life. This may be used time and time again to combat Satan's attempts at casting doubt in his mind.

Before you ask him to place his name on the card, it is wise to tell him that this will be for him to keep. Otherwise, he may think he is signing a commitment which will go into the records of your church. He might think there is some binding link to membership or a financial responsibility attached to it.

After the words on the card have been read, ask, "*Is* this the decision you have just made?" Do not say, "This is the decision you have just made." Let him tell you what has happened. If he says yes, then put the date on the card and ask him to place his name on the signature line.

When you put your name, address, and phone number on the reverse side of the card, you are indicating interest in your spiritual child and making yourself available. Be sure you follow through on this responsibility.

BIRTH THEN GROWTH

The opening paragraphs point out that growth should follow birth. Following the positive statement that "God wants you to enjoy a full and healthy spiritual life and has provided for this," you will find a word of caution. The "Decision card" is compared to a spiritual birth certificate. Birth certificates do not *bestow* life—they merely *record* life's existence. If life is present, it will show itself. Likewise, when there is genuine spiritual life, it will be apparent. Of course, this does not mean instant perfection, but it does mean that the desires of the heart demonstrate themselves with new interests for life. Using this word of caution will greatly assist you in the overall discipling process. These signs of life are clearly indicated as valid in the first epistle of John.

THE MEANS OF GROWTH

After the word of caution the five means for spiritual growth are listed.

THE BIBLE

As you look at the booklet you will notice we have skipped a paragraph dealing with Scripture. It contains general comments about the Scripture and can be used if dealing with someone who has absolutely no understanding of what the Bible actually is. In that omitted paragraph the reader is urged to obtain a version of the Bible that he can understand. You may not need to say anything about this during the immediate follow-up, but you should be sure by the end of the seven-day contact that he has a Bible of his own.

The dialogue urges the new convert to begin reading in the Gospel of John. John is identified as an eyewitness to most of the events recorded in his book. Then Scripture is described as food for the soul. Give the convert a copy of the Gospel of John. Challenge him to read a chapter a day, and try to get an actual commitment from him to do this. Ask him to underline verses through which God "impresses truth on him." Be cautious about saying God speaks to us. Some new believers expect to hear an audible voice. Urge him to place question marks in the margin by any passage he does not fully understand.

SEVEN-DAY CALL BACK APPOINTMENT

If you have expressed the need for growth following birth, voiced the word of caution, gotten a commitment from the new convert to read a chapter in the Gospel of John each day with underlining and question marks, you will stand a very good chance of getting a seven-day call back appointment at this time. He will understand you want to meet with him *so that he can grow.* He will not have suspicions that you are after his money or trying to force him into church membership. Do not abbreviate any of these things up to this point or you will find fewer people making and keeping call back appointments. Notice the wording in the request for the appointment. Do not ask *if* you may come back. Rather ask for the best day and time.

ABBREVIATION

If the presentation of the gospel has taken a great deal of time and it does not appear that it would be wise to go for another ten minutes or so, you may abbreviate the immediate follow-up from this point forward. Abbreviate does not mean terminate. You have already mentioned the five means of growth. If you do not feel it would be wise to briefly explain each, then move to the promise of salvation (John 3:16) and ask him to learn this by heart. Try to get him to commit himself to attend the Bible study group and worship next Sunday and ask if you can bring the cassette tapes by. Then turn his attention to the page entitled, "How to grow in the Forever Family." This lists each thing he should do in brief, easy-to-understand terms. Ask him to follow the suggestions and indicate you will check next week to see how he has done.

REGULAR, UNABBREVIATED

If you do not need to abbreviate, continue by briefly explaining each means of growth as suggested in the printed conversation. Again you will notice that only portions of the *Welcome* booklet are quoted in the textbook guide. You should be very familiar with the total content of this booklet so that you can use the information in it according to what you believe the needs actually are.

BAPTISM AND THE LORD'S SUPPER

Baptism and the Lord's Supper are included in the *Welcome* booklet because Scripture indicates they are important. However, Christians sometimes widely differ as to their proper interpretation. Most evangelicals agree water baptism is to be performed in the local church and that it indicates visible relation with the body of Christ. Details you share beyond this will vary according to your particular denomination.

Baptism and the Lord's Supper are definite, distinct elements of worship.

When you mention baptism be sensitive and do not press too hard on the matter of church membership. Ask God to give you a balance. On the one hand do not press the person so that he wants to avoid both you and the church. But on the other hand, do not leave the impression that church membership is unimportant or that you do not care whether he is a member of your church or not.

FELLOWSHIP

The comments on fellowship can be used with a person who may be opposed to the church as an institution. As he gets involved in the life of other believers, his attitude toward the church should improve.

WITNESS

Witness is briefly mentioned in order to begin shaping his new life.

SATAN

Satan is referred to so that the new profession will not be caught off guard when he is tested. Be positive in emphasizing that God the Holy Spirit is greater than the devil. What God starts, he finishes! Urge the person to learn God's promises by heart in order to be able to deal with the devil. Let him write his own name in the blanks of John 3:16 as you show this to him. Ask for a commitment from him to learn this promise of salvation by heart by the time you get together next week.

GROUP BIBLE STUDY

The group we are referring to here is the basics class dealing with feeding, cleansing, and relationships for the new believer.

For a new believer, studying the basics of the Christian life in a small group is a very important thing. The teacher will be able to answer questions. Others in the class will raise questions that will greatly benefit him. Remember not to publicly call the class "Basics," "New Christians' Class," or anything like this. Rather give it an exciting name like, "Discovery Group" or "Christian Adventure Class." If your new convert has been attending the church for many, many years, do not tell him that this is a class for *new* Christians. Get him there and let him absorb the information that he needs.

CASSETTE TAPES

Listening to cassette tapes is very beneficial for all Christians, but especially for new believers. Be sure that you have listened to the tapes you share with a new believer before you give them to him. As you ask for the best time to deliver the tapes, be sure you indicate this will take only a few minutes. If your gospel presentation has taken an hour or more, he may think you will spend the same amount of time when you come back with the tapes. Find out if there is a tape player in the house and provide one if it is necessary. Battery-powered players are best—provided the batteries are not weak. These can be listened to anyplace and their convenience will encourage more listening to tapes.

PERSPECTIVE

Your closing comments from the booklet deal with a twofold perspective: relationship to the family of God on earth now and the church triumphant in heaven where all things are new. The more this perspective is in the mind of a believer, the more he will seek to walk consistently with Christ.

WORSHIP NEXT WEEK

If your new convert is not actively related to another church he should be encouraged to attend yours next Sunday. Do not ask him *if* he will attend, rather ask him which service he will be attending or if you can meet him in the front of the church or would he like for you to stop by and pick him up on the way to church. Indicate you will be looking for him and want to sit with him.

As your team leaves, be sure to mention the day and the time that you are going to be getting back together for your seven-day call back. This fixes it in the mind of all so that there is less likelihood of misunderstanding.

FIRST WEEK FOLLOW-UP ACTIVITIES

A. CONTACT ANALYSIS

After the contact has been completed as your team is returning to the church, you should analyze what has actually happened by answering these questions:

1. What did we learn that will help us minister in the future to the person with whom we shared?
2. What did we learn that will help us be more effective in evangelizing in the future?
3. What did we learn that will be helpful or encouraging to other people in the discipleship training program?
4. What specific prayer needs arise from this contact? These will be for the team members' ability to share the gospel as well as requests for the person contacted. Some needs will be confidential and must be kept among the team members. Others should be shared in the public report time and/or with prayer partners. Particularly in the beginning of a training semester it is helpful to use the list of suggestions in the *Prayer Guide* booklet to determine what you, the team, the witnessing fellowship, and the prayerpartners will need to pray for.

B. TEAM PRAYER

Effective prayer and effective evangelism cannot be separated. When the team returns to the church after the contact they should have a time of prayer together. Each member of the team should briefly pray. Express gratitude to God for the great things he has done. Needs of the gospel presenters to be more effective in sharing in the future should be brought to the Lord. Intercede for the person contacted and those related to him at this time.

Trainers must be models in prayer as much as they are models in presenting the gospel. It is wrong to assume that all Christians know how to properly pray. Many Christians have difficulty praying aloud in the presence of other people. Trainers must be sensitive to this and seek to help any trainee having difficulty. If you are a trainee who has difficulty in praying aloud with someone else, you should tell your trainer.

Paul reminds us that no one is completely adequate in the matter of prayer. He says, "the Spirit helps us in our weakness. We do not know how we ought to pray, but the Spirit himself intercedes for us with groans that words cannot express" (Romans 8:26, NIV). Jesus promised, "If two of you on earth agree about anything you ask for, it will be done for you by my Father in heaven" (Matthew 18:19, NIV). Ask your trainer to claim this promise with you and apply it to praying aloud with others.

Some practical suggestions also might be helpful. *In your private devotions* when no one else is around, *pray aloud.* This helps you break the sound barrier and makes it easier to pray aloud when you are with someone else. **In the witnessing team** hold your prayers to *brief sentences.* Those who are able to pray lengthy, eloquent prayers sometimes overwhelm people who find it difficult to utter five words. Do not feel that you must pray with King James words such as "Thee," "Thou," etc. God understands contemporary English.

Another thing some have found helpful is for the team to occasionally pray in unison the Family Prayer (Our Father, who art in heaven . . .) before leaving the church for the contact.

C. INITIAL CONTACT RESULT REPORT

Written reports are absolutely necessary in this ministry! Completing this report on each initial contact will help you concisely crystalize the experience and more permanently impress it in your mind. Then you will retain the things that will help you be effective in sharing the gospel with others and ministering in the future to the person contacted. Turning this written report in to the evangelism office makes it possible for staff and other persons in the church to assist in the total discipling process. The first few weeks of the training semester, the trainer should fill out this form while trainees observe closely. Then trainees should alternate in completing this form and the trainer should check it each week to see that it is adequately filled out. (Appendix B).

D. PUBLIC REPORT BOARDS

Report board for witnessing in the program. As each team returns to the church, they should indicate the results of their contact on the public report board. (See Appendix D for suggested board layout.) This enables the report session leader to get an overview of the calling activities. He can call on people who indicate exciting results or particular problems to share with the group. Also this enables the report session leader to know which teams are still out. Prayer can be offered in the group for those who have not yet returned. The first few weeks of the training semester the trainer should put the report on the board. Trainees should closely observe and then alternate each week putting the report on the board. Each week the trainer should check the report to see that it is accurate.

Report board for witnessing in daily life. It is usually best to maintain a second board for witnessing in the daily life. This should give each participant an opportunity to record each attempted sharing of the gospel. By having two boards (one for witnessing in the program and a second for witnessing in the daily life outside the program) emphasis is placed on the program as a means to an end rather than an end in itself. Be sure that the report board for witnessing in the daily life includes opportunity for *every* attempted sharing of the gospel, not merely professions.

E. PUBLIC REPORT SESSION

The public report session keeps vitality in the Evangelism Discipleship Training Program. After on-the-job training, the teams return to the church for refreshments and for sharing. Morning groups may bring their lunch to report session, while evening teams might have light refreshment and coffee.

The purposes of the public report session are to inspire, to instruct, and to pray.

Inspiration. You might be on a team that spends two hours driving around looking for someone at home and, finding no one, returns rather discouraged. This may happen to your team a number of weeks in succession. If you never hear reports from those who have had glorious visits, you might conclude you would be better off to stay at home.

However, in the public report session you learn that while some had the same experience as you, others presented the gospel and had professions. You get an overall picture and sense that you are part of a mighty work that God is doing in your city. This inspires you to continue.

Instruction. Problems you encounter can be discussed and solutions shared. Specific objections raised by those contacted can be considered and answers discovered. In this way the instruction is very relevant to the actual situations. Everyone learns in the school of real life and the training does not degenerate into abstract theology.

Intercession. As victories are reported, praise God in prayer. As professions are reported, seal them with intercessory prayer. Teams that are late returning need to be upheld by intercession also.

How to make the reports count. Proper procedure in the public report session will enable you to gain a lot of inspiration and instruction in a little time.

Prepare for the public report time by closely observing what happens in the contact.

During the contact analysis, determine what is to be shared and who will be the spokesman.

Concentrate on what will be of value to all participants. Report on: (1) follow-up calls, (2) professions of faith, (3) new insights gained into effective witnessing and (4) problems encountered for which solutions are needed.

Each report should be about two minutes in length. Do not waste time telling what did *not* happen.

Prayer can be offered briefly after each report requiring it or in one period at the end of the report time.

Do not use people's last names in public. Word might get back to them that they were talked about in the group.

Do not make negative comments about people contacted by the team. We are to look at others through the eyes of Christ. Therefore, snide comments about people being fat or skinny or ugly, etc., are totally out of place in a public report session.

Do not make light of sharing the gospel. While it is obvious that God has a sense of humor, humor must be used with taste and discretion in public report sessions.

Trainers should make the public reports the first few weeks. Then trainees may alternate as they are able. Sometimes it helps new trainees make the report if the trainer will stand with them. New trainees should *not* be forced to speak before a group if this is very disturbing to them.

The public report session should begin and end at a designated time. It should not begin until teams return with positive things to share. It should end at a reasonable time so that participants are willing to stay for the last report. Those who return late can share their reports next week. At Coral Ridge report time for the morning group is from 11:45 to 12:15. For the evening groups, it is from 9:45 to 10:15.

F. NOTES TO INITIAL CONTACTS

A note written the same day as the contact from one team member to the person or persons contacted is a good thing. It will strengthen the personal relationships and reinforce spiritual decisions. Notes should be written to any person contacted who can be discipled into your church. These should be legibly hand written.

New Christian note. Express thanks for their hospitality. Mention that you and the other persons on the team (team members should be mentioned by name) are looking forward to seeing them in church Sunday. Be sure to mention the time of the service they indicated they would attend. Indicate you are looking forward to seeing them again next week (when you return for the seven-day call back.) Welcome them to the family of God, and tell them you are available to be of help any time you are needed.

Sample note to new Christian

Dear Chris:

Welcome to the forever family of God at First Community Church.

Thanks for your hospitality to George, Mary, and me.

We are looking forward to seeing you at the eleven o'clock service on Sunday. I am sure you will also enjoy the "Discovery Bible Group" at 9:15 Sunday morning.

I hope you are finding your Bible reading as exciting and helpful as I do. Remember to underline the things that stand out to you and put question marks by those things you want to talk about when we get together next Wednesday morning at 10:15.

Chris, please remember that we are available anytime you might need us.

Once again, welcome to the forever family of God at First Community Church.

Archie

Sample to no profession

Dear N.P.:

After leaving your home Wednesday morning, George, Mary, and I were talking about how much we enjoyed getting to know you. You are a very interesting person. We look forward to getting better acquainted in the weeks ahead.

I am sure you will find "The Truth and the Life" group next Sunday morning at 9:15 very interesting. We will be looking for you there and at the eleven o'clock service.

As you read the Gospel of John, be sure to put question marks by those things you want clarified when we get together next Wednesday morning at 10:15.

Remember that George, Mary, and I are available if we can ever be of any help to you.

Your friend,
Archie

Already Christian sample note

Dear A.C.:

Welcome to the forever family of God at First Community Church. George and Mary commented to me after we left your house how much they appreciated the opportunity to get acquainted with you. It's always good to meet another member of God's forever family.

I am sure you will find the couples' class next Sunday morning at 9:15 as exciting as I have found it to be. After the group is over maybe we can worship together in the eleven o'clock service.

In the weeks ahead, Mary and I are looking forward to getting better acquainted with you and your family.

Please remember that we are available if you ever need us for anything.

Your friend in Christ,
Archie

G. CHURCH MAILING LIST

The church office should add to the church mailing list those with a potential for future discipling into the local congregation. This includes professions of faith, Christians not actively related to another church, and people who do not make professions but are not hostile to the gospel.

They should receive any regular informational mailings about activities in the church life. Occasional mailings for special programs help to build attendance and good relations. Mailings concerning financial stewardship should never be sent to individuals who are not members of the church. There should be a systematic purging process so that names are not left on the list for unlimited, expensive periods of time.

H. PASTOR'S FOLLOW-UP LETTER

After the visitation team has made contact, the pastor should write a follow-up letter to those who show a potential for discipling into the local church.

When the pastor writes a person who has made a profession of faith his letter should be friendly, but general. *There should be no mention of the profession of faith with the visitation team.* It is not uncommon for very intimate and personal things to be shared with visitation teams. Professing one's faith is a very personal and intimate thing. If someone who was not on the team, even the pastor, indicates he knows about the profession of faith, the person contacted may think that other confidential things were shared as well. This can jeopardize the future relationship. The convert may be urged to use the services of the church and encouraged in Bible reading. The pastor may also indicate that the members of the church are looking forward to visiting again.

I. TWENTY-FOUR-HOUR FOLLOW-UP PHONE CALL

People who can be discipled into the local church should be contacted by phone by one of the team members within twenty-four hours. This should be brief and friendly. Remember to smile whenever you talk on the phone. This makes your tone of voice more pleasant.

If the phone call is to someone who has made a profession of faith, indicate that you are glad you had the opportunity to meet him, you are looking forward to seeing him at church on Sunday, you hope he will enjoy the Bible study group at church, and you are looking forward to getting better acquainted next week when you visit him again.

If the phone call is to someone who did not make a profession of faith but is still open, tell him how much you enjoyed getting a chance to meet him, and that you are looking forward to seeing him at church on Sunday. Say you hope he will enjoy "The Truth and the Life"* class, and you are looking forward to seeing him again and answering any questions he has after reading the Gospel of John.

If your team contacted a person who was already a Christian and he is not active in a local church, when you phone tell him (1) how glad you were to meet him, (2) you are looking forward to seeing him at church on Sunday, (3) you are sure he will enjoy the adult class in the School for Christian Living (use whatever name you have for that particular class rather than just "Adult Sunday school"), (4) you are looking forward to getting better acquainted with him in the weeks to come.

J. CASSETTE TAPES

Cassette tape recordings can be a valuable way of ministering to spiritual needs. But nonpersonal media, such as cassette tapes, must supplement personal, face-to-face ministering.

One advantage of cassette tapes over printed material is that voice inflection emphasizes things in a way that cannot be done in printed matter.

Quality cassette recordings can enable you to be more effective in follow-up than you might be otherwise. If you can effectively evangelize but are not a very good teacher, you can use material recorded by good teachers. Then you can discuss the material and both you and the tape listener will learn.

---

* A class designed to present evidence for the Christian faith and answer questions dealing with doctrine and life-style.

The best tapes for follow-up are not recordings of public presentations. A person speaking to a group gears his presentation to the group. When one person listens to a tape for maximum impact, the presentation should be geared to him as an individual.

If you can afford it, begin your own tape ministry. When you loan a tape and mention it is your personal tape, people are more likely to listen to it. However, if you cannot afford to develop your own tape ministry, urge your church to develop a lending library. For follow-up it is essential to have a number of tape players available for loaning. Of course if you loan tapes and players belonging to the church, you should assume responsibility to return them so others may use them.

When a new Christian begins listening to good taped Bible teaching within twenty-four hours of his profession of faith he will get off to a good healthy start. He will be more likely to continue growing and become a vital part of the local church. Many people will listen to tapes who will not complete written studies. Sometimes tapes have impact on other members of the household also.

Listening to the tape in private helps prepare for involvement in a small group later. Wisely selected, properly prepared tapes can be effectively used in get-acquainted coffees or home Bible study groups.

This Is the Life is a series of taped messages prepared for new believers. It contains six thirty-minute presentations on the following topics:

1. Knowing you are going to heaven
2. Staying right with God
3. Getting into the Bible
4. Practicing the art of prayer
5. Continuing in fellowship
6. Transforming the world

Ten-minute excerpts from these tapes have been collected on one sixty-minute tape. This is available with a student's workbook and can be used individually or in a Bible study group.

These tapes can be left at the time of the profession or within twenty-four hours. In some cases they can be loaned out during the seven-day call back.

The content of the tapes is also available in a book by the same title, *This Is the Life.**

Cassette tapes are also very useful with responsive non-Christians. If the person has a question, loan him a tape that deals in depth with that question. This can be an effective means of maintaining contact and witness. Offer to loan the tape with the understanding that you want to discuss it after he has listened to it.

Sometimes the person will listen with more attention to a tape than he will to you. He knows he cannot interrupt and argue with the tape. Therefore, most people tend to listen with more attention.

Be sure you listen to any tape you give away before you share it with someone else.

Delivering the tapes within twenty-four hours after a profession of faith also gives opportunity for brief face-to-face personal contact. This gives opportunity to affirm what has happened in the person's life the day before.

---

* Dr. D. James Kennedy, *This Is the Life* (Glendale, Cal.: Regal Press, 1974), 102 pp.

K. SATURDAY PHONE CALL

Saturday afternoon or evening is a good time to make a second phone contact with those who can be discipled into the life of your local church. A call should be made by a team member who has not written or phoned before. Probably it is best if the team member who is going to sit with him is the one who phones on Saturday. Briefly, pleasantly tell him you are looking forward to seeing him at church on Sunday and be sure about the time and place you are to meet.

L. SUNDAY MORNING WORSHIP

During your immediate follow-up conversation one team member should offer to transport the person to church or meet him at a particular place at the church so that you can sit together. Usually it is overpowering for all three team members to sit with the new person in the morning worship. But it is important for one team member and possibly his family to sit with the new person.

During the worship service help make the worship more meaningful to him. He may not bring a Bible, so share yours with him. He may not be familiar with the hymnbook. He may be embarrassed by ignorance of the worship. The more formal your worship is, the more important it is for you to sit with him and help him.

After the service introduce him to other church members. Help him develop as many personal relationships with Christians as possible.

M. BASICS CLASS FOR NEW BELIEVERS

New believers need to be informed very quickly in three basic things:

(1) how to properly feed on the Word of God

(2) how to keep their life clean before God

(3) how to properly relate to the family of God.

With an effective evangelism program you may have professions of faith almost every week. Therefore it is wise to have these three topics taught individually in self-contained classes. Each class should stand alone, without need of any prerequisites. Then a new believer may enter the class the Sunday following his profession of faith regardless of which of the three topics is being taught that week.

When he has finished these three basic classes he can enter the "This Is the Life" class. The content of the tapes and book is such that he can enter at any point.

The content of these nine weeks is "milk." After completing them he can pretty well fit into most other Bible study groups. New believers should not indiscriminately be placed into classes. Some classes must be taught sequentially so that the learner's understanding develops and he is able to handle heavier concepts.

Do not call the class by any name that indicates it is for "New Believers." Very few will attend if this is done. Instead, call it the "Christian Adventure Class" or "Discovery Class" or something of that nature.

N. SEVEN-DAY CALL BACK

If possible, the seven-day call back should be scheduled in the regular calling program one week from the time of the profession; and the same visitation team should make this call. By making the call back in the regular calling program, team members are not so overloaded with follow-up calls. Having the same team members makes it easier to reestablish rapport.

While driving to the call, a team member should read the seven-day call back checklist aloud. This helps everyone understand what they should be trying to accomplish in this contact. While driving back to the church, the checklist should be reviewed again by the team. Explanation should be given by the trainer as to why each thing was done as well as why some things were not done.

SEVEN-DAY CALL BACK CHECKLIST

Seven-day Call Back Checklist

I. Introduction
  A. Reintroduce team
  B. How has your week been?
  C. Church—last Sunday
  D. Personal Testimony—team member shares his New Christian testimony
  E. Two questions
    (1) God's "Why?"
    (2) Assurance
II. Growth
  A. Bible
    (1) Daily reading (underline, question marks)
    (2) Promise memorized
    (3) Tapes listened to
    (4) Bible group
  B. Prayer
    (1) *Prayer in the Forever Family*
    (2) (Prayerpartner)
  C. Worship—next Sunday
  D. Fellowship—Sunday dinner
  E. Witness—family and friends (Acts 16:31)
  F. Satan (1 John 4:4)
III. Parting prayer

Introduction. You will notice from the checklist that the introduction is similar to the initial contact introduction.

REINTRODUCE TEAM. At the home, the team should be **reintroduced** to make sure the new convert has the names clearly in mind. This helps to make the call more friendly. If the other contacts scheduled between the profession and the seven-day call back have been made, the new convert will have had some contact with each team member.

HOW HAS YOUR WEEK BEEN? When you ask, *"How has your week been?"* the new convert will usually respond, "It has been good." However, if he raises problems at this point do not press insensitively through the rest of your checklist. Pause and listen empathetically. If he raises questions dealing with assurance or God's "Why?" before you get to that part of your checklist, deal with it as seems best in the situation. If extensive discussion follows concerning family or financial problems or the like, do not consider your seven-day call back complete until you have gotten the person's response to God's "Why?" and the assurance question, even if this must be done in a subsequent call.

CHURCH—LAST SUNDAY. If the person attended, tell him how much you enjoyed worshiping with him. Talk about the positive benefits you received from the service. If he did not attend, do not scold him but let him know he was missed. Then share some of the positive benefits you received from the service. This will help motivate him to attend next Sunday.

PERSONAL TESTIMONY—TEAM MEMBER NEW CHRISTIAN. A team member should share a testimony of what things were like when he or she first received eternal life. If there were problems that have since been overcome, this may be shared. Do not give more detail than is necessary to identify with the new convert. In sharing testimony this way the new convert is encouraged to be more honest if he or she is having problems.

THE TWO QUESTIONS—(1) GOD'S "WHY?" (2) ASSURANCE. You will notice the two questions are in reverse order from their use in the initial contact. We deal with God's "Why?" first because it draws from the person an indication of whether or not he is basing his hope of eternity on faith in Christ alone. Not until that is established should you be concerned with the question of assurance. Once you know that he is trusting Christ, then raise the question of whether or not he knows he is going to heaven.

It is important to raise these questions in the seven-day call back. Experience has demonstrated that it is not uncommon for up to 10 percent of the people who profess faith on an initial contact to actually come to true faith during the call back.

Growth. The growth section of the seven-day call back parallels to some degree the outline of immediate follow-up from the initial contact. We talk about the Bible, prayer, worship, fellowship, witness, and Satan. Baptism and the Lord's Supper are not in the outline because they are included under worship.

BIBLE

(1) Daily reading (underlined, question marks). The previous week you asked the new convert to make the commitment to read one chapter a day in the Gospel of John. He was told to underline things that stood out so that he could find them more quickly and to insert question marks in the margin beside anything he wanted clarified.

Ask how he is coming with his Bible reading. If he has read the seven chapters, ask him to share with you verses that were meaningful to him. Talk together about this. Be cautious about criticizing any "unique" interpretation he might have. If there are verses that are meaningful to you in those same chapters, share these. Emphasize verses on assurance, such as John 1:12; 3:16, 18, 36; 5:24; 6:47.

Ask if he has any questions from the reading. Those you can accurately answer, do so. If you cannot accurately answer them, follow the procedure suggested under the potential problems in the seven-day call back.

Urge him to continue reading until he completes John's Gospel.

(2) Promise memorized. Last week you asked that John 3:16 be learned by heart. See if he can recite it with you.

(3) Tapes listened to. If the *This Is the Life* tapes were delivered during the initial contact or within twenty-four hours, ask the new convert if he listened to them. If he did, inquire about his reactions. If he has any questions, discuss them.

If the tapes have not been delivered previously they should be delivered at this time. This of course means that they must be picked up one week later.

(4) Bible group. If the new convert attended the basic Bible study group, see what his impressions were. If he did not attend, urge him to do so next Sunday.

B. PRAYER

(1) Prayer in the Forever Family. This booklet contains a brief explanation of "Our family prayer," usually called, "The Lord's Prayer." Remind the new convert that God speaks to us through the Bible. Then he wants us to talk to him through prayer.

Read Matthew 6:5–15. Explain that verses 9–13 are the words of the family prayer of all Christians. Notice it begins, *"Our Father,* which art in heaven." This prayer contains in seed form everything a person needs to know about prayer. Urge him to learn these five verses by heart so he says them with meaning with the family on the Lord's Day.

(2) (Prayerpartner). If the new convert is clear in his faith and enthusiastic you should try to enlist him as a prayerpartner for one person on the witnessing team. Briefly explain the prayerpartner portion of the booklet. Ask him to carefully read this after you leave. The team member seeking to enlist him as a prayerpartner should contact him a few days later to see what he has decided.

Parentheses are placed around this item in the checklist because you should not always try to enlist the new convert. If he is not clear and enthusiastic about his faith do *not* try to enlist him as a prayerpartner.

C. WORSHIP—NEXT SUNDAY. Assume that the new convert will be in church next Sunday. Ask if you can meet him again and sit with him during the service.

D. FELLOWSHIP—SUNDAY DINNER. In the early church Christians often broke bread together. You will find it easier to befriend your new convert if you plan for times of informal fellowship. One team member should invite him to come home with him after worship next Sunday to enjoy dinner together. If the new convert accepts this invitation, then the team should attempt to also invite another church member about the same age with similar interests. Encourage the church member not only to invite the new convert to his home for dinner at a later time but also to invite another church member to join them. This type of chain reaction dinner invitation can be very helpful in blending new converts and old members together in the body of Christ.*

E. WITNESS—FAMILY AND FRIENDS (ACTS 16:31). If the new profession has a deep concern for friends and relatives to hear the gospel, share the promise of Acts 16:31, emphasizing the last phrase, "and your household." Begin praying with him for God to open the door for witness. If the new convert is not too involved in other studies give him *Your Personal Influence and the Forever Family* to help him see God's attitude toward his relatives and friends. Offer to assist him in any way you can. (See Relational Evangelism, page 199.)

If the new convert is fearful of witnessing to his friends and relatives, remind him of the great difference it makes to trust Christ—not only for time but for eternity as well. But do not press him at this point. As soon as it is practical, according to his attitude and the other studies he is doing, give him *Your Personal Influence and the Forever Family* booklet to study. Be sure he understands that you are praying with him and are available to help.

F. SATAN—1 JOHN 4:4. Reference is made to Satan in the immediate follow-up booklet, *Welcome to the Forever Family.* Emphasize again that Satan will try to tempt but the Holy Spirit, who dwells within our hearts by faith, is more than sufficient for every need.

III. Parting prayer. After you have gone through the other items in the checklist, ask the new convert if you can have prayer together before you go. It is best that this be a time of sentence prayers with everyone on the team joining in. Team members should be very cautious not to use King James English if the new convert is not already oriented to it. Before you begin praying ask the new convert to name one thing for which he is thankful. When he indicates what he is thankful for, then ask him to simply tell God thank you for it. In this way you can start the new Christian praying aloud with others.

Remember, after the contact is completed, on the way back to the church you should read over the seven-day call back checklist again and discuss each thing on the card. Be sure you decide who is going to make the public report and what is to be shared with the group and with your prayerpartners.

SEVEN-DAY CALL BACK
(Possible Problems)

We note that there are ten basic problems that may be encountered in seven-day call backs. The following suggestions may help you in this very important area.

1. Does not attend church the following Sunday. Some people are just not in the habit of attending church and therefore need extra encouragement. Some

* Footnote: For other helpful suggestions on vital blending of new and old in the local church, see Lyle Schaller, *The Change Agent* (Abingdon). Also see "Fellowship Meals" below, page 145.

are shy. Not knowing very many people at church, they may feel uncomfortable. Some have had unpleasant experiences with churches in the past. They may be either turned off or hostile toward the institution.

Those who are shy or hostile should be invited to a small, informal group of people from the church. The first group they should associate with is the visitation team. Team members should introduce them to others in the church. This can be done by inviting the new Christian for dinner or for coffee and dessert along with other members from the church. As soon as it is practical, the spiritual parent should seek to involve the new Christian in a Bible study group. After becoming acquainted with other persons in the church in this way, the new Christian will be more inclined to worship with the larger family of God in the local church.

2. Does not keep the appointment for the seven-day call back. In some cases the new convert simply is not home when the visitation team calls. In other cases, he does not permit admittance to the team when they call.

Sometimes the person is not at home because he did not clearly understand that the team would return at a particular time or he may simply have forgotten the appointment. This can be avoided if the team leader clearly indicates the time and day of the week he will be returning as is indicated in the immediate follow-up dialogue. Team members should have several contacts before the seven-day call back: the new contact note, the twenty-four-hour phone call, delivering the tapes, the phone call on Saturday and church on Sunday. In each of these contacts casually mention that you are looking forward to getting together again next Wednesday morning at 10:15 (or whatever the day and time is). This avoids any misunderstanding and it increases the likelihood that the appointment will be kept.

3. Still trusting works. If the person responds with a works answer to God's "Why?" go over the gospel again. You may recall some of the questions or problems he expressed the week before. Your presentation should try to answer these as fully as possible and preclude their arising again. Do not be afraid of repeating what was said in the presentation of the gospel the previous week. It is important that the evangelist not show discouragement or disgust with the incorrect answer. It may be helpful to use the *Good News** booklet by explaining the visual illustrations.

If you have a number of persons making professions of faith who are still trusting in their own works when you make the seven-day call back, you should check the content of your gospel presentation with the textbook or another trainer or staff teacher in the program.

4. Lacks assurance. The convert may indicate that he is trusting in Christ alone for his salvation, but still not have assurance that he is going to heaven.

In this situation, probe the person's answer before trying to use Scripture verses to give him assurance. Ask, "Who, in your understanding, is Jesus Christ?" If he is clear on this, then ask, "When you use the words believe, trusting, etc., what do you mean?"

* The *Good News* booklet is described on page 185 of this book.

The Bible indicates that there are a number of **kinds of faith** a person may have in relation to God.

"There is a *blind* faith, where the person steps out into dark uncertainty, but there is no basis to his trust.

"There is a *head* faith, where the person believes about Christ as much as he believes about Napoleon or George Washington. He believes he was a historical person who lived a long time ago, but he is not trusting him to do anything for him now.

"There is a *now* kind of faith with which we actually trust God to do things for us now—to provide us with a place to live, food to eat, money to spend, etc.

"But the *faith that gains eternal life* for us is trusting Jesus Christ alone, not merely to satisfy our intellectual curiosity or provide for us in this life. It is trusting in Jesus Christ alone for my eternal life. Which of these kinds of faith is in your mind when you say you believe in Christ?"

Since the gospel was shared with him only a week before, it is possible he may be using words without understanding what they mean. Probing in this manner can help determine if the person truly understands.

If he has stated that he is trusting in Christ, then you might ask, "Is there anything else you would add to this?" Sometimes he is not trusting Christ alone. Asking this question will bring out that he is trusting in Christ and his own efforts. If this is the case, it must be pointed out, very graciously and clearly, that it is not Christ plus me—not grace plus works—but by grace alone that we receive eternal life.

Romans 11:6 is very helpful in this regard. Also, there are three illustrations that can be of value. In addition to the "Faith and Works Boats" and the "Rope or Thread" in the chapter on objections (page 101), you might find the following parachute illustration helpful.

FAITH AND WORKS PARACHUTES. Suppose you were in an aircraft flying at a high altitude. The engine fails. As you prepare to leap to save your life, you find that there are two parachutes available. One very quickly reveals that it is moth-eaten and that some of the lines are broken. The other appears to be in excellent condition. Which would you choose to save your life?

Our works are moth-eaten and tangled. They are not perfect enough to save us. We must take the perfect parachute of grace and rest in it if we will be saved.

THE LORDSHIP OF CHRIST. It is quite possible that the basic problem may be lack of yielding to the lordship of Christ, or God may be dealing with him about his morals, habits, or some relationship.

This may be determined by saying, "Last week when we were talking I mentioned that God requires that Jesus Christ be the Lord of our lives. When we give as much of ourselves as we can to as much of Christ as we know, he gives us assurance of eternal life. Is there anything you know that you are holding back from him?"

If he mentions something, then deal specifically with it. If he does not mention something specific but you detect by his tone of voice or attitude that there may be something, make this a matter of private, personal prayer.

EMPHASIZE GOD'S PROMISES. If he has understanding of what it means to trust in Christ alone and there appears to be no basic problem with the lordship of Christ, emphasize the promises of the present possession of eternal life. Open the Bible to the specific passage, place it in his hands and ask him to read it aloud. Following are some of the passages which may be used: Psalm 103:12; Isaiah 43:25; Jeremiah 31:34; Micah 7:19; John 6:39, 40, 47; 10:28, 29; Romans 8:38, 39; Philippians 1:6; 1 Peter 1:5; Jude 24.

HOLY SPIRIT GIVES ASSURANCE. The Holy Spirit alone gives assurance of eternal life (Romans 8:16). Never say to the person, "You have eternal life," or "You are going to heaven." No human being can be sure of this for another human being. What we can say is, "If you are trusting in Christ alone, he gives you eternal life." As we share the gospel, we are telling what Christ has done for man, but only the individual in whom the Spirit of God is working can tell you what Christ has done in him.

5. Not reading the Bible. If the new convert indicates that he has not been reading the Bible, be very patient and positive with him. He probably does not realize the importance of doing this. Do not merely tell him he *ought* to read and memorize the Word. Instead, share with him positive and exciting things God has given you from his Word. Turn in the Gospel of John to passages that have been exceptionally meaningful to you and share the Word and your experience of it.

6. Did not learn promise by heart. If he has not memorized the promise of salvation in John 3:16, take time to help him do this. Divide the verse at the punctuation marks and explain as you go. This will help him to understand how vital and important this really is.

Also you might share with him God's command to memorize his Word with our hearts (Deuteronomy 6:6–9; Joshua 1:8). Point to the example of Jesus Christ who overcame the temptations of the devil by properly quoting previously learned Scriptures (Matthew 4:1–11). Share with him the value of learning the Scriptures by heart (2 Timothy 3:14–17).

Share with him in a positive, enthusiastic manner benefits that you have derived in your own Christian life by hiding God's Word in your heart. Go over some practical suggestions on how he may better memorize the Word of God. Take one of the verses and apply the practical principles and work on it with the new Christian.

7. Questions. If he has been reading the Scriptures and has many questions about interpretation and application, do not be threatened by this. Answer as many questions as you can, briefly and accurately.

If questions that you cannot answer are asked, simply say, "I don't know the answer to that, but I will find out and share it with you." Then use books in your church library or talk with older Christians or a minister to find the answer.

Most questions coming from new Christians concerning the meaning of Scripture indicate a spiritual hunger. Therefore, these questions should not be ignored or put off and forgotten. As you seek to find answers for your new convert, you will grow as much as he will.

8. The new convert has problems. The Holy Spirit may be dealing with his personal habits or he may find new difficulties in his personal relationships with friends and members of his family.

The spiritual parent should be shockproof! Do not be surprised at the nature or degree of problems shared with you. Do not be overwhelmed by them either. If they are more than you can handle, ask an older Christian or minister for his assistance. In most cases the minister will first try to help you help your spiritual child. But, if the problem goes beyond what you are able to handle, he will do whatever is necessary.

Don't be too strict or judgmental. God is not through with him yet. He has a long way to grow.

Give as much personal support as possible to your new Christian. This is especially important when the person has no other Christian friends or very few Christian friends. Man was not made to live alone. God has placed us in families. It is sometimes a very traumatic experience to change from the family of Satan to the family of God.

If there are particular problems with a relationship between children and parents or husband and wife, or courting couples, the spiritual parent should offer to go with him to share the gospel with the other person or persons involved. It is important that the new convert realize that the spiritual parent will be the one sharing the gospel. By prayerfully going together, the spiritual parent is encouraging and supporting his spiritual child. If the other friend or member of the family receives eternal life, then there is the beginning of a nucleus for group follow-up. If the person to whom the gospel is presented does not respond positively, the spiritual parent is with his spiritual child when the trauma first sets in and he can help to explain why and how God is working. Thus the strength of the parent is shared with the child.

9. Another person present. Sometimes there will be another person with the new convert at the time of the first follow-up contact. This may be another member of the family, a friend, or a neighbor. If there is another person present, it is wise to try to determine his spiritual condition before attempting to obtain answers to the two questions from the new convert. This may be done by saying something such as, "Did John (the new convert) tell you about our conversation last week?" Regardless of his response, you may continue by saying, "We discussed some very important questions. I would be interested in your thinking on them." Then raise the questions in the normal order that you would use in an initial evangelistic contact.

Seek to get answers to both of these questions before raising them with the new convert. In this way, the new convert will not give away the answers to the other person. Before presenting the gospel be sure that you ask the questions of the new convert so that you know whether or not you are presenting the gospel to both of them.

If the new convert lacks assurance, present the gospel first to his guest and then deal with the point of assurance.

10. Priority of problems. The most important thing to determine in a first follow-up contact is whether or not the new profession is trusting in Jesus Christ alone for his salvation. The second most important thing is to discover if he has legitimate assurance of salvation. However, if he feels distraught over personal problems, the weight of them may be such that he will not be interested in simply dealing directly with salvation and assurance.

Be sensitive to his needs and the leading of the Holy Spirit. If he has problems, listen attentively with concern. Pray that the Holy Spirit will give him the ability to deal specifically with the problems, then, in the course of the conversation, raise the questions for an understanding of salvation and assurance. For his sake the work of the first follow-up contact should not be considered complete until these questions have been satisfactorily answered.

After dealing with the problems, salvation, and assurance, the other matters follow in this order of importance: Bible reading, questions of interpretation and application, memorizing the Scriptures, getting the person involved in the visible family of God.

When dealing with two or more new professions in one contact, seek to determine the specific needs of each and deal with them in this suggested order of importance.

SEVEN-DAY CALL BACK FOLLOW-UP REPORT

After returning to the church the seven-day call back follow-up report should be completed. This will provide another opportunity to briefly review the significant aspects of the call. The first few weeks of the training semester the trainer should fill out this report while trainees carefully observe. Then trainees should alternate filling out the report and let the trainer check it before it is turned in.

Be sure to note seven-day call back results on the report board for the program (Appendix C).

NINE
CONTINUING FOLLOW-UP

The first week of a new believer's life is extremely important. What happens then usually has great effect on his future development. But the work has just begun. Your responsibilities are not fulfilled until you have done everything possible to develop your disciple into a vital, reproducing member of the local church. The activities listed below are designed to help you, your team members, and your local church family transform your spiritual babes into functionally mature working members of the local assembly.

A. STAFF/MINISTER'S/OFFICER'S CONTACT

A full-time staff person, minister, or church officer contacts those who have made professions of faith or who were already Christians and have no active relationship in a local church. This should be done after the seven-day call back to be sure that time is being used to the best advantage.

The purpose of this call is to demonstrate interest in the person and to encourage him to become an active member in the church. This contact can be face to face or over the telephone.

B. GET-ACQUAINTED COFFEE

The get-acquainted coffee is an informal social situation to allow new Christians to become acquainted with each other and with older Christians. Also responsive seeking people who have not professed faith should be invited. This gives them opportunity to see more of the implications of the Christian faith. It may be all that is necessary to bring them to trust Christ. A get-acquainted coffee should have both a host and a leader. The coffee is held in the home of the host or hostess. The leader is a mature Christian with experience in working in small groups. The format is very flexible and spontaneous, but there are specific things that should be accomplished. The leader should set a very friendly atmosphere. Serving coffee and light refreshment helps people relax. The leader should steer the conversation so that Christians can share a word of personal testimony. For many new Christians this gives an opportunity to express their faith for the first time in a small group.

Prayerfully choose your host or hostess and leader. Work with only one group at a time and do not add additional groups until the need is obvious.

C. HOME BIBLE STUDY GROUPS

Early Christians often met in homes for the study of the Word of God. Home Bible study groups provide opportunity for Christians to experience the vital love of the family of God.* Individual Christians can talk over the Word and discover their gifts and abilities. They also give opportunity for the use of individual gifts in the body.

Small groups are always important, but whenever the church grows beyond one hundred regular attenders they become even more important. The average person can remember the names and faces of forty to sixty people he associates with on a regular basis. Therefore, if he is in a group of between 100–120 people, he will feel that he knows every *other* one and will still not feel lost in the crowd. However, when the number is larger he will lose his identity unless he is part of a smaller subgroup. Home Bible studies provide opportunity for local assemblies to have subcongregations without the great expense of elaborate buildings. They also add a warmth and unstructured accountability into the life-style of believers. A large church without small subgroups with properly trained leadership will lack strength for service and will become impersonal.

When Bible study groups are formed, they should agree that they will later divide. If this is not done, they may become a closed clique and defeat their vital function in the local church.

Bible study leaders should be trained in an apprentice relationship with a good home Bible study leader. Those with the gift of teaching should disciple others to teach.

There should be close communication between the leaders of the home Bible study groups and the church staff. Caution must be exercised not to allow people with doctrinal differences to infiltrate the group and do damage to it and eventually to the whole church.

D. SUPPORT GROUPS

Whenever one has an eager new believer who is open to a home Bible study "support group," the trainer should suggest one for a six-week period. A support group features sharing, counsel, prayer, and a Bible study on the basics of the faith usually lasting one and one-half to two hours. Suggest that the group meet in the new believer's home. This provides a comfortable, familiar setting into which his unsaved friends and relatives readily come. A sponsoring couple who are members of the local church should also attend. This, then, provides a bridge into the church.

Often at the end of six weeks several friends and relatives have been saved and the study can be moved and the process repeated. Rev. Bob Carl of Minneapolis reported

---

* *Your House and the Forever Family* is a booklet that helps Christians improve family communication and transform their homes into outposts of heaven. It is available from Evangelism Explosion III International, P.O. Box 23820, Fort Lauderdale, Florida 33307.

that one church had a chain of over fifty conversions and nearly 50% of these converts identified with the church through a combination of E. E. calls and support groups.

At a later point some of these groups may become "Growth Groups" into which still more church members can be added. Not more than 50% of the group should be church members. This discourages new Christians from asking questions and sharing.

Often new believers faithfully attend a support group for a number of weeks before identifying with the church. In the meantime they can be fed and overcome their hesitancy to enter the church.

E. FELLOWSHIP MEALS

Christians in the early church often broke bread together. This was a social time for them to get better acquainted with each other. This is still a good way for Christians to share one another's lives.

In some large churches the pastoral staff arranges for all the membership to entertain each other once a quarter. They are careful to see that new friendships are established this way rather than merely continuing old ones.

Getting new Christians and older Christians together around a table can be an effective manner of blending them together. When you lead someone to Christ, invite him to your home for dinner. Also invite another member of the church who has been a Christian for some time. Try to select the individual on the basis of his interests and age so that there will be something in common with the new Christian. Explain to the church member that you have someone else coming to dinner who has started attending church. Do not go into a lot of details about his profession of faith.

Ask the church member if he is willing to help you. Indicate that you would like for him to invite the new Christian to his home for dinner at a later date, if the two of them appear to be compatible. Also ask the church member to invite another church member when he invites the new Christian to his home. The church member in each case should be asked to do the same thing that you have done. This can cause a chain reaction that will beautifully blend the old and new members in your church.

Non-Christians who have heard the gospel and have not yet trusted need to be involved socially with believers. Invite them to dinner. Watch your friendships grow—and watch them come to Christ!

F. SCHOOL FOR CHRISTIAN LIVING

The school for Christian living, or, as many churches call it, the Sunday school, is a very important part of the church life. It provides not only an opportunity for more personalized education in the Word of God and Christian living, but also gives opportunity for dividing into small subcongregations. New Christians should be encouraged to attend adult classes after they have finished their three basic classes. (See M. Basic Classes for New Believers under first week follow-up.)

Participants in the Evangelism Explosion Discipleship Training Program should be regular attenders in a weekly class. It is impossible for anyone to know everything about the infinite God in one lifetime. So regular study is necessary.

G. NEW MEMBERS

1. PERSONAL INVITATION TO CHURCH MEMBERSHIP CLASS

As periodic new member classes are conducted the team members should personally encourage all those who have made professions of faith and are not actively related in other churches to attend the new member class. Of course, attending the class does not obligate the person to join the church. It does give him information so that he can determine God's will in the matter.

Those with whom you have shared the gospel who did not make a profession of faith but are open to the gospel may be invited to the new member class also. One of their problems may be that they misunderstand what it means to be a member of the church. By attending the classes many of their questions may be answered. Also it should be emphasized that no one should come into the church until he has had a personal interview with a staff member or officer of the church in which he indicates that he personally trusts Christ.

2. PASTOR'S LETTER INVITING TO NEW MEMBER CLASS

One week before the new member class begins the pastor writes a friendly letter to all possible candidates for church membership. He collects these names from the initial contact result report and from the call-back follow-up reports. All those who made professions, Christians not actively related in other churches, and those making no professions who are not hostile receive a letter.

Usually it is wise to circulate the list of names of people who will receive the letter among the trainers in the E.E. program before the letter is mailed. Sometimes they will add names to the list. They may also want to indicate names that should be removed from the list.

3. STAFF/OFFICER PHONE INVITATION TO NEW MEMBER CLASS

Allowing time for the pastor's invitation letter to the new member class to be received, a staff person or church officer should follow up with a phone call. After getting the right person on the phone, opening comments may go something like this:

> Pastor Kennedy asked me to give you a call. He wrote you a letter recently inviting you to the new member class. He wanted me to be sure the letter had been received and answer any questions you might have about attending the new member class.

There is a significant increase in the number of people attending the new member class when this telephone procedure is used. Sometimes all it takes is a few words to resolve an uncertainty in the mind. Other times you may have to ask the pastor himself to call at another time. Some people will be absolutely closed to membership in your church and this also is helpful information to have. Usually Friday and Saturday evenings and Sunday afternoons before the new member class begins are the best times to try to make telephone contact.

4. MEMBERSHIP APPLICATION

Membership applications should be personally given by the team member closest to the potential new member. Or they can be mailed by the church office to those who indicate interest. All persons who made professions and Christians not active in other churches should be urged to complete the application and attend the classes.

This should be completed before the new member class and brought to class or handed in during the first class session. The membership application should provide basic information about the person: where he lives, his family, his work, his church background, his general interests or areas of ability for service in the church, and how we will be uniting with the church. This varies in different churches. At Coral Ridge Presbyterian Church, new members are received by profession of faith, reaffirmation of faith, and transfer of letter. Do not use forms that go into great detail before people commit themselves to the local congregation. This basic information will help the church family properly minister to the new members.

If your church has a covenant or set of vows, these should be printed on the membership application.

5. MEMBERSHIP CLASSES

Those who are interested in membership are invited and urged to attend membership classes conducted by the pastor. At Coral Ridge we hold such classes for one hour following the Sunday evening service for four weeks. Other churches may find that other times are better. These classes are not absolutely compulsory but we do stress their helpfulness to the individual's familiarity with the church, her beliefs, and activities. The subject matter is

Session I. Doctrine

a. What all Christian churches believe in common

b. What all Protestant churches believe in common

II. Doctrine—What our church believes. During this class we give everyone a 3″ X 5″ card with the two diagnostic questions on it. We ask participants to take an inventory of their spiritual life. Each person is asked to place his name on the card so these can be attached to the membership application. Then a presentation of the gospel is made. While that presentation is in progress, the cards are sorted into three stacks.

a. Right answers

b. Wrong answers

c. Fuzzy answers

At the conclusion of the presentation the pastor reads some of the correct answers and asks the new member group to indicate whether the person writing that answer trusts in Christ or himself. Of course the group responds "He is trusting in Christ." After a few correct answers the pastor will read a wrong answer and ask the group to indicate in whom the person is trusting. No names are given publicly with the answers so that no one is embarrassed in public. However, there is a great impact when an answer is read and an entire group says it indicated that the person is trusting himself.

III. Baptism, the Lord's Supper and church government.
IV. Basic Christian duties. This is covered in conjunction with the vows of membership. Scripture reading, prayer, church attendance, stewardship of time, talents, and possessions, and witnessing are dealt with in detail.

Plenty of time is allowed for answering questions, but don't bog down in the meeting. Make personal appointments as you see the need, or deal with touchy points in the staff/officer new member interview. Due to your evangelism program you may expect to have people from varied backgrounds. The classes outlined will be a great help in clarifying any confusing issues for them. Of course you will have to tailor the content of these classes to your own church's position.

6. STAFF/OFFICER NEW MEMBER INTERVIEW

Prior to or during the time of the membership classes a staff person or officer meets with each one who has filled in an application for membership. Sometimes this is done in the prospective new member's home. Other times it may be done by appointment at the church. When the number of new members grows it is usually best for this to be done by appointment at the church. This makes the most efficient use of the interviewer's time and provides an atmosphere with less distraction.

The interview is a *must!* The purpose is twofold: for the staff person or pastor to get acquainted and, more importantly, to determine where the potential new member is spiritually. The interview takes much the same form as the seven-day call back mentioned above. It needs to be stressed again that this interview is a *must!* It is done before any new member is received. *We believe that the careful, private investigation of an individual's spiritual understanding of his faith by the pastor is the most important step you can take in building a spiritual church.* Usually at least one hour is necessary for this interview.

During this time the interviewer should see if the potential new member has any questions that have been generated by attending the classes. Then the assurance question and God's "Why?" are discussed. If the spiritual inventory card has been used and followed with the presentation of the gospel to the group, the interviewer may have a wrong answer on the card but find the person has now come to trust Christ. If he has not trusted Christ, the gospel must be presented. If the gospel is rejected, the person should *not* be received into church membership. If he is trusting Christ, you will want to discuss the method of uniting: at Coral Ridge we receive members on profession of faith, transfer of letter, and reaffirmation of faith. Those who were trusting Christ, and active members of other churches are received by transfer. Individuals who have trusted Christ in the past but have not been actively involved in a church recently unite by reaffirmation of faith. Persons who have only recently trusted Christ are received on profession of faith.

Balanced intake and output. During the new member interview it is important to discuss the need for balance in spiritual intake and output. One of the significant problems in the church today is that many new members do not change role when they unite with the church. Until a person trusts Christ and unites with the church he is an object for ministry. When he unites with the church be becomes a channel for ministry to others. In order to make this change in role it is important to discuss those things which will enable the new member to both give and receive.

7. NEW MEMBER PUBLIC RECOGNITION/BAPTISM

The keynote for this event is to make it meaningful. We follow this procedure:

a. The new member group meets with a staff person before the Sunday morning service. The individuals have been previously carefully catalogued by method of uniting so that proper acknowledgment may be made when they are introduced to the congregation. They are given reserved seats in a prominent place in the sanctuary.
b. Each individual is introduced during the service. As their names are called, they stand. When the group is formed, the pastor asks the questions related to their membership vows. After their very audible, positive response he welcomes the new members to the church family.
c. Each new member is given an attractively designed name badge, which he is to wear to all church functions. (This helps us always to be able to tell members from nonmembers and is a great assistance to developing body life among the members.)
d. Following the service, new members file out first and form a receiving line. Others may extend to them the right hand of fellowship as they leave the sanctuary.
e. Following the Sunday evening service, a reception is held in honor of the new members. Every effort is made to warmly welcome them and to make this a day which they will never forget.

Baptism should be scheduled in conjunction with receiving new members. Though Christians may differ as to some of the meaning of baptism, one thing most evangelicals agree on is: water baptism for adult converts is a visible sign of vital relationship to the local congregation. Since the Great Commission commands us to "baptize" we must seek to vitally relate to the church all those who receive Christ as a result of sharing the gospel with them.

Note: You may find a great source of responsive prospects in the relatives and friends of new members. Urge them to personally invite their relatives and friends to the service of public recognition and/or baptism. Then your visitation teams can make contact and evangelize. Some churches provide attractively printed invitations to new members for this purpose.

8. NEW MEMBER SPONSORS

After new members have been received into the church, their names may be assigned to mature members who agree to be their sponsors for a period of three months. Assignments are made by a committee who are well acquainted with the congregation. Tentative assignments should be made as soon as membership is applied for. All assignments should be checked with the minister before being finalized. Letters of final assignment should be mailed as soon as the members are officially received. A copy of the application for membership can be given to the sponsor to acquaint him with his new member.

A system of records showing who is sponsoring whom is important. It is also important that sponsors be supervised by an officer of the church or staff person. During the three-month period that they serve, they should meet with their staff-sponsor at least twice to share the results of their sponsoring activities. A checklist enclosed in the sponsor assignment letter should be turned in by each sponsor on each new member. The letter and checklist outlining a sponsor's responsibilities to new members and their families (pages 151, 152) are sent to each sponsor.

9. NEW MEMBER CLASS SOCIALS

As soon as possible following official reception of new members there should be a class get-together. This provides an opportunity for new members to become acquainted with each other in a way that is not possible during the periods of instruction. The new members may share in a potluck dinner or the church may provide a buffet or a coffee and dessert. Workers related to various church activities present the new members with specific program opportunities. After a time of getting acquainted, when each person states his name, where he is from, his occupation and family status, there is a time of spiritual sharing. Individuals at random tell how they came to know Christ and the results.

The meeting is closed with a time of prayer and with the word that there will be a similar gathering three months hence at which time each new member will be asked (1) How is the church meeting your need? and (2) How are you fitting into the ministry of the church?

A second get-together is scheduled for three months after the new member has been received. This is started with coffee and dessert. Then each new member is asked to put on paper his answers to the two questions announced at the first social. This is followed by discussion of the two questions.

10. UNDERSHEPHERD PROGRAM/PARISH PLAN

Anytime a church grows to more than 100–120 members it needs to be subdivided. The larger the church the more important this subcongregation structure is. The Sunday school, choir, and E.E. fellowship provide some opportunity for subgrouping by age and interests. As the church grows the need for pastoral attention increases. Therefore, some program is needed that groups members of the church and provides them with a mature Christian leader so that they may be properly shepherded. It has been properly said, "If shepherds would beget shepherds, then sheep would beget sheep." **The key to any successful undershepherd or parish program is the training of leaders.** The pastor needs to disciple lay pastors so that they can shepherd the flock. Many plans are available for this type of program. Select one that meets your needs, but be sure you train the leaders!

As new members unite with the church they should be assigned to specific officer-discipling groups. They should be told who their undershepherd or parish leader is and what his responsibilities are toward them and the church.

Side 1

Comments:

SPONSORS CHECK LIST

NEW MEMBER

Name______________________

Address______________________

Phone No.______________________

Side 2

Check the following items as you do them. This list is to be turned in at the first Sponsor's Meeting.

☐ 1. Pray for them daily by name.

☐ 2. Welcome them personally as new members.

☐ 3. Call on them in their homes. Be observant and note any interesting features about their home which will help you to know them better. Notice books and magazines, and any hobby indications.

4. Find out which morning service they are attending. Greet them at the church and introduce them to others. You may want to come to church together or sit together for the next few Sundays. When the member misses a service you should telephone—not as a truancy officer—but to inquire whether there is illness and to express regret that you did not see each other.

☐ 5. Invite them to attend the evening service with you.

☐ 6. Try to get the new member into church organizations and activities, perhaps arranging to go together or prodding an organization if it is negligent in its recruiting. Your relationship to the new member will help bridge the gap between joining the church and enlistment into its total ministry.

☐ 7. Give him an invitation to your home and/or arrange for social occasions at the homes of other church members.

☐ 8. Discover and try to use the new member's talents in the ministry of the church.

☐ 9. Give such guidance in Christian living as can be tactfully offered, i.e., suggestions for family and personal devotions.

☐ 10. Watch for any sign of failure to get a good start and try to correct it—calling on others to help as needed and notifying the pastors immediately if there are problems or difficulties you cannot handle.

Community Church

495 MAIN STREET
ANYTOWN, USA

DR. JOHN JONES
MINISTER

Dear John Doe:

You have been selected to be a sponsor for one of our new members.

The first 90 days in the life of a new member are most critical! It is important that they be made to feel that they are a part of the church family and that they find their place of service in the ministry of the church.

As a sponsor you will be expected to do the things listed on the enclosed New Member Sponsor Check List.

On Sunday, February 8, at 5:30 p.m.,* we would like for you to meet with all the other sponsors of new members in the church Fellowship Hall. At that time you will be able to share the problems and the joys you have encountered. Also at this meeting you will be asked to turn in your "Sponsor Check List" indicating what you have done with your new member.

I am enclosing a copy of a letter which was recently sent to each new member.

This is a silent service. The new member does not know that you are his sponsor. However, if he should ask you if you were assigned to him, tell him we do this with all new members so that they may quickly and meaningfully become a part of the church family.

If for some reason you are not able to serve as a sponsor of the person here named, notify me immediately.

Let me underscore again the importance of your relationship to the new member. Call me for any assistance I can provide.

Sincerely in Christ,

Minister of Visitation

---

*Sponsors should meet twice during the 90-day period.

H. SPIRITUAL BIRTHDAY CARD

The spiritual birthday card can be an easy way to reinforce a new Christian. Standard Christian birthday cards can be used with a brief handwritten note. Specially designed spiritual birthday cards are being developed by E.E. III International. Team members may send the cards to those they lead to Christ on the anniversary of the first, sixth, and twelfth month of their new life in Christ.

I. CORRESPONDENCE BIBLE STUDIES

When you are not able to personally follow up a new believer, correspondence Bible studies can be very helpful.

The "Living in Christ Series" produced by Grason Publishers has been widely used in conjunction with Billy Graham Crusades. Also many churches have found them helpful in relation to their local follow-up programs. This series consists of four booklets: *Knowing Christ, Growing in Christ, Obeying Christ,* and *Sharing Christ.*

"Project Philip" of the World Home Bible League is being used by more and more churches. For information write: World Home Bible League, Project Philip Division, P.O. Box 11, South Holland, Illinois 60473.

J. CHURCH GROUPS

People in local congregations have a way of gravitating together according to mutual interests. This may be a particular ability, age, or sex grouping. "Balanced involvement" is what is important. If a person is overcommitted to many groups he may simply drop out of them all. If he is not involved in any group he will not feel he belongs. It is important that members in the various groups actively enlist new people. Otherwise they may come in the front door, bounce off one group after another, and then bounce out the back door, never to return again.

The following is a list of some groups that may exist in your church.

Choir
Women of the Church—circles
Men of the Church
Midweek school of the Bible
Sunday school teacher training
Special weekday Bible classes
Bible memory groups
Boy Scouts or Christian Service Brigade
Girl Scouts or Pioneer Girls
Youth activities

K. SPIRITUAL ADOPTION

Occasionally a new Christian and his spiritual parent may not get along well together. There may be personality differences that make it difficult for the discipling process.

On some occasions the age difference between the spiritual parent and the new Christian works against this also. If the new Christian is of the opposite sex and approximately the same age also, problems may develop. When these factors are present, the spiritual parent should take the initiative to place his new Christian for adoption. First you should attempt to have another person on your witnessing team take this responsibility. If this is not feasible, then check in the group of which your team is a part. In any case, do not merely leave your spiritual offspring wandering without anyone to guide him.

L. EVANGELISM EXPLOSION TRAINEE

Most of the things mentioned thus far provide intake for the new Christian. As soon as he is vitally involved and grounded—and this usually takes about six months, he should be enlisted as an E.E. trainee. For fuller information on this process, see the chapter on enlistment.

M. EVANGELISM EXPLOSION TRAINER

Most people who are enlisted into the E.E. program should at least attempt to be a trainer. Not all have the gift of evangelist, but all do have the role of witness. Ninety percent of those who are *now* effective trainers in the E.E. ministries around the world once felt they could never do this. Personally I doubt that one half of one percent of the participants in E.E. have the gift of evangelism. But most witnesses find they produce more fruit when they are part of the training fellowship.

Many churches consider Evangelism Explosion training a prerequisite for any potential leader before he takes on other responsibilities. Every choir member, Sunday school teacher, and leader in any position will be able to perform better when he is equipped to verbally share the gospel.

N. TEACHER TRAINING

For a church to be functionally healthy it must have both evangelism and education. Not many are called to be teachers, says James, so E.E. participants with this gift should be encouraged to use it. Some will be teachers in the E.E. ministry itself. Others will be teachers in various aspects of the life of the church. After teachers have learned to share the gospel, they will be able to evangelize the people God brings to their classes. Also they will channel their students into Evangelism Explosion Discipleship Training.

O. LEADERSHIP TRAINING

This title covers a variety of responsibilities. One of the shortcomings of the church today is that it places people in positions of leadership without properly training them. Spiritual commitment is not a substitute for competence. The two must go hand in hand. Paul told Timothy to select leaders who were both faithful and able.

OVERVIEW OF FOLLOW-UP PROCEDURES

The suggested procedures listed above may be classified under the three headings of prayer, correspondence, and personal follow-up.

PRAYER

1. Team prayer
2. Public report session prayer
3. Prayerpartners
4. *Prayer Pact*

CORRESPONDENCE FOLLOW-UP

1. New contact notes
2. Church mailing list
3. Pastor's follow-up letter
4. Pastor's letter inviting to new member class
5. Membership application
6. Spiritual birthday card
7. Bible studies—Living in Christ Series, Project Philip, etc.

PERSONAL FOLLOW-UP (telephone)

1. Twenty-four-hour phone call
2. Saturday phone call
3. Invitation to new member class by spiritual parent or prayerpartner
4. Staff or officer call about new member class

PERSONAL FOLLOW-UP (face-to-face)

1. Immediate follow-up
2. Tape delivery
3. Bring to or meet at worship
4. Worship together
5. Accompany to basics class
6. Seven-day call back
7. Enlist as prayerpartner
8. *Prayer Pact*
9. *Your Personal Influence and the Forever Family* contact
10. Get-acquainted coffee
11. Home Bible study group
12. Fellowship meal
13. School for Christian living
14. Invitation to new member class by evangelist or prayerpartner
15. Staff/officer new member interview
16. Undershepherd/parish plan
17. Sponsor
18. New member socials
19. Church groups
20. Spiritual adoption

Viewed from another perspective, personal follow-up may be divided according to that which is done by the individual, the cell, the subcongregation, or the whole assembly.

INDIVIDUAL

1. New contact notes
2. Twenty-four-hour phone call
3. Twenty-four-hour tape delivery
4. Saturday phone call
5. Bring to or meet at worship
6. Worship together
7. Enlist as prayerpartner
8. *Prayer Pact*
9. *Your Personal Influence and the Forever Family* study
10. Membership application
11. Invitation to new member class
12. Sponsor
13. Spiritual birthday card

CELL

1. Immediate follow-up
2. Prayerpartners
3. Seven-day call back
4. Seven-day call back report
5. Get-acquainted coffee
6. Home Bible study group
7. Fellowship meal
8. Memory groups
9. Spiritual adoption
10. Enlistment to E.E.

CONGREGATION/SUBCONGREGATION

1. Public report
2. Basics class
3. School for Christian living
4. New member class
5. Undershepherd/parish plan
6. New member social
7. Church groups

WHOLE ASSEMBLY/CHURCH STAFF

1. Worship
2. Mailing list
3. Pastor's letter
4. Staff/minister contact
5. Pastor's letter inviting to new member class

6. Staff/officer phone calls about new member class
7. Staff/officer new member interview
8. New member baptism
9. New member public recognition
10. Bible studies

DISCIPLING CHARTS

The purpose of the discipling charts is to give an overview of all the things that can be done to disciple the person contacted to a place of responsible reproduction within your church. It shows you the *total* process and your part in it. Discipling is the responsibility of the entire local church. One person cannot do it alone in isolation.

When there is potential for future discipling, whether the contact is in the program or the daily life, a discipling chart should be completed. This should be a team effort under the direction of the trainer. The chart shows many procedures for discipling. Some of these are done by the church office, some are by small groups, some are by staff members. Items designated for alternating team members should be specifically assigned by the trainer. Some duties can be performed best by the trainer. Other responsibilities should be assumed by different team members.

Select the discipling chart that relates to the type of response received in the contact. Christians actively related to other evangelical churches and outright rejections are *not* open for future discipling. For one who has not made a profession of faith but has not rejected, complete the "no profession" chart. For the person who makes a profession with your team, complete the "profession" chart. For a Christian who is not actively related to a church, complete the "Christian" discipling chart.*

When responsibilities are assigned to specific team members, the trainer is responsible to see that these are done.

---

* The three Discipling Charts are available from E.E. III International, P.O. Box 23820, Fort Lauderdale, Florida 33307.

DISCIPLING CHART—New Profession

WHAT?	WHEN?	WHO?
1. Immediate follow-up	When "commitment" completed	Team leader
2. Contact analysis	While returning to church	Whole team
3. Team prayer	After "analysis" at church	Each team member
4. Initial contact written report	After "team prayer" at church	*
5. Public report board	After written report	*
6. Discipling chart	After "board" at church	Team directed by traine
7. Public report session	After "discipling chart" at church	*
8. New profession note	After "discipling chart" at church	*
9. Contact/pray with prayer-partner	Within 24 hours	Each team member
10. Place on church mailing list	Within 24 hours	Church office
11. Pastor's letter	Within 24 hours	Church office
12. 24-hour phone call	Within 24 hours	*
13. Tape or book delivery	One to seven days	*
14. Saturday phone call	Saturday after profession	*
15. ☐ Bring to ☐ Meet at worship service	Sunday after profession	*
16. Sit with during worship	Sunday after profession	*
17. Accompany to "basics" class	Sunday after profession	*
18. Seven-day call back	Usually 7 days after profession	*
A. Questions to research	As raised in 7-day call back	Each team member
B. Problems to solve	As raised in 7-day call back	Team leader
C. Enlist as prayerpartner	When convert is clear on his faith After 7-day call back	Mutually agreed upon team member
D. Written report	After 7-day call back	*
19. "Your Personal Influence and The Forever Family"	After 7-day call back Within 8 weeks after initial contact	*
20. Enter prayer pact	As needed and desired	Prayerpartner/team member
21. Staff/officer follow-up contact	2 weeks after 7-day call back	Staff/officer
22. Get-acquainted coffee	One-two weeks after initial contact	*
23. "This Is The Life" class	After completing "basics"	*
24. Home Bible study group	After completing "This Is The Life" class	*
25. Fellowship meal	Within 10 days to 3 weeks after profession	*
26. School for Christian Living	After completing "This Is the Life" class	*

*Alternate team members
Write in name of person responsible.

WHAT?	WHEN?	WHO?
7. NEW MEMBER A. Personal invitation	2 weeks before class begins	Prayerpartner/team member
B. Provide "application"	When personal invitation is given	Prayerpartner/team member
C. Church invitation letter	2 weeks before class begins	Church office
D. Staff/officer phone call	1–3 days before class	Staff/officer
E. Attend classes	As scheduled	Encouraged by team
F. Interview	Before uniting with church	Staff/officer
G. Public recognition	When publicly received into membership	Pastors/officers/church
H. Baptism	As prescribed by local church	Pastor
I. Placed in officer discipling group	First week as new member	Staff or committee
J. Sponsor	First week as a new member	Assigned by committee or staff
K. Group social	Within two weeks after class became members	Church officers and other leaders
8. Spiritual birthday card	3rd, 6th, and 12th month anniversaries	Team members
9. Correspondence Bible studies A. Living in Christ B. Project Philip C. Other: ________	When personal contact is NOT possible	Team notifies church office. Church office mails material.
0. CHURCH GROUPS A. Choir B. Women of the Church C. Men of the Church D. Midweek School of the Bible E. Bible memory F. Christian Service Brigade/ Awana/Boy Scouts G. Pioneer Girls/Girl Scouts H. Youth activities I. Others: ________ ________	According to interest and need—for the contact and his/her family	Team members
1. Placed for spiritual adoption	As needed	Prayerpartner/spiritual parent
2. Evangelism Explosion A. Trainee	Usually not before six months as a Christian	Prayerpartner/team member
B. Trainer	12–18 months after profession	Trainer/Lieutenant
3. Teacher trainer	18–24 months after profession	Staff/Christian education enlistment committee
4. Leadership training	24–36 months after profession	Leaders in various groups/Staff

CHRISTIAN—Not Active in Local Church

WHAT?	WHEN?	WHO?
1. Gospel for assurance	Initial contact	Team leader or trainee
2. Gospel for recommitment	Initial contact	Team leader or trainee
3. Gospel for trainees	Initial contact	Team leader or trainee
4. Contact analysis	While returning to church	All team members
5. Team prayer	After "analysis" at church	All team members
6. Initial contact results report	After "prayer" at church	*
7. Public report board	After "results report" at church	*
8. Discipling chart	After "report board" at church	Members—trainer in charge
9. Public report session	After discipling chart at church	*
10. Same day note	Same day	*
11. Contact/pray w/prayerpartner	Within 24 hours	Each team member
12. Place on church mailing list	Within 24 hours	Church office
13. Pastor's letter	Within 24 hours	Church office
14. 24-hour phone call	Within 24 hours	*
15. Tape/book delivery	1–7 days	*
16. Saturday phone call	Saturday after initial contact	*
17. ☐ Bring to ☐ Meet at worship A.M.	Sunday after initial contact	*
18. Sit with during worship	Sunday after initial contact	*
19. Accompany to School for Christian Living	Sunday after initial contact	*
20. Tape/book follow-up contact	About 7 days after delivery	*
21. "Prayer in the Forever Family"	2 weeks after initial contact	*
22. Enlist as prayerpartner	3 weeks after initial contact	Mutually agreed upon team member
23. Enter prayer pact	As needed and desired	Prayerpartner/team member
24. "Your Personal Influence and the Forever Family"	4 weeks after initial contact	Trainer or jr. trainer
25. Staff/officer follow-up contact	2 weeks after initial contact	Staff or Officer
26. Get-acquainted coffee	1–2 weeks after initial contact	*
27. Home Bible study group	Within 6 weeks after initial contact	*
28. Support group	As desired and needed	*
29. Fellowship meal	By 3rd week after initial contact	*
		*Alternate team membe[r] Trainer assigns and writ[e] name of person respons[ible]

HAT?	WHEN?	WHO?
). NEW MEMBER A. Personal invitation	Week before new member class	Team member closest to him
B. Provide "application"	When personally invited	Team member closest to him
C. Pastor's invitation letter	10 days before new member class	Church office
D. Staff/officer phone call	1–3 days before new member class	Staff or officer
E. Attend classes	As scheduled	Urged by team
F. Interview	Before church membership	Staff or officer
G. Public recognition	Day of public reception	Pastor/officers/church
H. Baptism	Day of public reception	Pastor/officers/church
I. Placed in officer discipling group	First week as new member	Assigned by pastor
J. Sponsor	First week as new member	Assigned by pastor or committee
K. Group social	Within two weeks after public reception	Officers
1. Spiritual birthday card	Annually on spiritual birthday	Team members
2. Correspondence Bible studies A. Living in Christ B. Project Philip	When personal contact is NOT possible	Team notify church office. Church office mails lessons
3. Church Groups A. Choir B. Women of the Church C. Men of the Church D. Midweek School of the Bible E. Bible memory F. Christian Service Brigade/ Awana/Boy Scouts G. Pioneer Girls/Girl Scouts H. Youth activities I. Others: ______ ______ ______	According to interest and need for the contact and his family	Team members
4. Evangelism Explosion A. Trainee	Usually not before 6 months as a Christian	Prayerpartner/team member
B. Trainer	Preferable 12–18 months after profession	Trainer/lieutenant
5. Teacher training	If qualified, 18–24 months after profession	Staff/Christian education enlistment committee
6. Leadership training	As qualified, 24–36 months after profession	Leaders in various groups/staff

NO PROFESSION FOLLOW-THROUGH CHART

WHAT?	WHEN?	WHO?
1. Follow-through appointment	Initial contact	Team leader
2. Contact analysis A. Questions to research B. Problems to solve	While returning to church As raised in initial contact As raised in initial contact	All team members Trainer or jr. trainer Trainer or jr. trainer
3. Team prayer	After "analysis" at church	All team members
4. Initial contact results report	After "team prayer" at church	*
5. Public report board	After "results report" at church	*
6. Follow-through chart	After "report board" at church	Team under trainer direction
7. Public report session	After "discipling chart" at church	*
8. Note	After returning to the church	*
9. Contact/pray with prayer-partners	Within 24 hours	Each team member
10. Place on church mailing list	Within 24 hours	Church office
11. Pastor's follow-through letter	Within 24 hours	Church office
12. 24-hour phone call	Within 24 hours	*
13. 24-hour tape/book delivery	1 to 7 days	*
14. Saturday phone call	Saturday after initial contact	*
15. ☐ Bring to ☐ Meet at worship	Sunday after initial contact	*
16. Sit with during worship	Sunday after initial contact	*
17. Accompany to "Truth and Life" class	Sunday after initial contact	*
18. Follow-through contact	Usually 7 days after first contact	All team members
19. Follow-through contact written report	After "follow-through contact"	All team members
20. Get-acquainted coffee	One or two weeks after initial contact	*
21. Home Bible study	Within 6 weeks after initial contact	*
22. Fellowship meal	By third week after initial contact	*
23. School for Christian Living	After completing "Truth and Life"	*
24. Profession of faith	This may occur as a result of involvement in one or more of the groups above. It may happen in individual conversation. If it does not happen before the new member class, encourage him to attend. His problem may be lack of understanding church membership. Of course he will not be received as a member until he has professed faith.	When the profession is made known, the team members who made initial contact shoul[d] work with other church membe[rs] who have become involved to complete the remaining follow-up activities.
25. Immediate follow-up	As soon after profession as possible	Trainer or jr. trainer—Possibly whole team
26. Contact analysis	At next training class after profession	Whole team
27. Team prayer	At next training class after profession	Whole team
28. Written report	At next training class after profession	Team member closest t[o] the convert
29. Public report board	At next training class after profession	Team member closest t[o] the convert
30. Public report session	At next training class after profession	Team member closest t[o] the convert *Alternate team membe[r]. Trainer assigns and writ[es] name of person respons[ible]

WHAT?	WHEN?	WHO?
31. New profession note	As soon after profession as possible	Team member closest to the convert
32. Contact/pray with prayer-partner	As soon as you hear about it	All team members
33. Tape or book delivery	1 to 7 days after profession	Team member closest to the convert
34. Accompany to "basics" class	First week after profession	*
35. Seven-day call back A. Questions to research B. Problems to solve C. Enlist as prayer partner	Usually 7 days after profession As raised in 7-day call back As raised in 7-day call back When convert is clear on his faith. After 7-day call back	Whole team Each team member Trainer/jr. trainer Mutually agreed upon team member.
36. Staff/officer follow-up contact	Two weeks after 7-day call back	Staff/officer
37. "Your Personal Influence and the Forever Family"	Between second and eighth week after profession	Trainer or jr. trainer
38. Enter prayer pact	As needed and desired	Prayerpartner/team member
39. "This Is the Life" class	After completing "basics" class	*
40. NEW MEMBER A. Personal invitation B. Provide "application" C. Church invitation letter D. Staff/officer phone call E. Attend classes F. Interview G. Public recognition H. Baptism I. Placed in officer discipling group J. Sponsor K. Group Social	 2 weeks before class begins When personal invitation is given 2 weeks before class begins 1–3 days before class As scheduled Before uniting with church When publicly received into membership As prescribed by local church First week as new member First week as new member Within two weeks after class became members	 Prayerpartner/team member Prayerpartner/team member Church office Staff/officer Encouraged by team Staff/officer Pastors/officers/church Pastor Staff or committee Assigned by committee or staff Church officers and other leaders
41. Spiritual birthday card	3rd, 6th, and 12th month anniversaries	Team members
42. Correspondence Bible studies A. Living in Christ B. Project Philip C. Other ______	When personal contact is NOT possible	Team notifies church office. Church office mails material.
43. CHURCH GROUPS A. Choir B. Women of the Church C. Men of the Church D. Midweek School of the Bible E. Bible memory F. Christian Service Brigade/ Awana/Boy Scouts G. Pioneer Girls/Girl Scouts H. Youth activities I. Others: ______ ______	According to interest and need—for the contact and his/her family	Team members
44. Placed for spiritual adoption	As needed	Prayerpartner/spiritual parent
45. Evangelism Explosion A. Trainee B. Trainer	 Usually not before six months as a Christian 12–18 months after profession	 Prayerpartner/team member Trainer/lieutenant
46. Teacher trainer	18–24 months after profession	Staff/Christian education enlistment committee
47. Leadership training	24–36 months after profession	Leaders in various groups/Staff

*Alternate team members. Trainer assigns and writes name of person responsible.

TEN
THE GOSPEL FOR THE SECULAR MIND

It is estimated that in 1977 approximately forty million Americans could be classified as pagans. They have neither read the Bible nor been to church. Their world view is strictly secular.

Additional millions of Americans have read the Bible and gone to church, but they function as though there is no God. They claim to believe in him but live as though he did not exist. They are practical atheists. They have a form of godliness but deny the power.

Secularism is a life-style that flows out of a world view. For the gospel to be effective it must deal with the basic elements in a person's world view.

"The Gospel for the Secular Mind" presentation attempts to do this. It was developed over a period of more than six years. We began with the standard E.E. presentation for the church-oriented person. As we encountered the same questions and objections over and over, answers were developed and incorporated into the presentation. The following is the content as it stands today. It begins with the questionnaire introduction and concludes with assurance.

THE OUTLINE

I. THE INTRODUCTION (ASSURANCE QUESTIONNAIRE)

- A. The approach
- B. Appeal for help
- C. The five questions
- D. Thanks
- E. Follow-through

II. THE GOSPEL

- A. GRACE
    1. Eternal life is a free gift.
    2. Eternal life is not earned or deserved.

B. GOD
   1. There is only one true God.
   2. Made man in his own image because he loved man and wanted man to love him.

C. MAN
   1. Did not love God so he disobeyed him and became guilty and polluted.
   2. Cannot clear himself of his guilt or cleanse himself of his pollution.

D. CHRIST
   1. Lived the perfect life, died, came out of the grave alive.
   2. When Jesus came out of the grave alive it proved:
      a. he is true God and true man
      b. that the penalty for man's disobedience had been paid
   3. Then he returned to the Father and sent the Holy Spirit to cleanse the heart.

E. CHANGE YOUR MIND/TRUST
   1. Changing your mind
      a. Is not merely feeling badly for getting caught doing wrong.
      b. Causes sorrow for doing wrong and turning from it.
   2. Trust
      a. Is not a blind leap in the dark, or mere head or now belief.
      b. Is trusting in Jesus Christ alone for your eternal life.

III. THE COMMITMENT
   A. God removed my guilt, brought me into a new relationship with him that gave me purpose, power, and personal peace.
   B. (Qualifying question) "Does this make sense to you?"
   C. (Commitment question) "Would you like to receive the gift of eternal life?"
   D. Clarification of commitment
   E. Prayer of commitment

IV. THE IMMEDIATE FOLLOW-UP
   A. Assurance of salvation
   B. *Welcome to the Forever Family*
   C. Spiritual Birth Certificate
   D. Means of growth (seven-day call back appointment)
   E. Satan

SAMPLE PRESENTATION

ASSURANCE QUESTIONNAIRE

Hello, I am Archie. This is Dan and Diane. We're from the Greenhouse. We're trying to determine people's religious thinking and to assist anyone looking for a faith. Will you help us by giving your response to five brief questions?

I'm not religious.

We are particularly interested in the thinking of people outside our own group. Would you help us by giving us your thoughts in response to these questions?

> I don't have much time.

It will only take about two minutes for the questions. It would be of help to us, and we are interested in your thinking. How about it?

> Well, OK.

The first question is, "Of what religious group are you a member?"

> None.

The second question is, "What local church do you attend?"

> None. I only go to churches for weddings and funerals.

Have you come to the place in your thinking where you know for certain that you have eternal life? If you were to be killed in an accident today do you know for certain that you would go to heaven?

> No, I'm not even sure there is a heaven.

If you were to be killed today and you stood before God and he said to you, "Why should I let you into my heaven?" what would you say?

> I'm not sure there is a heaven.

For the sake of discussion, assume that there is a heaven. If you were to be killed and you were standing before God and he said, "Why should I let you into my heaven?" what would you say?

> That's a pretty hard question. I don't know what I would say.

I know you don't have any formal paper prepared on the subject, but just off the top of your head, what do you think you would say?

> Well, I haven't given it a lot of thought. Sometimes I do think about what death is going to be like. But I have never really thought too much about what I would say to God if he should ask why I should get into heaven.

You've heard sermons over the radio and television, I'm sure. Probably you've been in discussions on religion and the Bible at one time or another. In the light of what you have heard and studied and thought on the matter, what do you think the general requirements would be for anyone to get into heaven?

> I think a person's got to treat people right and do the best he can. You know a person can't just go to church and think he is going to get into heaven because of it, there's got to be something in the life too.

That's very interesting. Since you say the general requirements for anyone to get into heaven are to treat people right and to do the best we can, do you think that if you were standing before God you would say to him something like, "I've always done the best I can and treated people right"?

> I can't say that I've *always* done the best I could or that I have really never hurt anybody, but generally I have tried to do the best I could and haven't intentionally hurt anybody.

OK, then, what you would say to God is, "I have tried to do the best I could and I've never intentionally hurt anybody." Is that right?

> Yes, I guess that is what I would say.

This completes the questionnaire. Your answers are interesting. Thank you for your help. May we have a few more moments of your time to share with you how we came to know that we have eternal life and how you can know it too?

> Yes, I'd be interested in your thinking on this.

By the way, what is your first name?

> John.

Do you mind if I call you John?

> No.

John, there's so much bad news in the world today that it's refreshing to find some good news. I would like to share what I consider the best news I ever heard! It is possible to have a personal relationship with God. This will result in life that has purpose, power, and personal peace. It is a life that will never end and is even better after death. God calls this eternal life. He says, "This is eternal life, that they may know Thee the only true God, and Jesus Christ whom Thou hast sent."[1]

God makes this life available now.

(TESTIMONY)

I am experiencing this life now. I find that it gives me an unshakable security. Since I received eternal life, I've found real, genuine love! God himself loves me, and through his love he has given me the ability to love others. I can be open and honest with other people without being afraid. I've found a way to get rid of guilt for things

I've done that I shouldn't have done. Life is a real adventure! And I'm not afraid of dying because I know that when I leave this life I'll be with God in heaven.

There was a time when I felt like I was treading water in the middle of the sea of life. Most people feel this way sooner or later. You know, like you're in the middle of an ocean and there's no help in sight. You swim as far as you can, and you tread water as long as you can. You try floating, and then comes the time when you can't even float anymore! At that point, I think I would have given almost anything for some sort of life preserver that would enable me to rest and not work so hard to keep from drowning. That's what eternal life is—a life preserver in the sea of life. *How can a person get it?*

(THE GOSPEL—GRACE)

This is the amazing thing. God says that eternal life—his presence in my life now and heaven in the world to come—**ETERNAL LIFE IS A FREE GIFT.** "The free gift of God is eternal life in Christ Jesus our Lord."[2] A gift is something a person is not obligated to give.

IT'S NOT SOMETHING WE EARN OR DESERVE. Wages are paid for work that is done. A just wage means getting exactly what is deserved. God declares, "The wages of sin is death." Eternal life "is the gift of God; not as a result of works, that no one should boast."[3] You see, it's not a matter of personal opinion. One man's opinion is just as good as another's. *This is true because God said it.*

(GOD)

God is not an abstract cosmic blur.

THERE IS ONLY ONE TRUE GOD.

He is personal because he thinks, feels, and makes decisions.

He is not limited by other beings.

"He is Lord of heaven and earth . . . neither is He served by human hands, as though He needed anything, since He Himself gives to all life and breath and all things."[4]

He created "heaven and earth." All men everywhere can look at the creation and see his wisdom and power. "That which is known about God is evident within them; for God made it evident to them. For since the creation of the world His invisible attributes, His eternal power and divine nature, have been clearly seen, being understood through what has been made."[5]

We can know some things about a person by looking at his work. But only when a person reveals himself can we know him fully—as he is in his inner being. God reveals himself fully and accurately in the Bible alone. **He reveals that he exists in three persons: Father, Son, and Holy Spirit. Among these three persons there is perfect love and communication.**

GOD MADE MAN IN HIS OWN IMAGE. Stamped on all men is the likeness of their Creator. The Bible says, "God created man in His own image, in the image of God He created him; male and female He created them."[6] This is why man is a personal, spiritual being with the ability to worship, love, and communicate.

He gave us intelligence and feeling and the ability to make decisions. These faculties make man like God in contrast with lower animals. We are meant to use these faculties to worship and serve God. No creature other than man has ever been observed building chapels.

Because God is a person and we are persons, communication between us is possible. In fact, it is only when I am in a right relationship with God that I can fully understand what I am as a person. Then I can *properly* use my mind. I can properly love and feel with my heart. Then I can make the right decisions for my life.

God also gave man the responsibility for all the other creatures and the world itself.

Since God is the Creator, he is in charge. It's God's world and God's heaven. I'm his creature—totally dependent on him for my whole existence.

(Love's requirement). GOD LOVED MAN. He says "I have loved you with an everlasting love."[7]

HE WANTED MAN TO LOVE HIM. He told us, "You shall love the Lord your God with all your heart, and with all your soul, and with all your mind."[8] But genuine love requires a choice. It has to flow freely from a willing heart. It can't be the action of a robot or of a person who has no other choice. In order to give man the ability to truly love, God put him in an ideal situation and gave him the genuine option not to love. Man was told that he should obey God. **If he obeyed, this would show that he did love God.**

(Man's original condition). At first, the man and woman knelt in willing submission to God. They accepted the responsibilities he had given them. His love flowed down to them. Their love flowed up to him. While they were in this loving relationship with God, they also were able to love each other and communicate with each other perfectly. They were able to properly care for God's creatures and his world.

But one day the devil came. Through one of the lower creatures he said, "God knows that in the day you eat from it [the tree of the knowledge of good and evil] your eyes will be opened, and you will be like God, knowing good and evil."[9]

(MAN)

MAN DID NOT LOVE GOD, SO HE DISOBEYED HIM AND BECAME GUILTY AND POLLUTED. Instead of kneeling in submission, he stood and turned his back on God in rebellion. God says, "All have sinned and fall short of the glory of God."[10] He made us so that we could worship him and love and communicate with him and with others. When man failed to love God supremely, he lost his ability to properly love himself and others, and so he stands guilty and polluted.

He gave the man and woman responsibility to care for his creation. When they let one of the creatures be used to encourage their disobedience, they ran from responsibility. The man blamed the woman and God for his disobedience. The woman blamed the creature. But they both knew they were wrong. Their conscience told them so.

Conscience is the moral monitor God has placed in every person. Even though people vary as to what they think is right and wrong, I have yet to meet anyone who would say he has *always* done exactly what his conscience said was right and has *never* done what his conscience said was wrong.

(The greatest sin). Man's rebellion and lack of responsibility shows itself most clearly when he comes up against God's moral law. This was impressed into the heart of man when God first made him. Later **God had the Ten Commandments written as an expression of his own moral goodness.**

Jesus said the first and greatest commandment is to love God with all our heart, soul, and mind. As I look at my own life, I see that there have been times when I went days, weeks, months without even thinking about God—let alone consciously loving him. Since loving God is the greatest commandment, not loving him is the greatest sin.

God says, "None of you carries out the law."[11]

(Violating God's law). If I violate God's law, in reality I violate him—the holy God who made me. This can be done by specific acts, but it also can be done by attitudes and even thoughts. Jesus said that whoever is angry has committed murder in his heart already, and whoever lusts commits adultery in his heart.[12] In the eyes of God, adultery in the head is as bad as adultery in the bed. God tells me that when I violate these laws I sin.[13]

You'll notice I didn't say, "I *break* the Ten Commandments." They cannot be broken! The moral laws of God are as unbreakable as the physical laws of God. If I jump off a very tall building and say, "Look at me! I'm going to break the law of gravity," you know what's going to get broken. It will be *me.* I will be a mass of broken bones and bloody, mutilated flesh on the pavement below.

Well, **when a man violates the moral laws of God, he gets broken too.** It may seem that he gets by with it, but in reality he's broken inside. This is the reason people feel empty and fearful and guilty. This is why people can't get along with each other—husbands and wives, parents and children, nations, and races! This is why man misuses God's creatures and abuses God's world. These are symptoms of shattered souls!

Since sin is a violation of the very moral nature of God, it must be punished. God's wrath is the response of his justice to our sin. This is why he threatens to "visit transgression with the rod, and iniquity with stripes."[14] There is no doubt about it—God will certainly punish all sin.

Because God is loving, he didn't immediately destroy the man and woman the instant they first sinned. God's failure to destroy did not mean that he condoned the rebellious rejection of responsibility. The Bible tells us not to "think lightly of the riches of His kindness and forbearance and patience, not knowing that the kindness of God leads you to repentance."[15]

If God had destroyed me the moment I first sinned, I would never have had an opportunity to turn back to him. This explains the presence of so much evil in the world today. It comes from the rebellious hearts of individuals like me and you. God is not permissive, but he is loving and patient. He gives us time to turn back to him. One day his patience will run out. Then he will judge all sin and balance the books once and for all! Violating God's moral laws breaks man and must be punished. Violating God's moral law results in loss of purpose, power, and personal peace.

MAN CANNOT CLEAR HIMSELF OF HIS GUILT. God says, "The wages of sin is death."[16] This is spiritual death. If I receive what I deserve for my sins I will be eternally separated from God's love. He says, "Cursed is every one who does not abide by all things written in the book of the Law, to perform them."[17]

Even one small sin is enough to condemn. The Bible says, "Whoever keeps the whole law and yet stumbles in one point, he has become guilty of all."[18] The penalty for violating God's law is death. The criminal is just as dead when he is executed for one crime as he would be if he were executed for ten crimes. When one link in a chain snaps, the whole chain is broken; one break in a telegraph wire and communication is lost; one puncture is sufficient to ruin a tire; one crack spoils a pane of glass. The point is not that a person has violated every part of the law, but that he is guilty of not keeping every part of the law.

MAN CANNOT CLEANSE HIMSELF OF HIS POLLUTION. The Apostle Paul said, "I know that nothing good dwells in me, that is, in my flesh; for the wishing is present in me, but the doing of the good is not."[19]

Separation from God corrupts our hearts, so that out of them come evil thoughts, murders, adulteries, fornications, thefts, false witness, slanders.[20] These are the things which defile us. Our problem is that we cannot change our own hearts.

(Do-it-yourself heart transplant). Suppose I had a severe pain in my chest and I collapsed. I'm taken to the hospital, and after the doctor takes extensive tests he says to me, "Your heart has been permanently damaged. The only thing that can save your life is a transplant."

Suppose on the one hand there is a skilled surgeon available who has transplanted many hearts and never had a failure. On the other hand, I might attempt a do-it-yourself heart transplant. What do you think the outcome would be if I attempted to transplant my own heart? It would be suicide!

I found I was committing spiritual suicide by trying to change by myself the spiritual core of my life. The more I tried to change, the weaker I became. I found I could not be in a right relationship with a holy God while my heart was unholy. Since I could not relate to the God who made me, I found it very difficult to properly relate to others around me.

(Summary of man's problem). So you see, there are two parts to this problem of man relating to God. He is a holy God and I have violated him by violating his law; therefore, he is my judge and I stand guilty and condemned before him. He is also a loving Father—the source of all life. But the corruption within my heart produced a spiritual deadness within my soul, making it impossible for his powerful life to flow through me.

God's answer to this problem is Jesus.

(Christ)

JESUS LIVED THE PERFECT LIFE. This is a fact of history!

He once challenged his enemies with these words, "Which one of you convicts Me of sin?"[21] And there was not one flaw they could point to.

Simon Peter, the big fisherman, who lived very close to Jesus for three and a half years, said that Jesus "committed no sin, nor was any deceit found in His mouth; and while being reviled, He did not revile in return; while suffering, He uttered no threats, but kept entrusting Himself to Him who judges righteously."[22]

He healed the sick, fed the hungry, gave hope to the downtrodden, and taught man to love even his enemies. By living this perfect life, he proved that it is possible to live a life of love in tune with God in an ungodly world.

This also shows us that he was qualified to pay for the sins of others.

This was promised in the Bible and then actually happened in history. After thirty-three years of living perfectly, what did Jesus do?

JESUS DIED. This is a fact of history.

On a hill outside of Jerusalem two thousand years ago, before a bloodthirsty mob, between two thieves, he was executed by professional Roman soldiers. It was a common practice in those days to break the legs of people being crucified in order to get the process over more quickly. An eyewitness of the crucifixion said the soldiers came to Jesus to break his legs and, "When they saw that He was already dead, they did not break His legs; but one of the soldiers pierced His side with a spear, and immediately there came out blood and water."[23] When the soldier ran the spear into Jesus' heart he had been dead long enough for the blood to separate into serum and corpuscles.

More than twenty specific details relating to the event of Christ's death were predicted in the Jewish Scriptures hundreds of years before they occurred. *Then what happened?*

JESUS CAME OUT OF THE GRAVE ALIVE. This also was promised in the Bible and is a fact of history.

Three days after Jesus was crucified he came out of the tomb alive. He is alive today! We do not worship a dead Christ, but a living Savior. This is the most important and the best attested fact of human history. "He presented Himself alive, after His suffering, by many convincing proofs, appearing to them over a period of forty days."[24]

Jesus showed himself alive to hundreds of people. The Apostle Paul said, "He was raised on the third day according to the Scriptures, and that He appeared to Cephas, then to the twelve. After that He appeared to more than five hundred brethren at one time, most of whom remain until now . . . and last of all . . . He appeared to me also."[25]

Sir Edward Clark, an authority on evidence, once wrote a prolonged study of the resurrection, and as a result he wrote: "To me the evidence is conclusive. Over and over again in the high court I have secured a verdict on evidence not nearly so compelling. A truthful witness is always artless and disdains effect. The Gospels' evidence for the resurrection is of this class. As a lawyer I accept it unreservedly as the testimony of truthful men to facts they were able to substantiate."

On April 9, 1929, Chief Justice Ben C. Hilliard, of the Colorado Supreme Court, presided when the evidence concerning the resurrection of Jesus was presented. He advised on the legal value of each piece of evidence and eventually summed up as follows: "Overwhelming evidence has been given to us tonight of the fact of the resurrection of Christ, and we must decide that Christ did rise from the dead, in deed and in truth."

In Jesus' resurrection from the dead we see God as man declaring that death is not the final word. We see the God-man overcoming man's alienation and despair. We see him becoming whole again and offering life to man.

When Jesus came out of the grave alive, what did this prove?

WHEN JESUS CAME OUT OF THE GRAVE ALIVE IT PROVED WHO HE WAS. Scripture explains "He was declared to be the Son of God with power, according to the Spirit of Holiness by the resurrection from the dead."[26]

JESUS IS TRUE GOD AND TRUE MAN. He is the Creator of the whole universe! This comes as a real surprise to many people. They don't realize that he is God the Son.

The historical fact that God became a man in the person of Jesus of Nazareth is what we celebrate at Christmas. When, where, how, and why he would be born were predicted hundreds of years before it happened.

In one place in the Bible, Jesus is called "the Word." Words express thoughts which could not otherwise be known. Jesus Christ expresses God, who cannot be known apart from him. We are told, "In the beginning was the Word (Jesus) . . . and the Word was God . . . All things came into being through Him . . . And the Word became flesh, and dwelt among us, and we beheld His glory, glory as of the only begotten from the Father, full of grace and truth."[27] Jesus Christ is in reality the eternal Creator who clothed himself in human flesh and walked among us.

When Jesus came out of the grave alive it also indicated that the penalty for man's disobedience had been paid and he could be cleared of this guilt. *"He was raised for our justification."* Justification means to be made just as if I'd never sinned.

The Bible says, "He made him who knew no sin to be sin on our behalf, that we might become the righteousness of God in Him."[28]

After Jesus came out of the grave alive and appeared to different people for forty days, *then what did he do?*

JESUS RETURNED TO THE FATHER AND SENT THE HOLY SPIRIT TO CLEANSE THE HEART. The night before he was crucified he explained, "I am going to Him who sent Me; . . . if I do not go away, the Helper [the Holy Spirit] shall not come to you; but if I go, I will send Him to you."[29]

God says, "I will cleanse you from all your filthiness . . . I will give you a new heart."[30] This is what Jesus had in mind when he promised, "I give eternal life to them; and they shall never perish."[31]

To receive eternal life you must change your mind about doing wrong.

(CHANGE YOUR MIND/TRUST)

THIS DOES NOT MEAN MERELY TO FEEL BADLY FOR GETTING *CAUGHT* DOING WRONG—like a small child caught with his hand in the cookie jar. He says he's sorry but has every intention of stealing cookies the next time he has the chance.

This change of mind will cause you to be sorry for doing wrong and to turn from it. We recognize sin is a violation of the holy God and we are sorry enough to turn from the sin. It is like making a U-turn on the road of life. God says, "He who conceals his transgressions will not prosper, but he who confesses and forsakes them will find compassion."[32]

Changing your mind is necessary! God's holy nature will not allow him to forgive sin without it! But to be sorry for past wrong cannot undo it.

With God's help we can turn from our sin; the *gift of eternal life is received by trusting.*

Trust is the key that opens the heavenly door to eternal life. You know, you can have a key ring with a lot of keys on it, like this (if you have a ring of keys, it can be used as a visible object lesson). They all look somewhat alike. But if you go to the front door of your home and try all of the keys except the right one, the door will not open. It's like this with trust.

One thing that people sometimes mistake for saving trust is **BLIND FAITH**—a blind leap in the dark. It is like a blindfolded man stepping off a cliff into the darkness of uncertainty, hoping that there is something out there, but not really sure. There is no substance to this idea of faith.

The evening of the first Easter Sunday, Jesus appeared to ten of his disciples. One of the disciples, doubting Thomas, was not with them. The ten told Thomas they had seen Jesus alive. Thomas replied, "Unless I shall see in His hands the imprint of the nails, and put my finger into the place of the nails, and put my hand into His side, I will not believe."[33]

Eight days later, Jesus appeared to the disciples again. This time Thomas was with them. The Apostle John was an eyewitness to this event, and he relates that Jesus said to Thomas, "Reach here your finger and see My hands; and reach here your hand, and put it into My side; and be not unbelieving, but believing."[34]

Thomas knew this was the same Jesus he had lived so close to for three and a half years. It was the same Jesus who had been crucified and buried. But he was alive. Facing the fact of the resurrected Jesus in the flesh, Thomas exclaimed, "My Lord and my God."[35]

Rather than being a blind leap in the dark, saving trust is built on the incontestable facts of the life, death, and resurrection of Jesus Christ. These were predicted in Scripture and the predictions were fulfilled in history!

If there had been only eight fulfilled prophecies, the chances that any one man might have fulfilled them is one out of one hundred quadrillion (1 out of 100,000,000,000,000,000).

Suppose this number of silver dollars were spread over the face of Texas. They would cover the entire state in stacks two feet deep. If you marked one, stirred them all up, blindfolded a man, and told him to pick the marked coin, he would have as much chance to pick the marked coin as the prophets would have had of writing eight prophecies and having them all come true in one man.

As a matter of fact, Canon Liddon, a great scholar, has stated there are 332 distinct predictions that are literally fulfilled in Christ. As mere chance, this is not a mathematical possibility!

Another thing that saving trust is not is a **MERE HEAD BELIEF.** It is not a mere abstract idea in the brain—a mere intellectual assent. Even the demons had this. They cried out, "What do we have to do with You, Son of God?"[36] They acknowledged Jesus to be the Son of God, but obviously they do not have eternal life, nor will they ever be in heaven.

Merely knowing about food in the mind will not satisfy hunger. Merely knowing about Jesus in the mind will not give eternal life.

There is one more thing that people sometimes mistake for saving trust. It's what we might call a **MERE NOW BELIEF.** This is where we trust God to provide things for us now, like a place to live, food to eat, money to spend, and clothes to wear. It is not wrong to trust God for these things. In the Lord's Prayer, Jesus taught us to pray, "Give us this day our daily bread."[37] God wants us to look to him for the provision of things that we need for this life. But there is more to life than the things that are seen. He tells us that "the things which are seen are temporal [temporary], but the things which are not seen are eternal."[38] Most of these things are for our physical existence. God wants us to realize that within our bodies there is a soul that will exist forever. Therefore, merely relying on him for the things of time will not take our souls to heaven.

What then is trust?

SAVING TRUST IS RELYING ON JESUS CHRIST ALONE FOR YOUR ETERNAL LIFE. "God so loved the world that He gave His only begotten Son, that whoever believes in Him should not perish, but have eternal life."[39]

Suppose a man was in a small boat many miles out to sea. It's an old boat and it begins to leak and finally sinks. The distance is too great for him to swim back to the shore. He treads water as long as he can. Suddenly, as if by a miracle, a boat appears alongside him. A man in the boat throws him a life preserver with a line on it. He knows that he cannot swim to shore; his only hope is to put the life preserver around him and be pulled into this boat. This is the only reasonable thing to do, isn't it? If he does not trust the man in the boat, he will drown.

Saving trust is similar to this. We cannot get out of the sea of life by our own efforts without drowning. We cannot work our way to heaven any more than we can swim across the ocean by ourselves. But Jesus Christ appears in the boat of salvation. He reaches out a powerful hand of love and offers us the life preserver of eternal life. He says to us, "I am the way, and the truth, and the life; no one comes to the Father, but through Me."[40] He urges us to trust in him, not merely for things of this life, not merely to satisfy our minds, and certainly not as a blind leap in the dark. On the basis of the evidence of his life, death, and resurrection he says, "Trust in me and I will give you eternal life. I will take you to heaven!"

"The free gift of God is eternal life."[41]

I trusted the Lord for all kinds of things in this life, but when I got right down to what I was trusting in for eternal life—I was trusting in myself. I tried not to intentionally hurt anybody and to do the best I could. You see, it was I, I, I.

Remember when I asked what you would say to God if he were to ask why he should let you into heaven? Do you remember what you said? You said, "I try to do the best I can, and I don't intentionally hurt anybody." When you said that, in whom were you trusting to get into heaven?

I was trusting in myself.

To receive the gift of eternal life you must trust the Giver. The Lord Jesus Christ died on a cross and rose from the grave to provide this gift. He paid for it. Now he freely offers it to you. To receive it you must extend the empty hand of faith. Saving trust then, is putting confidence in Jesus Christ alone for eternal life. A number of years ago my trust was transferred from myself to Jesus Christ, from what I had been doing for God to what he had done for me on the cross. By a simple act of faith I transferred my trust from what I had done to what Christ had done for me. Just as a drowning swimmer would have to transfer his trust from his weak efforts to the man in the boat, so I had to transfer my trust to Jesus Christ. No longer am I trusting what I have done: rather, I trust what he has done for me. *What happened when I trusted?*

(COMMITMENT). God removed my guilt and entered into a new relationship with me. This resulted in life with power, purpose, and personal peace.

God provides life with power. Sin had killed my human spirit. This made it impossible for me to do what I ought to do. But God, the Holy Spirit, caused my dead human spirit to be reborn. "That which is born of the Spirit is spirit."[42] This new birth gave new power—power to be and do what I ought—what God intended when he made me. Scripture exclaims, "If any man is in Christ, he is a new creature; the old things passed away; behold, new things have come."[43]

Christ is at the right hand of God making intercession for me.[44] The night before he was crucified he prayed, "I do not ask Thee to take them out of the world, but to keep them from the evil one . . . Father, I desire that they also whom Thou hast given Me be with Me where I am, in order that they may behold My glory."[45] There can be no doubt that God the Father will answer this prayer of his Son.

To do this he promised, "I will put My Spirit within you and cause you to walk in My statutes."[46]

God provides life with purpose. I found the purpose for life is properly loving God, myself, and others and doing the things God has planned for me. He tells us that we are to "love the Lord our God with all our heart, and with all our soul, and with all our mind, and to love our neighbor as ourself."[47] Trusting Christ makes it possible for me to rightly relate to God, myself, and others.

God has a particular plan for each of us that fits together into his great master plan for all time and eternity. Doing his will gives purpose to my life. "We are His workmanship, created in Christ Jesus for good works, which God prepared beforehand, that we should walk in them."[48]

Using God's power to do his purpose gives me personal peace.

(QUALIFYING QUESTION) DOES THIS MAKE SENSE TO YOU?

Yes, it makes a great deal of sense.

You have just heard the greatest story ever told about the greatest offer ever made—the Good News, the gospel of Jesus Christ. Now the question God is asking you is simply this **(COMMITMENT QUESTION) WOULD YOU LIKE TO RECEIVE THE GIFT OF ETERNAL LIFE?**

Yes, I would.

Let's be sure you're very **CLEAR ON THIS COMMITMENT.** This is the most important decision any person can ever make. It actually makes the difference between heaven and hell for all of eternity. **We receive the gift of eternal life by entering into a personal relationship with God.**

God, the Holy Spirit, convicts us of our sins and calls us to receive Christ as our personal Savior. **This means that we turn from our sin and trust in him alone for eternal life.** By the Holy Spirit he comes into our lives to forgive and cleanse us from our sin. This means that we must be willing to turn from whatever is not pleasing to him and follow him as he reveals his will to us in his Word. Is that what you want?

Yes, it is.

(God in the driver's seat). God, the Son, desires and deserves to be our Lord. This also means giving control of your life to Jesus—making him your Lord. He insists on being in control of our lives. It is as though at this point as you travel down the road of life in your automobile, you move from behind the wheel and become a passenger. You say to God, "You take the wheel, Lord, and I'm with you. Anywhere you want me to go, I will go. Anything you want me to do, I will do."

The first time I thought about God taking control of my life, it frightened me. The idea of anyone else, even God, controlling me just didn't make me too comfortable. But then I thought of two things. First I remembered that the one who wanted to come in and take control of my life was Jesus Christ. He is the only being in the whole universe who loved me so much that he left heaven and came into this confused world so that he could make it possible for me to have eternal life. If he loved me that much it just didn't make sense that the first thing he would do when I gave him control of my life was make it miserable and disrupt it.

The other thing I thought about was this: Jesus Christ is true man and true God. That means he knows everything, everything that is happening in the world now and everything that will ever happen! He knows it all. With that knowledge he can guide my life better than I ever could. Many times it's been as though I've gone down dead-end streets or blind alleys in my life. Then, I've had to back up and start all over again. But when Christ has been in control of my life this has never happened.

Are you willing to yield your life, to surrender your will to him out of gratitude for this gift of eternal life? **Is this what you want?**

Yes, it is.

God, the Father, wants you to rely on him as your heavenly Father. **This means having a childlike confidence in him and seeking to be a responsible growing member in his forever family. Is this what you want?**

Yes, it is.

(PRAYER OF COMMITMENT) All right. The Lord is here right now. He said, "Where two or three have gathered together in My name, there I am in their midst."[49] Prayer is God's appointed means for giving expression to faith. I can lead us in prayer and then together we can tell him what you have just told me: that you have sinned and are sorry for it—that you want to turn from your sin and turn to Jesus Christ alone for your eternal life—that you want him to take control of your life. The Lord is looking at your heart more than he is listening to your lips. If this is really what you mean, then the Lord will hear your prayer and grant you eternal life. Let's pray.

Father, I pray that now you would give John the gift of eternal life. By your Spirit draw him to yourself. Grant him faith to believe your promise and in repentance to turn from his sins. Hear us as together we ask you to come into his life.

Now John, pray after me.

Lord Jesus, I know that I have sinned.

Lord Jesus, I know that I have sinned.

I am truly sorry for all my sins.

I am truly sorry for all my sins.

With your help I want to turn from all my sin.

With your help I want to turn from all my sin.

I put my trust in Jesus Christ alone for my eternal life.

I put my trust in Jesus Christ alone for my eternal life.

Take complete control of my life.

Take complete control of my life.

Do with me as you please.

Do with me as you please.

Help me to be a responsible growing member of your forever family.

Help me to be a responsible growing member of your forever family.

Give me now, the gift of eternal life.

Give me now, the gift of eternal life.

In Jesus' name.

In Jesus' name.

Father, you have heard the prayer which John has prayed and I ask that by your Holy Spirit you will give him the assurance of eternal life. Cause him to hear in the depths of his soul your voice saying, "I give eternal life to them; and they shall never perish, and no one shall snatch them out of My hand."[50] In Jesus' name we pray. Amen.

(IMMEDIATE FOLLOW-UP—ASSURANCE)

John, Jesus says something very important to them who trust in him alone for eternal life. I'd like for you to read it with your own eyes.

"Truly, truly, I say to you, he who hears My word, and believes Him who sent Me, has eternal life, and does not come into judgment, but has passed out of death into life."[51]

John, these are the words of Jesus Christ. Can he lie?

Of course not!

Notice, John, what he says, "Truly, truly, I say to you, he who hears My word, and believes Him who sent Me has eternal life, and does not come into judgment, but has passed out of death into life"—the good news of trusting in Jesus Christ alone for eternal life is his word. Do you believe that Jesus is the God-man who was sent by his Father to die for your sins?

Yes, I do.

The one who has eternal life is in good hands. Jesus promised, "I give eternal life to them; and they shall never perish, and no one shall snatch them out of My hand."[52]

(Extend your right hand, clasp his right wrist, and ask him to do the same with your right wrist.)

Let my right hand stand for Christ's nail-pierced hand. As we cling to Christ with our hand of faith we will sometimes find it to be weak. We can even lose our grasp on him. But his nail-pierced hand is all-powerful. He never weakens and he never turns loose of the one who trusts in him. Nothing can snatch you out of his hand when you trust in him. The nail-scarred hand of Jesus holds the one who trusts him.

On the basis of what Jesus said, and your response, do you now have eternal life?

Yes, I do.

Then John, if you should die tonight in your sleep, where would you wake up?

In heaven.

And if God said to you, "John, why should I let you into my heaven?" what would you say to him?

I would say, he should let me into heaven because I am trusting in Jesus Christ alone for my eternal life.

When a person truly trusts in Jesus Christ, he is born into the forever family of God. The Bible says, "As many as received Him, to them He gave the right to become children of God, even to those who believe in His name."[53]

John, welcome to the family of God.

ANALYSIS

Let's take a brief look at the reasons behind the content included in the presentation as it stands today.

VOCABULARY

You will probably notice that the vocabulary is less theological. Instead of "intellectual assent," we speak of "head faith." "Now faith" is used instead of "temporal faith," "came out of the grave alive" instead of "resurrected," "returned to the Father" instead of "ascended." While we could not completely adopt a nontheological vocabulary, we did feel it was important, wherever possible, to use words that were clearly understood to the secular mind. Where theological terms are used we try to define them in context so that they are easily understood.

ETERNAL LIFE

Eternal life has a present and future dimension. The gospel deals with both the future judgment of our guilt on the last day and the present regenerating of new life. Both dimensions are emphasized throughout this presentation. In the personal testimony, eternal life is defined as being in a present personal relationship with God that results in power and purpose and personal peace. This is further expanded by showing that we as persons find full life only in proper relationship with God our Creator. Sin is seen not only as bringing guilt but also as polluting the life so that it is diminished in its meaning. Christ's perfect life is the model even as his death is the atonement. God cleanses the heart and gives new power for living.

When we state that eternal life is a free gift, it is important that this *not* be understood in terms of modern Madison Avenue gimmicks. The gift is free because the giver (God) is not obligated to give it. That's what grace is all about—getting what is not deserved.

GOD

The secular mind is skeptical. It questions the existence of the supernatural. When it is stated that eternal life is not earned or deserved it is not uncommon to be challenged with, "Who says so?" Therefore, we state that "it's not a matter of personal opinion. One man's opinion is just as good as another's. This is true because God said it."

For most secularists God is like a cosmic blur. The popular concepts of naturalistic evolution have robbed modern man of an understanding of God as his personal Creator. If you ask one what comes to his mind when you mention the word God, most will merely stare at you in blank silence. So we define him as the one true God who is personal, not limited by anything outside himself, and existent in three persons—Father, Son, and Holy Spirit. His self-revelation is uniquely in the Bible. Later in the presentation at the point of Christ, we reinforce this uniqueness of Scripture by the statement of detailed predictions fulfilled in history.

When we make simple statements about God we are presupposing that he has put a sense of the eternal in the heart of every man (Ecclesiastes 3:11, ASV margin), and that the Holy Spirit is bearing witness in man's conscience (Romans 2). Even when someone says he does not believe in the existence of God, we assume that God knows what he is talking about. Only the *fool* says in his *heart* that there is no God (Psalm 14:1).

USE OF BIBLE

Usually it is best not to pull out your Bible and point to specific Scripture verses. Nor will it help your communication to quote the reference when you use the Scripture. To use the Bible or the references turns you into a teacher and your contact into a student. It is assumed that the teacher is the superior and the student is the inferior. To establish greater rapport, keep it conversational. Only use your Bible when you need to establish an external, objective authority for what is being said.

MAN—THE IMAGE OF GOD

Man has the faculties of personality because he is made in the image of the personal God. Emphasis should be made on his capacity for worship which no other creature has. This he demonstrates in his construction of chapels and shrines.

God's purpose for man is love—God desires to love man and be loved by man. This desire required that man be made with freedom of choice to love or not to love. This explains why man is in the trouble he is in today. He voluntarily chose to disobey and thus brought sin into the human race. His soul was ruined and his relationship with God was ruptured. He has become guilty and polluted.

THE SIN OF IRRESPONSIBILITY

One aspect of original sin is particularly relevant in our generation—it is irresponsibility. This irresponsibility showed itself in personal relationships—Adam blamed

Eve, and Eve blamed the serpent. No one was willing to accept his own responsibility. This irresponsibility also shows itself in man's lack of care for the creatures and the creation. Adam had responsibility for all the creatures, yet he let the devil use one creature (the serpent) to accomplish his evil deed. With the power given him by God, man could have forbidden that. In our day of ecological crisis, this is a point that is very relevant to many.

All men everywhere violate their consciences. This moral monitor of conscience functions even in the most secular mind. Paul greatly expands this thought in Romans 2.

Many secularists pride themselves on their morality. Actually, morality is a mockery if there is no God. The only logical alternative to Christianity with its morality is Nihilism and no morality. But in order to pierce to the heart in the matter of sin, we point out that the greatest sin of all is failure to love God with all the heart, soul, and mind. This does not carry with it inferences of socially unacceptable sins, i.e., murder, stealing, etc. The Holy Spirit uses this to convict.

ILLUSTRATIONS WITH NEGATIVE SUBJECT

Any time an illustration is used that puts the subject of the illustration in a negative light, you should use yourself or some hypothetical third person. Do not use as an example the person with whom you are speaking. This is why in the illustration on violating the moral and physical laws of God we use the first-person pronoun "I." The person with whom you are speaking might resent the suggestion that he would leap from a tall building. The same thought is contained in the "do-it-yourself heart transplant" illustration. Your contact might get so involved with the physical danger that he misses the spiritual truth. So instead, use yourself as the subject of the transplant.

One question encountered often is, "If there is a good God, how do you account for this bad world?" This we explain on the basis of God's gracious patience. He is giving us time to change our minds about our sin so that we can be brought back into a right relationship with him. But one day he will balance the books and judge sin once and for all.

THE DELICATE ISSUE OF SIN

Sin is a touchy matter. Is there any way to get the point across that a person is a sinner without making him unnecessarily angry at us?

The portion of the gospel presentation dealing with the fact that man is a sinner and cannot save himself is one place where prospects can sometimes get a little bit disturbed with us. We begin laying the groundwork to avoid that problem in the sharing of personal testimony. If we share the difficulties we have encountered and make it clear that we are not self-righteous Pharisees, they are much less inclined to be hostile toward us. They will feel an empathy and identification with us.

When you come to the part dealing with man as a sinner you will find it helpful to use the following six-point procedure.

1. State the general principle that all have sinned.
2. Clearly define what sin is.
3. Describe sin's symptoms.
4. Talk about your own sin.

5. Indicate that others you have talked to have the same problem.
6. Ask the prospect if he has ever felt this problem in his own life.

If only the general principle is stated it will be so vague that it will have very little impact. Most people agree that all have sinned. Therefore, it is necessary to clearly define what sin is. Point out that it is a transgression of God's law—stepping over the line; that it is a falling short of God's ideal for us; that it consists of acts, thoughts, and words; that it is even sin for us to know what we should do and not do it.

Sin's symptoms are described in the presentation as "fear, frustration, shame, guilt, ruptured relationships between husbands and wives, parents and children, races and nations." Some might not admit that they are sinners in the abstract theological sense, but there are few who will say they have never had any of these psychological symptoms.

It is essential to define and describe sin before you talk about it in your life. Communication may break down if your prospect's concept of sin differs from yours and he defines your words with his understanding. For example, if he thinks sin is only murder and adultery and you say that you have committed many sins, don't be surprised if he appears shocked. After you have clearly and comprehensively defined sin, then you can talk easily about what it has been in your life and he will understand what you mean.

Be sure that you do not convey a flippant attitude toward sin. This might leave the impression that God's forgiveness gives a license to practice sin with immunity.

After talking about your own sin, mention that others you have talked with have indicated they had the same problem. Then casually ask, "Have you ever felt the impact of this problem in your own life?" By asking, rather than telling, usually there is a deeper work of conviction that takes place in the heart of the prospect.

CHRIST

When presenting the truths about Jesus, it is best with the secular mind to inductively describe his unique life, death, and resurrection. Then from these facts conclude that he is true God and true man. If you first state that he is true God and then present the evidence, often you will encounter resistance to the evidence because of rejection of the original premise.

The pagan and religious secularists view religion as a subjective mystical experience for the simple-minded. But Christianity has solid objective historical evidence to substantiate its claims. Therefore, in presenting the gospel to them, it is essential to put emphasis on the evidence—the historical-objective evidence that God actually invaded time in the person of Jesus of Nazareth. The predictions fulfilled in his life, death, and resurrection present an overwhelming case. The resurrection of Christ is the keystone in the arch of faith. Without it the entire Christian system would fall apart. This was the central truth in the apostolic proclamation of the gospel, and it must be emphasized very strongly with the secular-minded person.

When you state that Christ came out of the grave alive, be prepared for someone to ask, "Then where is he now?" Scripture tells us that he returned to the Father. When this is stated some will say, "What good can he do me now?" Scripture tells us he sent the Holy Spirit to cleanse our hearts and to provide power for our lives. This pattern of proclamation is found in the Acts of the Apostles, and it is well to emulate it today. Without the ascension and the sending of the Spirit the resurrection would be declared null and void. But since Christ came out of the grave alive, returned to the Father, and sent the Holy Spirit, all power and authority that are needed to accomplish his will are available.

CHANGE MIND ABOUT WRONG

When discussing faith we found it necessary to present the other side of the issue—being sorry for our sin. If this was not discussed before the commitment question we found that many people misunderstood. They thought this was a veiled hook. Therefore, we have found it wise to make this clear prior to entering the commitment section. Before eternal life can be received by trusting, we must be sorry for our sins and be willing to turn from them.

TRUST

To emphasize again the evidential aspect of our faith, we indicated first off that the trust that enables us to receive eternal life is not a blind leap in the dark. The evidence of the resurrection must be emphasized over and over to the blind mind of the secularist. This can be done, as in the presentation, by using the concept of mathematical probability as it relates to fulfilled prophecy.

Head belief and temporal belief are not to be discouraged as bad things unless they are *all* a person has. Instead we strive to show that saving trust brings eternal life: it involves knowledge, assent, and does trust God for things in this life. But it also goes beyond this world and trusts God for eternal life.

With the secularist we found it essential to deal with the motive for godly living (gratitude) and also to explain the power for the new life. Often they ask, "What happens if I trust in Christ?" In the presentation we preclude this by answering the question before it is asked. We explain that God provides life with purpose and with *power.*

CLARIFICATION

Many seemed fearful at the thought of turning control of their life over to the Lord. So we have sought to alleviate that concern by pointing out that giving Christ the wheel and moving into the passenger's seat is the only reasonable thing to do in the light of his love and his knowledge as God.

Also, in clarifying the commitment we found it to be essential to be very specific about the responsibility to be a part of God's forever family. We ask if they desire to "have a childlike confidence in him and seek to be a responsible growing member in his forever family." Since most secularists have no relationship with the church, or else a very unfunctional relationship, this needs to be crystallized before the actual prayer of commitment.

PRAYER OF COMMITMENT

The brief prayer of commitment found in the *Good News* booklet is a good one to memorize and use almost identically with each person.

ASSURANCE

The visual illustration of the Roman handshake emphasizes the new relationship with an all-powerful Christ. Visual illustrations utilize more senses and therefore make greater impact. They should be used whenever possible.

After the person has prayed to receive eternal life and you are dealing with the question of assurance, it is wise to repeat the two diagnostic questions from the introduction. Say to the person, "And now do you know for certain if you were to die tonight that you would open your eyes in heaven?" and if God should ask 'Why should I let you into my heaven,' now what would you say?" In some cases he will still not be clear and therefore you will need to deal with the particular problem. You will find that by raising these questions at the end of the presentation you will avoid many problems in your future ministry to the person.

USE OF GOOD NEWS BOOKLET

The relationship of the *Good News* booklet to "The Gospel Presentation for the Secular Mind" needs to be clearly understood. This *Good News* is *never used in the initial presentation of the gospel.* Sometimes people are insulted if simple printed pieces are read to them. Witnesses tend to develop dependency on printed pieces and so are not able to share the gospel unless they have them. The *Good News* booklet is used as a learning tool for the trainees and to visually clarify the gospel *after* it has been verbally presented. The *Good News* booklet is also used as a follow-up piece so that the person making the profession can read the concepts and crystallize them in his mind.

NOTES

1. John 17:3 2. Romans 6:23 3. Ephesians 2:8,9 4. Acts 17:24,25 5. Romans 1:19,20 6. Genesis 1:27 7. Jeremiah 31:3 8. Matthew 22:37 and Deuteronomy 6:5 9. Genesis 3:5 10. Romans 3:23 11. John 7:19 12. Matthew 5:21,22,27,28 13. 1 John 3:4 14. Psalm 89:32 15. Romans 2:4 16. Romans 6:23 17. Galatians 3:10 18. James 2:10 19. Romans 7:18 20. Matthew 15:19,20 21. John 8:46 22. 1 Peter 2:22, 23 23. John 19:33,34 24. Acts 1:3 25. 1 Corinthians 15:4–8 26. Romans 1:4 27. John 1:1,3,14 28. 2 Corinthians 5:21 29. John 16:5,7 30. Ezekiel 36:25,26 31. John 10:28 32. Proverbs 28:13 33. John 20:25 34. John 20:27 35. John 20:28 36. Matthew 8:29 37. Matthew 6:11 38. 2 Corinthians 4:18 39. John 3:16 40. John 14:6 41. Romans 6:23 42. John 3:6 43. 2 Corinthians 5:17 44. Romans 8:34 45. John 17:15,24 46. Ezekiel 36:27 47. Matthew 22:37,39 48. Ephesians 2:10 49. Matthew 18:20 50. John 10:28 51. John 5:24 52. John 10:28 53. John 1:12. All Scripture quotations in this presentation are from the New American Standard Bible, Lockman Foundation, used by permission.

ELEVEN QUESTIONNAIRE EVANGELISM

BY DIVINE APPOINTMENT

April, 1976, the people on this planet to be discipled number more than four thousand million. How is that entire group to be reached with the gospel and discipled into a vital relation with local congregations?

There are two things for certain:

1. We must go to where these people are to reach them for Christ.
2. When we go with the gospel, the Holy Spirit goes before us and establishes divine appointments.

WE MUST GO TO WHERE PEOPLE ARE TO REACH THEM FOR CHRIST

If we wait for people to come into our church buildings before we go to them with the gospel, the task will never be done. In the Great Commission, our Lord commands us to *go!* The apostles set the pattern.

As the number of trained evangelists increased at the Coral Ridge Presbyterian Church, a new challenge confronted us. How do you provide enough responsive contacts for the training ministry? There were many first-time visitors each week at the worship services. But the growing number of people in the organized training ministry became so large that it was impossible to provide good contacts for every team.

At first we tried casual calling door to door. We were able to get into many homes this way. But once we were inside the home, we found that we had an even greater challenge. Many of the people who invited the teams into their homes were absolutely not interested in the gospel. Our trainees were being exposed to one difficult situation after another, and this was discouraging.

The trainees need to see the basic presentation repeatedly shared with people who are spiritually open. Without this they never really learn how to share their own faith.

As a result of this challenge we started using a questionnaire as a screening tool.

The questionnaire helped separate those people who were sincerely interested from those who did not have an openness to the gospel.

At first it was long and cumbersome. By regular review and revision, the questionnaire and the procedure for using it have been refined into the brief form in this book.

The assurance questionnaire has become a main source of providing meaningful contacts for the evangelism discipleship training program. With the church as the center we move out in all directions.

Wherever you go you will find people who need Jesus Christ. The questionnaire is a means for discovering your "divine appointment." You aren't limited to those who come to your church or ask you what they must do to be saved.

Our church and many others have maps marked to show apartment complexes and residential sections for door-to-door comprehensive evangelism using the questionnaire approach. We have marked all public centers for the questionnaire program.

When our teams call on people who have first visited the church and the "first timers" are not home, the team will usually use the questionnaire and make contact with someone else in the same community.

In all of these ways our trainees usually see the gospel presented each week and there is less time spent traveling between calls. We find divine appointments everywhere!

WHEN WE GO WITH THE GOSPEL, THE HOLY SPIRIT GOES BEFORE US AND ESTABLISHES DIVINE APPOINTMENTS

When we go with the gospel, the Holy Spirit goes before us and establishes divine appointments. He did this for Peter with Cornelius. He did this for Philip with the Ethiopian eunuch. The Holy Spirit is the same yesterday, today, and forever. He still establishes divine appointments.

A white-haired, eighty-four-year-old man sat alone on a bench in a shopping center in Atlanta, Georgia. Three people approached. One of the trio smiled and spoke to the elderly gentleman. "Hello, I'm John. This is Mary and George. We are from First Church. We're trying to determine people's religious thinking and to assist anyone looking for a faith. Would you help us by giving your thoughts in response to five brief questions?"

The man looked up in astonishment. "I'm eighty-four years old. At least twenty times this year people have told me that I should trust Christ as my Savior. They have told me that he was God, clothed in human flesh. They have told me that if I put my faith in him alone, he will give me eternal life and take me to heaven when I die. I think it's about time I did that. Can you tell me how to do it?" The team quickly explained how a person puts his trust in the living Christ. The aging patriarch found new life while sitting on a bench in a shopping center. **That was a divine appointment!**

It was a bright, sunny day. A handsome young man had nothing better to do, so he was picking burrs out of his dog's fur in front of his apartment. Three young people walked up to him. A lady said, "Hi, I'm Dottie. Meet

> Fran and Jim. We're trying to determine people's religious thinking and to assist anyone looking for a faith. Would you help us by giving your thoughts in response to five brief questions?"
>
> He had not been in church for a long time. He had not given too much serious thought to spiritual things. But in that moment God moved upon his heart in an overwhelming fashion.
>
> When the questionnaire was completed, Dottie asked if she could share how she came to know that she had eternal life and how he could know it too.
>
> He was eager to listen. After the gospel was presented he prayed to receive the gift of eternal life.
>
> A few weeks later he entered the Evangelism Explosion III Discipleship Training Program. Six months later he was studying for the ministry. **That was a divine appointment!**

These stories can be repeated over and over. The names change, the places change, but the fact that God the Holy Spirit goes before his people and establishes divine appointments is the same.

A word of caution: The questionnaire is very brief and simple. Because it looks so easy, eager trainees want to use it too soon. The questionnaire *is* simple. But the judgments that must be exercised in determining the course of action following the questionnaire are not so simple. Trainees are not qualified to make those judgments until near the end of a four-and-one-half-month training program. They will sometimes rush in where angels fear to tread—and then panic. Always be sure that an experienced trainer is in charge of the witnessing team.

One more thing needs to be considered. The more caring personal association an evangelist has with a contact before the profession of faith, the easier the follow-up will be. On the other hand, the less caring personal contact an evangelist has with a contact before he shares the gospel, the more difficult the follow-up will be.

When using the questionnaire in public places and door to door, you will find two interesting phenomena. First, you will usually make more contacts, but there will be less professions per number of contacts than when calling on church visitors. Secondly, you will find that fewer of those who make professions with the questionnaire will be discipled into vital, visible relation with the local church.

Don't let these facts throw you. Enlist prayerpartners and ask them to pray that you will be led to prepared people who will be abiding fruit. The number of presentations and genuine conversions will both increase.

Remember, also, that you are training soul winners. The use of the questionnaire in a training program will help equip a trainee to effectively share the gospel. Once he has learned to effectively present the training program, he will be much more able to do this in his daily life. So to get a proper picture of what can happen when the questionnaire is used, you must consider not only the number of people discipled in the training program. You must add to this the number of new disciples the evangelists can have in their daily lives.

I. BASIC INFORMATION YOU SHOULD KNOW BEFORE USING THE QUESTIONNAIRE APPROACH

The assurance questionnaire is a small, printed form containing introductory comments and questions, concluding comments, and six options for follow-through. (See Appendix A for sample assurance questionnaire.) Because this is a somewhat formal approach, it is best used with people with whom you have no opportunity to first cultivate a friendship or relate to casually. It is best used in public places, door-to-door, or over the telephone.

FIVE FUNCTIONS

The five specific functions of the assurance questionnaire are:

1. It helps to obtain information on an individual's religious thinking.
2. It provides a means for measuring the spiritual climate of your community.
3. It provides opportunity for conversation on spiritual matters.
4. It provides opportunity to assist any who are looking for a faith.
5. It provides a screening device to keep trainees from exposure to too many difficult cases.

People generally appreciate someone else being interested in their thinking. This helps you to establish rapport with them. Also, you become more aware of the true spiritual condition of the people around you.

Jesus said, "Enter by the narrow gate; for the gate is wide, and the way is broad that leads to destruction, and many are those who enter by it" (Matthew 7:13). You will never realize this more than when you widely use the questionnaire approach in public places and door to door. You will find there are very many people who do not know the truth. We have a responsibility to reach them.

The questionnaire provides opportunity for conversation on spiritual matters by asking questions about the individual's relation to religious organizations, the degree of involvement in these organizations, his assurance of eternal life, and the basis of that assurance. This raises the subject. If he is interested in continuing the conversation, you can share your testimony and the gospel.

Looking for a faith. As you talk with him, his need will be indicated by his religious affiliation or lack of it, and so will the basis for his faith and assurance. However, his attitude, reflected in the tone of his voice and his facial expressions as he responds to the questions, will let you know if he is looking for a faith.

A screening device. Many people who answer the questions will not be prospects for hearing the gospel. Asking these questions helps to separate the prospects from the suspects.

A prospect is someone who does not have eternal life but is interested in knowing how to receive it. He will be seeking or at least be open.

A prospect will not be doctrinally difficult—like for example, a Jehovah's Witness who goes to Kingdom Hall eight times a week.

A prospect will not be philosophically argumentative and argue with a closed mind about the existence of God.

A prospect will not be emotionally hostile and unreasonably antagonistic.

A suspect is the opposite of a prospect.

Keep in mind that the training of a soul winner is more important than merely getting one profession. And it is infinitely more important to train a soul winner than it is to win an argument! Trainees need to see the basic presentation repeatedly in order to be able to share it themselves.

Even if the "suspect" wants to continue a discussion beyond the questionnaire, don't. Try to make a future appointment. When you approached him, you asked for permission to get his response to five questions. You are not under obligation to continue beyond that point unless you feel God wants you to.

Also, remember that we have no right to try to force somebody to submit to our presentation of the gospel if he does not want to hear it. Jesus told us, "The field is white unto harvest" (John 4:35). Do not try to pluck green fruit.

THINK!

As you use the questionnaire, you should think about yourself, your teammates, the circumstances, your prospects, and the procedure that you are going to use. Give serious thought to your attitude toward the Lord and your appearance before people.

Your attitude toward the Lord is the most important part of the whole witnessing process. It should be one of loving obedience and trust. Jesus said, "If you love me, keep my commandments" (John 14:15). He commanded us in the Great Commission to "go into all the world" (Matthew 28:19). We are to go into the highways and the hedges and compel them to come in (Luke 14:23).

The Apostle Paul, constrained by the love of Christ, went into the marketplace in Athens and personally shared the gospel with those who were willing to listen (Acts 17:17). In the city of Ephesus, he went from house to house, door to door, finding those who were interested, and with them he shared the gospel (Acts 20:20).

Trust expects the Lord to establish divine appointments and to go with you to keep them. Trust is willing to joyfully accept whatever role God gives in bringing others to him.

DIVINE APPOINTMENT

A divine appointment is when God brings you in contact with a specific individual that he intends to bring to himself through the contact. What he did with Philip and the Ethiopian eunuch (Acts 8:26–38), Peter and Cornelius (Acts 10), and for many, many others since then, he will do for you as you trust him.

The Lord promised that when you go with the gospel he will go with you (Matthew 28:19,20). He cannot lie (Titus 1:2). He has all power and authority in heaven and on earth (Matthew 28:18), so nothing can keep him away. You can be sure he is with you, not because of your feelings, but because he is faithful to his promise. He wants to use you to draw others to himself. He will use you to accomplish his will in their lives, and he will use them to accomplish his will in your life. He will already be working in the life and circumstances of the individuals to whom he guides you (Acts 10:1–7).

He may use you to plant the word in their hearts. He may use you to water the word that has already been planted (1 Corinthians 3:6). But do not be satisfied with *only* planting and watering. You are commanded to make disciples.

As you faithfully witness, he will give fruit (Psalm 126:6).

Your faith is important for witnessing. Recall the story of the four men who brought the paralytic to Jesus Christ. They could not get through the crowds, so they climbed on the roof, tore a hole in it, and lowered the cripple into the presence of Christ. Jesus said because he saw "their faith" he healed the man (Mark 2:5).

When you go out to share the gospel, believe that God will use you to bring people to him. He will honor your expectant faith.

PERSONAL APPEARANCE

Your appearance attracts or repels. Watch your facial expressions and what you wear.

The number one thing you should wear is a smile. It will attract, and it will usually cause others to be more interested in talking with you. If you are wearing sunglasses, take them off. Eye contact is important for good communication.

Dress for the occasion. When you are using the questionnaire in a public park or on a beach, wear casual clothes. Ladies using the questionnaire on the beach should wear modest garb. In a shopping center, don't wear clothes that are too formal or too casual. When calling door to door, generally it is best for men to wear coats and ties. Clothes express a great deal about you. Sometimes they can break down lines of communication. When you are witnessing for Christ, direct attention to him. It is a poor witness who draws attention to himself.

The Bible gives basic principles on your appearance. Be modest and moderate. Be as winsome and attractive as possible. Your appearance should always be a credit to Christ. The length of a lady's skirt and the fashion of her apparel should indicate that she is a Christian woman with a meek and quiet spirit (1 Peter 3:3,4).

TEAMMATES

Remember that you have been brought together by God to help each other learn to more efficiently share the gospel. The trainer is always in charge. Trainees are to rely on and follow the direction of the trainer.

When you are not leading the interview you should watch and pray—not with bowed heads, closed eyes, and folded hands, but with eyes open and wearing your most pleasant smile.

Observe the presentation carefully so that afterward thoughts can be compared. In that way, every member of the team will grow in understanding and ability to share the gospel.

Always look at whoever is talking in the course of the conversation. Don't stare at the prospect; he may become frightened and run away.

Stay alert for opportunities to prevent disturbances. Notice, for example, if a crowd begins to gather, and let the presenter know.

CIRCUMSTANCES

As you consider the circumstances watch your *public visibility.* Whether witnessing in a public place or in residential areas, it is important to *keep low visibility.* There should never be more than one witnessing team in the same place at the same time. Those who don't like Christians to witness will spread rumors. If this happens, people will be less willing to talk to you. Keep your questionnaire pad concealed until you are ready to use it in a public place or apartment building.

Consider the best *time* for the contact. Some places are better at certain times than they are at others.

In most places there are *strategic locations.* A good location will be close to the flow of traffic to allow you to watch the people go by. There you can pray for God to guide you to the person to whom you should speak. Ideally, your "good location" will also be a place where you can get out of the mainstream of traffic and have a degree of privacy as you talk. This will help the person not to feel embarrassed, especially when he prays to receive eternal life.

The *weather* is something else that you need to watch. If it's wet or cold, be sure you pick a sheltered place. Some people are so eager to share the gospel that they pay no attention to the circumstances around them.

Cold or wet weather can work in favor of teams calling in homes. More people will usually be home, and they will be more inclined to invite you in.

Avoid overlapping or skipping homes. On the back of the form there is a place for the name and address of the prospect and the recording of attempted contacts. The name and address can be filled in before the contact is attempted. This information can be obtained from a city directory or a cross reference telephone directory. In apartment complexes it can be obtained from the mailboxes. One form should be used for each apartment or residence. After the contact is completed, the form should be filled out and removed from the group.

When contact is attempted but not completed, this should be noted in the section in the lower left corner on the back of the form. Note the day of the week and the time of the day the contact is attempted. Then the questionnaire should be placed back with the incompleted contacts. When contact is unsuccessful on a particular day or time of day, the call should be rescheduled for a different day and time. If attempt at personal visit is repeatedly unsuccessful, then contact should be attempted by telephone on various days and at different times.

Always keep low visibility! Do not send a team into a complex every week on the same day or time of day until everyone has been contacted. Skip a week and, if possible, move to a different section of the complex. If you blitz the target you will contact a number of resentful people. They will spread rumors and you will be greeted with a tidal wave of resistance from people who otherwise would at least listen to the presentation of the gospel.

Consider the prospect. When in a public place, notice the prospect's age, sex, and whether or not he is in a group.

AGE. Usually, but not always, when you are witnessing in a public place, it is best to select a prospect that is near your age. Older people will sometimes patronize a younger person who is trying to witness to them. And young people sometimes will not listen to an older person.

Be cautious about talking to young children. This is especially true if the child is of another race or the team is made up of all men. People tend to be protective, and if they see three men talking to a small child, sometimes they will stand by to see what is going on. They may even interrupt and try to find out what you are doing.

If you lead a child to Christ, before telling the parents what the child has done, try to discover the parents' spiritual condition. If they are not Christians and reject the gospel, they may resent the child's spiritual interest and your involvement. If so, it may be best not to tell the parents what the child has done.

SEX. Usually it is best to pick someone of your own sex. When you witness to a member of the opposite sex who is about your own age, you will sometimes find that he or she may misunderstand your intentions or get more interested in you than in the gospel. This is not a hard, fixed rule. Christ witnessed to women as well as to men. But whenever possible, the principle should be kept in mind. Having both men and women on the team will help keep this from being a problem.

IN A GROUP. If you approach three or more persons and attempt to share the gospel, you will find it extremely difficult. This is especially true with younger people. Most of the time there will be at least one who will try to argue. That will turn the situation into an argument rather than a presentation of the gospel. Therefore, choose a person who is alone or with only one other person. If more people move into the situation after you have started the questionnaire and it turns into a debate, then politely leave as soon as you can.

TWO OR MORE PEOPLE AT THE SAME TIME. Use a separate form for each person. Ask each question of everyone being surveyed before going on to the next question.

When you come to the last question (God's "Why?") ask it first of the person who seems least likely to have a correct answer. This will avoid having someone give a correct answer which others will simply parrot.

The prospect's name and address. Do not attempt to learn the prospect's full name and address in advance of taking the questionnaire. Most of the time this would cause a person to be reluctant about participating. Usually it is all right to ask for a first name after you have given him your first name in the introduction.

ASSURANCE QUESTIONNAIRE OUTLINE

The five points in the introduction using the assurance questionnaire are:

A. The approach
B. The appeal
C. The five questions

D. Thanks
E. Follow-through

THE APPROACH

Do not say: "We are taking a religious survey. Will you answer some questions for us?"

Do fill in the blanks that are in the printed copy on the assurance questionnaire, and say the following.

"Hi, I'm Archie. Meet Gladys and Jerry. We are from the (name of your church or group). We are trying to determine people's religious thinking and assist anyone looking for a faith."

This helps the team relate more personally to the contact. It usually takes too long, initially, to give the first and last names of each team member.

By mentioning the group you represent, you help to promote the ministry of that group in the community and you let the contact know that you are not a Jehovah's Witness or a member of some other radical cult.

Saying, "We are trying to determine people's religious thinking and to assist anyone looking for a faith" explains the purpose of the contact. First you are trying to find out what their religious thinking is. You should have a genuine interest in this. Secondly, you are clearly and honestly saying that you are available to help anyone looking for a faith.

THE APPEAL

"Will you help us by giving your thoughts in response to five brief questions?"

Use these exact words. Asking for assistance puts us in the position of needing the contact person's help. Jesus used this approach when he talked to the woman at the well (John 4:7). He asked if she would give him a drink.

Asking for the person's response to five *brief* questions lets him know you want only a small amount of time.

THE FIVE QUESTIONS

We ask what religious group or church the person is a member of in order to discover his general religious background and orientation.

We ask what local church he attends so that we may know if he has any local relationship.

We ask him how often he attends to see the degree of his activity and involvement.

We ask if he knows for certain he would go to heaven to find out if he thinks he has eternal life. NOTE: this does not tell us he knows for certain he has eternal life.

You can rephrase this question for people under thirty and relate more effectively to them. People under thirty are concerned about dying, but they do not plan on doing it right away. So bring in the idea of accidental death. This is the number one cause of death among younger people. The reality of death is brought home to them more specifically with this idea. Rephrase the question in this way: "Have you come to the place in your thinking where you know for certain that you have eternal life? That is, *if you were to be killed tonight in an accident,* do you know that you would go to heaven?"

We ask what he would say if God asked why he should let him into heaven to discover the *basis* of his hope of heaven.

General procedure. Move through the questions quickly. Don't go off on tangents.

Indicate the response to the question by underscoring the printed answer when it is on the form or by printing it where this is needed.

Interact very little with the prospect. Ask the questions and record the answers without additional comments unless you find it necessary to do so briefly for additional rapport. Be sure that your comments are not judgmental when you do interact. The conversational introduction is very casual. The questionnaire introduction is somewhat formal. If you combine the two, it will usually be less productive.

Don't react negatively to his answers by what you say, by the tone of your voice, or by facial expressions. That will cause him to react negatively to you.

Stay very close to the wording on the questionnaire. Many generations of field testing have proven these words to be very effective.

THANKS

After you've gotten answers to the questions, express appreciation for his cooperation and then determine your course of action for follow-through.

Do not expect to share the gospel with every person who is willing to answer the questionnaire.

Many people are willing to answer the questionnaire who are not ready for you to share the gospel. You should not feel that you have to share with every person who responds to the questionnaire. This will help remove some of the pressure from you.

The trainer is to handle difficulties that may arise at any point in the contact. The trainer has experience and the trainee can learn from him or her how to deal with difficulties in the future. Until the trainee has mastered the variations and difficulties, he should depend on his trainer to handle them.

After the interview is completed, clearly print the numbers, corresponding to the answers, in the computer boxes in the column on the right side of the form. This makes manual or computer tabulation easier.

The results of the conversation following the questionnaire should be recorded as fully as possible on the back of the form.

Initial contact results reports should be filled out only if the person makes a profession or if there is to be some specific follow-through. (See Appendix B for Results Report.)

Questionnaires should be handed in each week so that they can be tabulated and studied.

FOLLOW-THROUGH

The six possible courses for follow-through are:

1. Share your testimony and the gospel.
2. Establish a future appointment.
3. Gain permission to send a letter and get the address.

4. Gain permission to make a future phone call and get the phone number.
5. Give an invitation to your church or group.
6. Give literature.

SHARE TESTIMONY AND GOSPEL

Jesus said the field is ripe unto harvest. Proper use of the assurance questionnaire will help you discover the "ripe fruit." After the contact answers the questionnaire you should usually try to share testimony and gospel when:

1. He appears pleasant and responsive.
2. He is not a militant member of a radical religious group.
3. He indicates he is not trusting Christ alone.
4. He lacks assurance.
5. The circumstances permit you to present.

Lead into sharing the gospel by using the words printed on the questionnaire. If you are on a witnessing team, say "we" instead of "I." "May we have a few more minutes to share with you how we came to know that we have eternal life and how you can know it too?"

If he gives permission to do this, then proceed with a brief testimony (about one minute) before going into the gospel. Personalize the presentation as much as you can.

How long should the presentation be? When the gospel is being presented in a public place or by telephone, it should be brief, clear, and to the point.

Usually the testimony and presentation should be about ten minutes. Remember that the qualifying question and the commitment question provide the opportunity to discover particular points of the gospel that need to be expanded for the contact.

FUTURE APPOINTMENT

Sometimes you should try to make a future appointment for the sake of the person being contacted. Other times you should try to make a future appointment for the sake of trainees.

If the contact is pleasant, responsive, unsaved and seeking but has no time to listen, try to make a future appointment—for the contact's sake.

If the contact is a militant member of a radical religious group, philosophically argumentative or emotionally hostile, try to make a future appointment. Trainers should shield trainees from too many difficult cases. When difficult people are encountered, the trainer may try to make a future appointment to present the gospel when the trainees are not along.

It is wrong to simply drop difficult people. Sometimes they are seeking. But trainers must not run the risk of harming their trainees. Try to make a future appointment.

Future follow-through appointments for responsive open contacts should be in the regular witnessing program if at all possible. This helps avoid overloading with too much work.

Future follow-through appointment for a difficult case would *not* be in the regular witnessing program. Set it at a time when you can go back with more experienced witnesses.

If the contact agrees to an appointment, get his name and address and phone number. Establish the location, the date, the day of the week, and the time of the day when you will visit. It is wise, when possible, to phone the day before the appointment to verify the time and place of the appointment.

If he refuses a future follow-through appointment you may do one or more of these four things:

1. Try to gain permission to send him a letter
2. Give him a phone call
3. Invite him to attend your fellowship group or worship at your church
4. Give him printed material

SEND A LETTER

Try to get permission to send a letter if the contact is hesitant to let you present or is in a rush.

Be sure you get his name and address.

FUTURE PHONE CALL

There are times when people are not willing to talk about religion in a public place, but are willing to talk in private over the phone. If you feel that this is the case, try to obtain permission to call later. Be sure to get the name, phone number, and the best day and time to call.

INVITE TO CHURCH OR FELLOWSHIP GROUP

Almost any time that you make contact with someone, it is all right to invite him to church or to a fellowship group. If the person sounds anti-church, it would be wise to invite him to the fellowship group first.

A printed invitation is very helpful. Members will invite more nonmembers to the church or fellowship group if they have a printed invitation to give. The impact of the invitation has a longer lasting influence when it is in printed form.

If it is possible to plan ahead and have specific topics printed on the invitation, even more invitations can be distributed. It can appear that a member is nagging a nonmember if he keeps giving a general invitation to his group. But if there are different titles given each month or each week, there is always something new to invite nonmembers to attend.

For example, Dr. Kennedy, at Coral Ridge Presbyterian Church, determines his sermon title two weeks in advance. This title and a few provocative questions are printed on a 3″ X 5″ card as an invitation to the service. Two of these printed invitations are inserted in the bulletin for services the Sunday before the message will be preached. Each person who attends is urged to give the invitations to his friends. Some take quantities of the invitations and place them in restaurants, coffee shops, motels, etc.

GIVE LITERATURE

Do not give literature *instead* of talking to a person about the gospel. Try to at least get in a brief presentation and then give the printed material. This gives the person something to read to reinforce what you have said.

Whenever you give literature, put the title on the back of the assurance questionnaire so that you can keep a record of what has been given.

The *Good News* booklet is a twenty-four-page gospel presentation. It contains twenty-three drawings illustrating the truth of the gospel. It was developed and field tested for five years in Fort Lauderdale by the witnessing fellowship of the Greenhouse ministries. It is most effective for follow-up of those with whom the gospel has been verbally shared. The comprehensive content of *Good News* makes it especially helpful for new believers who have a non-Christian or very little Christian background.

You should always make sure that the literature you distribute is well written and attractively printed. There are many very colorful and well-produced pieces available today.

Do not give literature until you have first read it yourself. The content of the printed piece should always speak to the need of the individual receiving it.

It is always wise to have some literature in your hand ready to give to any person that you approach for the questionnaire. In case he is not willing to talk at all, you can at least give him the printed gospel presentation that he can take with him.

Methods for dealing with the basic problems you may face as you use the questionnaire are dealt with in the Learning Kits.

TWELVE
RELATIONAL EVANGELISM

As the phrase relational evangelism is used here, it means using existing relationships and developing new ones as channels through which to communicate the message that God has done all that is necessary to reestablish man in a right relationship with himself and his people.

Every human being is the center of a network of relationships. For example, consider yourself. You were born into a family and thus are related to your mother and father, brothers and sisters, grandparents, aunts and uncles, cousins, nephews, and nieces. When you marry, this network is enlarged. Not only would you be related to your new husband or wife and the children and possibly grandchildren that will come from your union. Your marriage also brings you into your marriage partner's family. You then have a whole network of inlaws.

Many relationships develop from your work. You are an employer or an employee. A number of people are your fellow workers.

When you select a place to live, the residence comes with a set of neighbors.

Over the years, you develop some special friendships.

When God the Son became a man in the person of Jesus of Nazareth, he entered in to most of the same relationships that you and everyone else has. Mary was his mother. Joseph was his stepfather. He had brothers and sisters, cousins and uncles. He worked in the carpenter shop in Nazareth. He, too, developed special friendships. He loved his family. Even as he died on the cross he made arrangements for John, his special friend, to take care of his mother. While Jesus loved his earthly family and friends, he was most concerned that they be in God's heavenly family.

God desires to use your relationships as bridges to reach those close to you so that they might be brought into his forever family. You are the salt of the earth and the light of the world. Salt prevents corruption. It adds taste. It makes one thirsty. Light helps people see where they are going. God wants to use your life to show others the way, to cause others to thirst for him, to add taste to life and curtail the corruption of sin that is in this world.

Each of us exerts personal influence for good or evil. But a paradoxical situation can develop as you grow in the grace and knowledge of Christ. The more spiritual you become, the more you may be *lifted* right out of normal contact with unbelievers.

The longer you are a believer, the more opportunity you have for spiritual growth. The more you grow spiritually, the more involved you become in the life of the church. The more you are involved in the life of the church, the less opportunity you will have to be involved with non-Christians.

On the other hand, the less time a person is a Christian, the less opportunity he has for spiritual growth. The less spiritual growth he has, the less he will be involved in the life of the church. When he is involved less in the life of the church, it is likely he will have more opportunity for involvement with non-Christians.

From this we see two things.

1. A new Christian who has regular contact with many non-Christians will probably feel a lack of ability to evangelize and disciple them.
2. An older Christian who has the ability to evangelize and disciple will probably have little regular contact with non-Christians.

The greatest potential for abundant fruitfulness is realized when the new, less mature Christian and the older, more mature Christian blend their strengths to overcome their weaknesses. The Father is glorified as you "bear much fruit," but your fruit is to last (John 15:16).

Christian	Evangelistic ability	Evangelistic contacts
Newer, less mature	Weak	Strong
Older, more mature	Strong	Weak

Quantity and quality must go hand in hand! When you lead someone to Christ you increase his ability to grow as you help him evangelize his relatives and friends. You will also discover that his family and friends are more likely to become lasting fruit. The more proper personal relationships unbelievers have with Christians before they profess faith, the more they understand the implications of receiving eternal life. When a convert has a number of vital personal relationships with believers before receiving eternal life, it requires less effort to integrate him into the local church. Because of this, more converts who have prior proper personal relationships with Christians become responsible reproducing disciples.

Knowing when to merge your evangelistic know-how with the potential contacts of a new believer requires sensitivity and tact. Some new Christians are eager to share their new life. But with their ignorant zeal they sometimes can do more harm than good. Their enthusiasm needs to be guided by someone with experience and sensitivity. Studying *Your Personal Influence and the Forever Family** may encourage the eager

* *Your Personal Influence and the Forever Family* is a study booklet designed to help Christians understand what God says about their personal relationships and how to team with other Christians to effectively evangelize their non-Christian family members and friends.

new believer to seek your guidance. Then together you can more effectively witness to his friends and relatives.

Some Christians are hesitant to share their new life. They may be afraid of personal rejection. They may be concerned about inaccurately or incompletely presenting the gospel. Studying *Your Personal Influence and the Forever Family* may encourage a hesitant new Christian to talk about his fears and concerns with you. Then you can encourage him by praying with him and offering to help.

WHEN SHOULD *YOUR PERSONAL INFLUENCE AND THE FOREVER FAMILY* BE GIVEN TO A NEW CHRISTIAN?

Not until after the seven-day call back. It is important that the new Christian truly trusts Christ and has assurance of eternal life. Usually you should not wait longer than five weeks to give the booklet. The sooner he sees his responsibilities for his family and friends, the more opportunity there will be to share the gospel with them.

When you give this booklet be sure that you are aware of the other studies the new Christian is involved in. Do not overload him.

WHAT SHOULD THE NEW CHRISTIAN SAY TO RELATIVES OR FRIENDS TO ESTABLISH AN APPOINTMENT?

It is important that the relatives or friends not feel that they are being "set up." They should be told the purpose of the contact and that others will be present.

You might suggest that the new Christian say something like the following:

"Some friends recently told me something that gave me a whole new perspective on life. I'd like you to meet them and hear what they have to say. How about coming over for coffee next Thursday evening at eight?"

If the friends ask "What did they tell you?" suggest that he say something like, "I'd rather you hear it from them. I might leave out something important."

If the friend should ask "What new perspective for life did you receive?" the new Christian can respond with something like, "I received eternal life. I know God is working in my life in a new way and I know I am going to heaven when I die. I'd like for you to hear from them how they came to know this also."

It is important that the new Christian not say too much. This might unnecessarily frighten his friends away.

WHAT SHOULD I TRY TO FIND OUT FROM THE NEW CHRISTIAN ABOUT HIS FRIEND OR RELATIVE BEFORE MAKING THE CONTACT?

The general instructions for the conversational introduction earlier in this text will give you guidance in this matter. The questions normally used to discuss a person's secular life and church background will usually provide adequate information. Try to find out if the person has had any involvement in a cult or non-Christian religion. If he has, this will require some special preparation on your part, or you will need to arrange from someone who is knowledgeable in the cult or non-Christian religion to accompany you. It is wise to ask the new Christian what he has told the friend or relative about his new experience of eternal life.

Much prayer should go into the establishing of the appointment. Share the specific needs with your prayer partners and other team members.

If possible, try to establish the appointment in the time you usually participate in your church evangelism training program. Whenever it is possible, have your team involved in making the contact. This will give you support and provide training for them.

Try to set the appointment for a place where the best possible communication can take place. Avoid disturbances and distractions. Sometimes the friend can be invited to the home of the new Christian. Other times it may be appropriate to go directly to the friend's home. It might be best to meet in a neutral spot like a quiet restaurant.

When you meet the relative or friend, be sure to use the conversational introduction. Don't jump immediately into the gospel. If the person being contacted has little or no previous contact with your church, it is good to find out what he knows about it and to discover his attitude toward it.

Sharing church testimony is very important when the person has not been to your church. This may cause him to want to come. When he becomes involved in the church, the follow-up will be easier.

Before you or your team members share a personal testimony, make reference to the new Christian and ask if he has shared what you discussed with him about eternal life. Whether he has or not, your question raises the subject of eternal life and gives a very natural situation for you to share your testimony.

GROUP PRESENTATIONS

If the new Christian gathers a small group to hear the gospel, certain adjustments need to be made. It's best if light refreshments can be served first. During this time you and the other team members can circulate among the people and get acquainted with them. Rapport can be established in this way. After a reasonable time of mixing in the group, the new Christian should briefly explain why he asked all of you together. Then the team members can briefly share their own personal testimonies. In a sizable group, new trainees should not be forced to give testimonies. This might cause them to drop out of the training altogether.

After testimonies have been shared, give each person a 3″ x 5″ card. Make it easy to be honest. Tell them you are *not* going to collect the cards, but you would like them to answer two questions for their own benefit. Ask the assurance question and God's "Why?" Have them write their response on the cards. Do not collect the cards. Share the gospel, and at the point of faith, contrast the correct answer to God's "Why?" with the common errors that many people hold. Then briefly go through the commitment, pointing out that if anyone would like to put his trust in Christ and receive the gift of eternal life, he can do so silently in his heart as you lead in prayer. Suggest that any who have done this speak to you before they leave. Indicate that anyone who is interested in talking further about this need only tell you so. Having more refreshments after the presentation makes it easy for individuals to talk to you and other team members.

It is always wise to have some good literature available to give to anyone with whom you share the gospel. If you cannot afford to purchase the literature, your church will usually be able to help.

If the new Christian's friend or relative makes a profession of faith, use the regular procedure for follow-up with him. If he does not make a profession of faith but is still open, try to get him into the worship services of the church as soon as it is practical. Enroll him in an appropriate Bible study class. Also try to get him into a Christian social situation where he can see that Christians are normal and, if needed, into a small caring group.

EVANGELIZE BY MAIL

If your new Christian desires to send a letter to a friend or relative, suggest that he try to crystallize what his life was like before he received eternal life and what it is like now. Then enclose a brief printed gospel presentation like the *Good News* booklet to explain how an individual actually receives eternal life.

Your Personal Influence and the Forever Family can be a very helpful study for new church members and new trainees in your evangelism program. This will show them the biblical teaching on their responsibility to witness to friends and relatives. It will also show them the subtle *lift* that is taking place in their lives.

THIRTEEN
THE OCCASIONAL WITNESSING SITUATION

Witnessing is to be a way of life! This is one of the goals of Evangelism Explosion Discipleship Training. If we follow the example of Christ and his apostles we will find an opportunity to bear witness in almost every occasion.

Christ used the most ordinary things to lead people to himself that they might have life. At a well, he spoke of himself as the water of life that quenches deep thirst. To the hungry he presented himself as the bread of life. To the crippled and the sick, he presented himself as the One who could make whole.

There are opportunities for witness all around you. Ask God to give you the ability to see them. Ask him for a heart that is bold enough to use them for his glory.

EXAMPLES:

Sometimes you can use *a person's name* as a springboard into the gospel. To a woman named Grace, you can say, "With a name like Grace you probably know for sure you are going to heaven. Am I correct?" If she says yes or no ask God's "Why?" and then seek to share the gospel.

The name Irene means peace. Timothy and Dorothy mean "a gift from God." The names of any of the saints of Scripture can be used to spring into the gospel. To a man named Jim, you can say, "You know you are named after one of the apostles, James. He is in heaven now. Do you know for sure that you will go there too?"

Cigarette smoking can be used to get into the gospel. When a person lights up, you can say, "Haven't you noticed all the ads by the Cancer Society on television? Cigarette smoking can kill you." If he responds by saying, "Yes, I know it, but I want to smoke anyway" or, "I'm not worried about that," then you can say, "Oh, you mean you have come to the place in your life where you know for certain if you were to die today, you would go to heaven?"

Elevators can be used to get into the gospel. I once stood outside an elevator with a friend. When another person approached, he reached for the button to call the elevator and said to the lady, "Are you going up?" "Yes" she responded. "Are you going *all* the way up?" he inquired. "No, just to the third floor," said she. "I mean when God's sweet chariot swings down low to take his people home to heaven, do you know for sure that you are going all the way up to heaven?" he continued. Her response was, "No, I'm not sure of that," and as we entered the elevator, he began sharing the gospel with her.

I know an *insurance* man who shares the gospel with his customers. After he has finalized their policy, he says, "This will take care of you until you die, but what's going to happen to you then? Do you know for sure that you are going to heaven?"

The *seasons of the year* can be used to spread the Good News. In the fall, as things are dying, you can use death in nature around you as a springboard into the topic of death. In spring, as new life buds out of the deadness of winter, this can be used to speak of eternal life that even death cannot overcome.

Special *holidays* can be used, especially Christmas and Easter.

There are so many opportunities to which we are oblivious. May God give you eyes to see them and boldness to use them.

THE OCCASIONAL INTRODUCTION

The occasional introduction has three parts:

1. The occasion
2. The two diagnostic questions
3. Permission to share the gospel

The occasion is the specific situation you use to raise the subject of eternal life.

The two diagnostic questions (assurance and God's "Why?") help you diagnose the person's spiritual condition.

Permission to share the gospel should always be sought. If it is granted, this usually means the person you have contacted is open and willing to listen.

Share in your public report session every opportunity you use to present the gospel. Make note of the occasions others report. This will keep you alert to new opportunities and increase your effectiveness in using them.

E.E. CERTIFIED TRAINER PIN (??)

The special pin given to all Certified E. E. Trainers is designed to provide opportunities for witness. Its two question marks symbolize the two diagnostic questions (assurance, God's "Why?").

When you wear the pin, someone will ask what it means or what the two question marks stand for.

Reply with something like:

"There is a great deal of uncertainty in the world today. People have so many questions. But when certain key questions are correctly answered, things come into focus. Two key questions have helped me greatly. Before I found the answers to these questions my life was . . . (personal testimony). Now that I know the answers to these key questions my life is . . . (personal testimony). Would you like to know what the questions are?"

If the answer is yes, raise the questions and proceed according to the person's need and response.

If the answer is no, back away from the situation with a brief presentation of the gospel. Your testimony brings eternal life into the conversation. The person contacted may not want to talk "religion." So say, "One thing I've always appreciated about God is his patience with us. He knows we are sinners and can't save ourselves. And even though he came into the world in the person of Christ, died for our sins, and came out of the grave alive, he said, 'I stand at the door and knock. If anyone hears my voice and opens the door, I will come into him.' He doesn't knock the door down. Since he doesn't force himself on us, I don't feel I can force him on someone either. It's been nice meeting you. Hope I'll see you again in heaven."

Then give him a tract and be on your way. Pray that God will use this brief encounter to draw the person to Christ.

FOURTEEN
ENLISTMENT FOR ENLARGEMENT

In the ongoing witnessing ministry it is necessary to have a specific time to recruit new persons into the training program. Without regular periodic enlisting of new trainees, the witnessing ministry will certainly diminish and may die. We will consider this in three aspects.

I. Basic principles
II. The practical procedures
III. The verbal presentation

BASIC PRINCIPLES

There are some *basic principles* that should be kept in mind as you consider your role in the next Discipleship Training Course.

1. WE EXIST TO GLORIFY GOD

"Man's chief end is to glorify God, and to enjoy him forever." This is the underlying theme of all the Bible. Paul exclaimed, "From him, and through him and to him, are all things: to whom be glory forever" (Romans 11:36). We must consciously seek to glorify God through our lives. Only as we thus relate to God does life have real and lasting meaning.

2. IN THIS WORLD WE BEST GLORIFY GOD BY ABUNDANT RESPONSIBLE REPRODUCTION OF DISCIPLES

In this world we glorify God as we willingly seek the work of the Spirit of God through his Word to change us from "glory to glory" (2 Corinthians 3:14–18). Paul prays that we may "accept one another" and "with one voice glorify the God and Father of our Lord Jesus Christ" (Romans 15:6, 7). Unity in the body of Christ glorifies God. He is glorified as individual believers employ their God-given gifts in "serving one another, as good stewards of the manifold grace of God" (1 Peter 4:10). Jesus said, "Let your light shine before men [in such a way] that they may see your good works, and glorify your Father which is in heaven" (Matthew 5:16). We are to glorify God in our bodies (1 Cor. 6:20). In fact, Paul tells us, "Whether, then, you eat or drink or whatever you do, do all to the glory of God" (1 Corinthians 10:31).

Perfect in heaven. In heaven the Spirit of God will have his perfect way in our lives. There will be perfect harmony and unity in the whole family of God. All that we do will perfectly glorify God. However, there is one thing that we will not be able to do in heaven that we *can* do in this present world—produce disciples!

Fruitfulness here and now. Jesus explains, "Herein is my Father glorified, that you bear much fruit; so shall ye be my disciples . . . You have not chosen me, but I have chosen you, and ordained you, that ye should go and bring forth fruit, and that your fruit should remain; that whatsoever ye ask of the Father in my name, he may give it you" (John 15:8,16). This has reference to total fruitfulness. The fruit of the Spirit which shows itself in Christian character—love, joy, peace, patience, kindness, goodness, faithfulness, gentleness, and self-control (Galatians 5:22, 23), is assumed by the emphasis on the "abiding" relationship without which Jesus says we can do nothing (John 15:4).

But Jesus is also saying that, as a properly pruned, healthy branch in right relation to the vine will produce an abundant visible harvest of grapes, so *the properly disciplined, healthy believer in right relation with him will produce an abundant harvest of visible fruit—disciples.* Thus Jesus commissions us to "Go therefore and make disciples of all the nations, baptizing them in the name of the Father and the Son and the Holy Spirit, teaching them to observe all that I commanded you" (Matthew 28:19, 20, NASB). We are not merely to obtain professions, but we are to bear visible fruit that "remains" (John 15:16).

Discipleship is demanding. Jesus makes very clear the demands of discipleship. Read Luke 14:26–33.

In the early church the martyrs were called disciples of the Lord. It was said as long as a Christian's blood had not been shed, he was only a beginner in discipleship. Throughout the Scriptures the word disciple implies that the person not only accepts the views of the teacher, but that he is also in practice an adherent. The disciple of Christ today may be described as "one who believes his doctrines, rests upon his sacrifice, imbibes his Spirit and imitates his example."[1]

3. WE CAN REPRODUCE DISCIPLES MOST RESPONSIBLY AND ABUNDANTLY WHEN WE ARE IN A WITNESSING FELLOWSHIP OF A LOCAL CHURCH WHERE EXPERIENCED TEACHERS AND TRAINERS HELP THE LESS EXPERIENCED WITH CLASSES AND ON-THE-JOB TRAINING

The local church[2] is God's primary base for evangelistic activity in this world. It is the visible family of God. Having children outside a family situation is a violation of God's order. It can mar and scar a child's total health. The church is the bride of Christ (Ephesians 5:23–32). As the bride the church is joined "to Him who was raised from the dead, that we might bear fruit for God" (Romans 7:4, NASB). The Great Commission is not obeyed simply by discipling and teaching. We are also commanded to baptize "in the name of the Father and the Son and the Holy Spirit" (Matthew 28:19). Baptism of adult converts is a public identification with the visible family of God. Reproduction is not responsible unless we also do everything in our power to meaningfully relate the new believer to the visible family of God.

In the family of God they should find love, protection, and increasing knowledge of the truth. They should be strengthened and encouraged by the one who is their spiritual parent. They should also be greatly helped by older brothers and sisters within the family of God. As they mature they should learn to accept responsibility for those who enter the family of God after them.

Mixed multitude. Ideally the whole church should be a witnessing fellowship, but it is not. One reason is because the church in this world is always a mixed multitude of believers and unbelievers. In the parable of the wheat and the tares, Jesus indicated this condition would continue to the end of time. In the world to come at the judgment the distinction will be made. It is interesting that Jesus draws a contrast between wheat and darnel. The darnel looked exactly like wheat through all stages of growth until the time of harvest. Then it had no "fruit." Perhaps there is the implication here that those who do not bear fruit are not true believers.

Levels of maturity. Another reason the whole church is not a witnessing fellowship is that there are varying levels of maturity and commitment within a local congregation. Thus it is vital to have within the church a group of men and women committed to God, to the all-important task of world evangelization, to each other and to the church.

A witnessing fellowship develops moral and spiritual strength. It encourages each individual and provides opportunity for united expression of the life produced by the gospel.

Scripture encourages such fellowship. "Iron sharpens iron, so one man sharpens another" (Proverbs 27:17). "Two are better than one because they have a good return for their labor. For if either of them falls, the one will lift up his companion. But woe to the one who falls when there is not another to lift him up . . . And if one can overpower him who is alone, two can resist him. A cord of three strands is not quickly torn apart" (Ecclesiastes 4:9,10,12). "If two of you agree on earth about anything that they may ask, it shall be done for them by my Father who is in heaven. For where two or three have gathered together in my name, there I am in their midst" (Matthew 18:19,20, NASB).

Multiplication through fellowship. In a fellowship of this nature the potential multiplication of reproducers is greatly increased. The souls of men are more valuable than anything else in this world. Jesus asks, "For what will a man be profited, if he gains the whole world, and forfeits his soul?" (Matthew 16:26). Being used of God to channel his grace to individual souls is the most important thing for us in this world. However, winning one soul is like picking an apple. Training a soul winner is like planting an apple tree, cultivating it, and harvesting from it bushels of choice apples for years and years. It is possible to win souls and not train soul winners. However, it is *not* possible to train soul winners without winning souls in the process.

Classes led by experienced, able teachers provide opportunity for in-depth understanding of the truth of the gospel and the best means of communicating it. However, classes alone do not tend to produce soul winners. Usually a student enters a class because he is aware of his ignorance. After attending classes for awhile he discovers there is a greater gap in his knowledge than he suspected. Add to this the seriousness of soul winning—the realization that the gospel can make the difference between heaven and hell for all eternity—and the witness may choke up. His mouth will remain closed. He may become a "theoretical expert," knowing more and more about less and less until he knows everything about nothing! But he seldom becomes a soul winner through classes alone.

On-the-job training with a qualified trainer provides the experience necessary to break the sound barrier—to open the mouth and actually verbalize the gospel. Experience in real situations removes fears. It inspires one to begin using the simple gospel and depend on the power of God for results. It short-circuits the fears that classes alone cannot dispel. For this reason Christ "appointed twelve, that they might be with Him, and that He might send them out to preach" (Mark 3:14, NASB).

Spiritual mathematics. The application of the principles had a very dramatic effect on the growth of the apostolic Church. Vergil Gerber describes it in these words:

> The New Testament gives us a thorough, well-documented report on the origins of growth of first century churches. Sometimes it is easier to spiritualize such a report than to document the conclusions with hard statistics. But the New Testament report is carefully documented with precise numerical figures:
>
> The First Church in Jerusalem began in an upper room with a small band of 120 disciples.[3]
>
> On the Day of Pentecost 3,000 were baptized, instructed in the Word, and added to the Jerusalem community.[4]
>
> With careful detail Dr. Luke records the growth pattern from the Day of Pentecost to the imprisonment and questioning of the early disciples. The membership of the Jerusalem Church now stands at 5,000.[5]
>
> In Acts 5:14 the emphasis is upon the fact that multitudes of men and women were added.
>
> In Acts 6:1,7 the number of disciples was multiplied.
>
> From this point on both the Book of Acts and the New Testament Epistles underscore the multiplication of churches as well as church members. New congregations were planted in every pagan center in the then-known world in less than four decades.
>
> In Acts 9:31 church multiplication is not in terms of a single church, i.e., the First Church of Jerusalem, but in the collective sense of geographical multiplication of believers in all Judea, and Galilee and Samaria. It focuses on the

> transition from the mother church to emerging congregations in other places.
> In Acts 16:5 here again is the change from church (singular) to churches (plural). *Churches* were planted. *Churches increased in number daily.* The Great Commission cannot be divorced from visible, structured, organized churches. In order to function and fulfill the Great Commission, there has to be some kind of structure.
> In Acts 21:20 Paul uses the word "myriads" in his report. A myriad is a measurement of 10,000. So the apostle reports tens of thousands of Jews alone who turned to Christ and became identified with local churches.[6]

There was an evangelism explosion!

From Gerber's observations, it may appear that you have a variety of options in spiritual mathematics. From one point of view it may be said that Christians add, multiply, or subtract. The incidents in Acts say that "*God* added to the church." But from another perspective it may be said that Christians only multiply. In creation of man God established the principle that we "multiply after our kind." Therefore, only two choices are open to you.

1. The *kind* or quality of your multiplication
2. The *degree* or quantity of your multiplication

You will invariably multiply others like yourself. If you are a functionally mature, responsible, reproducing Christian, you will produce others like yourself. To a great extent the spiritual **quality** of life in those who were multiplied through your ministry will depend upon the spiritual quality of your life.

The **quantity** of multiplication is determined by your passion for spiritual reproduction. Jesus said, "You did not choose me, but I chose you to go and bear fruit—fruit that will last. Then the Father will give you whatever you ask in my name" (John 15:16, NIV). "This is to my Father's glory, that you bear *much* fruit, showing yourselves to be my disciples" (John 15:8, NIV). The Apostle Paul believed that God was "able to do immeasurably more than all we ask or imagine, according to His power that is at work within us" (Ephesians 3:20, NIV).

Whether you are in the Evangelism Discipleship Fellowship or not, these principles remain true. You are constantly producing missionaries or mission fields, strong saints or crippled Christians, a pitiful few or an abundant harvest.

THE PRACTICAL PROCEDURES

Enlistment is best accomplished by personal, prayerful, private contact between people who are in the witnessing ministry and those who are not.

Public pulpit enlistment? It might appear that it would be better to have the pastor publicly enlist people from the pulpit on Sunday, but it is not. Some of the people to be called on during the week would be present in the congregation. If the pastor harangues the people to get into the witnessing program to go out and win poor lost souls, the "poor lost souls" are going to be on their guard when a team knocks at their door.

EGO DEFENSES ARMED. When Christians are urged publicly from the pulpit to enter the witnessing ministry, they arm their ego defense mechanisms. You might think that they would feel very guilty if they were not a part of the witnessing ministry. In most cases that is not what happens. They remember rumors they have heard about visitation teams. Someone who was visited said he would never, never come back to church, the team treated him like a heathen. So the silent saints remain in their pews on Sunday. They sit in their homes the nights the teams go out and say to themselves, "I am serving God better here watching my television than those fanatics who are out driving people away from Christ and our church."

I'M NOT A PREACHER! Another factor is that many laymen may not identify with the pastor. Let me illustrate it this way.

Suppose you were in a large group gathered to hear a very famous and distinguished four-star general lecture on "The Principles of War." The printed program informs you that the general has graduated from West Point with highest honors. He has completed post-graduate work at the War College in Washington, D.C. When he stands to speak he is the perfect picture of the model soldier. His words flood forth with an overwhelming eloquence. For twenty minutes you listen in awed silence to his masterful oratory. You are astonished at the breadth and depth of the man's knowledge and his command of the English language. It is obvious that he has thoroughly mastered the principles of war and knows very well how to communicate them to large crowds.

In concluding his speech, the general says, "Now I want you to be a soldier like me. Of course, you will not be able to attend West Point or the War College, but I will give you a twelve-week course which will expose you to everything I have learned in my twelve years of higher education. If you are not a yellow craven coward you will enlist today."

The wheels of your mind begin to turn. You think, "I wish I were like that general—but I am not like the general. He has an exceptionally alert mind and a natural ability to speak. He has had so much formal education. He is one in a million and I am just one of a million common people.

"I don't want to be a coward, but what he is talking about is dangerous. I am not like him so I cannot do it. Besides I am sure that many others here are much more qualified than I and they surely will respond. Anyway, somebody has to stay home. We can't all be heroes."

On the other hand, suppose you are sitting in your living room one pleasant afternoon. The doorbell rings. When you respond you are greeted by the smiling face of an old friend whom you have not seen for a number of years. You invite him into your living room so that you may reminisce over old times and catch up on what's been going on since you were last together. Your friend tells you that he has been in the army for the past three years. Enthusiastically he relates one adventure after another. Then he says, "I know I'm not a general, but the general couldn't fight the war without me and many others like me. I know what I do is dangerous, but I'm fighting for what is right and it has given meaning to my life.

"You and I are very much alike. Wouldn't you like to enlist with me and see your life really count for something?"

Once again, the gears in your mind are in motion. Your thoughts say, "My life sure hasn't had the meaning or excitement that his has. We are a lot alike. If he can do it I think I can too."

Who is the best recruiter? In the army of Jesus Christ the experienced lay evangelist can be a much more effective recruiter than the "professional general in the pulpit." The ongoing work of evangelism depends on the laymen enlisting and assisting in the training of other lay evangelists. The Apostle Paul told Timothy, "You therefore, my son, be strong in the grace that is in Christ Jesus, And the things which you have heard from me in the presence of many witnesses, these entrust to faithful men, who will be able to teach others also. Suffer hardship with me, as a good soldier of Christ Jesus. No soldier in active service entangles himself in the affairs of everyday life so that he may please the one who enlisted him as a soldier" (2 Timothy 2:1–4, NASB).

You are in touch on a regular basis with soldiers in the army of Jesus Christ who are "absent without official leave." Pray that God will enable you to be his instrument to make them good soldiers of Jesus Christ who can fight the forces of evil by verbally sharing his gospel with the lost.

Everyone is to enlist. Everyone in the witnessing program is responsible for enlistment of new trainees. That includes the leader and every trainer, junior trainer, and trainee in the program.

Though many people at the end of their first training program are ready to become trainers, some are not. They may think, "If I am not going to be a trainer next time, then I shouldn't try to enlist anybody." If you are in that particular situation, let me remind you that you have contact with some people that nobody else has. You should encourage them to come into the witnessing ministry even if you are not going to be their trainer. Don't feel that you are exempt from the enlistment effort because you don't feel you are going to be a trainer. Serve as a scout. Help others who will be trainers to enlist people you know.

Purpose to be a trainer. If you are now a trainee or junior trainer you should purpose to be a trainer. Possibly you are thinking that you don't have sufficient experience in sharing the gospel yet. Maybe you have not had another person profess faith in response to your presentation of the gospel, so you think you should not try to be a trainer. That is not the case. If you are able to pass the end of the course checkup and willing to invest your life in two trainees, in most cases you can begin to function as a trainer. You will learn much more as a trainer than you will ever learn as a trainee or even a junior trainer. You can increase the number of people brought to

Christ by being a trainer and enlisting others in the witnessing force in the next training course.

Train without trainees? Sometimes people let their participation in the next training program depend on whether or not they enlist trainees. If you will commit yourself to God to be a trainer with or without trainees, this will cause you to be more zealous in getting trainees. Then when you talk with potential trainees you will communicate more of the urgency of being in the program.

Seasoned trainers—best recruiters. Seasoned trainers are usually more able to enlist trainees than people who are becoming trainers for the first time. First-time trainers are sometimes nervous and uncertain about their ability to function as trainers. This uncertainty may cause hesitancy in seeking trainees, and may even cause people to be hesitant about working with the trainer as his first trainees. Therefore, seasoned trainers should seek to enlist trainees not only for themselves but for those they have trained who are becoming trainers for the first time.

Some trainers are more able to enlist people into the training program than others. If you happen to be in this group, work with others who are less able to get their trainees. If you know others in the program who are good recruiters, encourage them to work with you to help you get trainees.

Finding your disciple

PRAY! The first thing to do to find the right trainee is to pray. The Scripture says, "Beseech the Lord of the harvest to send out workers into His harvest" (Matthew 9:38, NASB). Ask God to lead you to the people he wants you to have as your trainees. Ask him to lead you to people in the congregation who need to be in the witnessing ministry whether they become your trainee or not. Then pray for him to touch their hearts and draw them in.

Faithful and able. The two basic qualities you should look for in a trainee are that he be faithful and able. "These things which you have heard from me in the presence of many witnesses, these entrust to faithful men, who will be able to teach others also" (2 Timothy 2:2, NASB).

"Faithful" in very practical terms means an *active member* of your local church who is *generally supportive* of its work. He should not hold major doctrines contrary to your church. If he does and brings them up in the calling situation it will certainly distract from presenting the gospel and can create serious problems.

When you look for "ability," look for a person who is somewhat *like you.* Don't necessarily look for a person who is a supersalesman with public relations background. Sometimes these people depend more on their natural abilities than on the Holy Spirit. The basic abilities to look for are availability and a willingness to learn. In many cases these will be quiet, meek, humble, shy individuals. If you do get someone who is a supersalesman, make sure he understands that his abilities must be yielded to the Lord and sanctified by him. Otherwise he will fail.

Don't automatically eliminate people that are *different from you.* Your trainees may be older or younger than you, more or less educated, of a different race or cultural background.

Teen-agers. Do *not* enlist teen-agers with the thought that they will be able to function as trainers in the next regular adult training program. Very few adults are willing to be trained by a teen-ager. If there is an adult on the team and the call is made on adults it will be very awkward for the teen-ager to take the lead and function as a trainer. If the team is composed of all teen-agers they will usually find it difficult to present the gospel to adults in a home situation. The adults will dominate the conversation or patronize the young people.

When teen-agers are trained it is best that they function as trainers of other teen-agers. In addition they need to be trained to use the assurance questionnaire so they can go in public places and witness to their peers.

Both men and women. Try to enlist both men and women. Women usually are more sensitive and gentle as they deal with others. Men usually are more direct and forceful. Having both men and women on the team will lend a balance that increases the capacity for communication.

Married couples. If possible a husband and wife should be enlisted for the same training period. Sometimes, when one is in the witnessing ministry and the other is not, a spiritual gulf can grow between them. It can be difficult to share what is not being experienced by both. Sometimes both are not able to be in the same training course due to pregnancy, small children, work schedules, etc. If a wife enters the training and her husband is hostile toward it, she will have difficulty completing the program.

Usually it is not wise for husbands and wives to be trainees on the same team or try to train each other. Normally one is more dominant than the other. This can cause problems. The dominant person will learn the gospel, the other one will remain dependent. When married couples start calling together they hesitate to divide after they get trained. This short circuits the multiplication. If there are exceptions, have a clear understanding in advance.

It is best to take your visitation team to enlist a couple. Explain that it is best to have them on separate teams. Indicate they can each be with one of your team members. If there is hesitation, ask if there is someone else in the program they would like to be with. Then notify him.

Women trainers. In this regard, *women serving as trainers* should not feel that they are going contrary to the Bible and usurping authority over a man. Peter, on the Day of Pentecost, declared, "But this is what was spoken of through the prophet Joel: 'And it shall be in the last days, God says, that I will pour forth of My Spirit upon all mankind; and your sons and your daughters shall prophesy, and your young men shall see visions, and your old men shall dream dreams; even upon My bondslaves, both men and women, I will in those days pour forth of My Spirit and they shall prophesy" (Acts 2:16–18, NASB). The first person to whom the resurrected Christ appeared was a woman. He specifically instructed her to go and tell his brethren. She was the first witness of the resurrection and proclaimed it first to the apostles (John 20:11–18).

Members of other churches. Generally, enlistment of a member of another church should be discouraged. Do not bring a layman from another church without his pastor. If a layman is from a liberal church where the gospel is not preached, he will grow so dissatisfied with his own situation that he will either create disharmony within his church or he will leave it. Then we get the reputation of "church splitter" or "sheep stealer."

If it is an evangelical church and the pastor says to the layman, "I'd like you to go and learn, and come back and start the program at our church," there will still be a problem. The layman will get excited and enthusiastic. Then he will wonder why his pastor does not participate. A layman without his pastor creates more problems than benefits.

When the pastor desires to come into the E.E. program of your church he must be interviewed by the minister in charge of the training program. He must commit himself to go through the entire training program, both the classes and the calling. He will assume the role of a layman in your church and be assigned to a trainer. He must also enroll in the first possible certified leadership clinic he can attend. This will provide the training he needs to certify his own lay people in an ongoing training program.

Usually not more than 10 percent of a total training program can be made up of people who are not members of the host church. More than ten percent would undercut the training base. It would put people in the program who will not be there to train others next semester. This would eventually be a case of suicide for the witnessing program.

A charge must be worked out for each person coming from another congregation. This pays for the materials and also is a token that encourages follow-through on the commitment.

Usually pastors and lay people discipled in a local certified E.E. program before attending a leadership clinic receive much more benefit from the clinic experience. After attending a certified leadership clinic, special alumni rates are available for subsequent clinics.

THE VERBAL PRESENTATION

By now you have discovered that having a well-learned presentation of the gospel makes it much easier to be an effective evangelist. This also applies when you enlist trainees. You will be much more effective in obtaining good trainees who in turn will become good trainers if you properly recruit them.

Proper recruitment requires that potential trainees be reasonably informed about the Evangelism Explosion Discipleship Training Program. The better informed they are the less likely it is that they will drop out.

An adaptation of the outline learned for presenting the gospel will help you enlist your trainees. You need not master the enlistment presentation to the same degree as the gospel presentation. Use the *Fishers of Men* booklet for that purpose. The following is an outline of the enlistment presentation.

I. Introduction
   Salutation
   With church member you know well—"Pastor Kennedy asked us/me to visit with you and see how you feel about the way the ministry of our church is now going."
   With member of your church you do not know—"Since we go to the same church, Pastor Kennedy thought it would be good for us to get better acquainted and share our thinking about our church's ministry."
   A. The person's secular life
      Ask, listen, note time involvement.
   B. His church background—before uniting with our church.
   C. Our church—attitude, time involvement.
   D. Testimony—church and personal (benefits others have received from discipleship training, and how you handle the time priority problem). (See *Fishers* booklet.)
   E. The two diagnostic questions
      "We use two questions to focus on spiritual things. I would be interested in your thinking on them."
      (1) Question one—(his answer). Do not deal with his answer until he has answered question two.
      (2) Question two—(his answer)
          Faith—move to enlistment
          Works—share gospel and begin follow-up.
II. Enlistment (See *Fishers of Men* booklet)
   A. Why are you still on earth?
   B. Left for a reason
   C. Here's how the ministry works!
   D. Here's how we share the Good News
   E. Commitment to the ministry
III. Commitment
   A. The qualifying question: "Does this sound like a workable training program to you?"
   B. The commitment question: "Would you be willing to let God tell you what your part should be in the next Discipleship Training Program?"
   C. Clarification
      1. Give *Fishers of Men*
      2. Read "How to Use the Book"
      3. Read "Six-Day Reading Schedule"
   D. Follow-up appointment
      "After you have read *Fishers of Men,* I'd like to check with you and see what you believe God wants you to do. Will this same day and time be best next week or is there another day that's better?" (date, day, and time).
   E. Prayer for guidance

SUGGESTIONS FOR ENLISTMENT PRESENTATION

I. Introduction

HIS SECULAR LIFE. When talking about the person's secular life, follow the same instructions you have had in the evangelism presentation. If you know him, ask questions to help you tune in to his present life situation. If you do not know him, ask questions that will enable you to get acquainted.

As your prospective trainee talks, listen for things that will give you clues to his present time involvement.

HIS CHURCH BACKGROUND. If you are not sure about his church background before uniting with your church, ask about it. This will give you interesting insights and may provide you with helpful information for future use in the evangelism program.

OUR CHURCH. When you talk about "our church" there are two basic things you need to discover: (1) his attitude toward the present ministry of your church and (2) his time involvement in the work of the church. You may casually ask, "How do you feel about the way things are going at the church?" If he is extremely negative, do *not* try to enlist him as a trainee. Do what you can to correct the situation. If you cannot correct it, be sure to inform the official leaders of the church so that they can try to help. This does not mean that the trainee must be a "yes man," in 100 percent agreement with everything that is happening. It does mean that he must be in basic agreement in the major areas of ministry.

THE PROBLEM OF PRIORITIES. Time involvement is the number one challenge that keeps people out of evangelism discipleship training. At least that is what they say. Really, it is not a matter of time, it is a matter of priorities. We usually make time for the things we feel are most important.

It is important to maintain balanced ministry. This requires that people utilize their Spirit-given gifts where they can best accomplish his work. In addition to personal evangelists, every church needs teachers, choir members, elders, deacons, etc. But it goes without saying that all of these other functions will be carried out better if the person doing them is striving to be obedient to the Great Commission.

Up to this point you are gathering information so that you will know what to try to preclude before you raise the question about participation in the training program.

CHURCH TESTIMONY. Church testimony ties in with the theme of discussing your local ministry. It is identical to what you have already learned for presenting the gospel.

PERSONAL TESTIMONY. Personal testimony in the enlistment presentation should share the benefits you have received from being in this work. Benefits others have received are listed in the *Fishers of Men* booklet. Select from these the ones that are true for you.

In your personal testimony you should include how you handle the time problem, that is, how you get your priorities in focus and follow through on them. Since the number one objection people give is not having enough time, you will be well ahead if you preclude that objection before it comes up.

THE TWO DIAGNOSTIC QUESTIONS. The two questions come at this point. You have been talking about the ministry of your church and now have focused specifically on the Evangelism Discipleship Training Ministry, so it is very natural to say, "In this training program we use two questions to focus on spiritual things. I would be interested in your thinking on them." Ask question one and get the person's response. It is important that trainees have assurance of eternal life. If they do not, they will never be persuasive with others. Also, the devil will constantly nip at their heels and defeat them at every turn in their own personal lives. Regardless of the answer gained to this first question, do not deal with it until after you have asked God's "Why?" and gotten the potential trainee's response. If his answer to question two is a clear statement of faith in Christ, move to the enlistment. If the answer to question two is clearly a works answer, then share the gospel and if he makes a profession of faith begin the follow-up. Do not be surprised if members of the church occasionally give works answers when approached as potential trainees.

II. The enlistment

Many things that can be said in this part of your enlistment presentation are contained in the *Fishers of Men* booklet. This is available in written form in order to lighten the learning load for you. It also provides a tool that can be left with the potential trainee so he can think the matter through. It is brief enough not to be a burden, but comprehensive enough to clearly explain what is involved in the training program.

You should study this booklet until you have its contents well in mind. When you are actually involved in the conversation with your prospective trainee you can open the booklet to the table of contents and use it as a cue sheet. Of course the cue sheet will do you no good if you are not familiar with the contents, so it is important to thoroughly understand what is contained in the *Fishers of Men* booklet.

The content of the enlistment presentation in *Fishers of Men* has been collected and refined over a number of years. It is designed to answer the basic questions and objections that Christians have about participating in this training.

III. The commitment

THE QUALIFYING QUESTION. This begins with the qualifying question, "Does this sound like a workable training program to you?" If you have properly described the training program the answer will be yes.

THE COMMITMENT QUESTION. Then the commitment question is posed, "Would you be willing to ask God to tell you what your part should be in the next discipleship training program?" Notice the question does not ask the individual to respond to you but rather to God. It is much easier to tell a man or woman "no" than to tell it to the Creator and Redeemer.

THE CLARIFICATION. If the response to the commitment question is yes, show him the *Fishers of Men* booklet. Turn to "How to Use This Book," and read that paragraph. Point out the "Six-Day Reading Schedule." Especially emphasize the importance of putting question marks in the margin beside anything that needs to be clarified. Urge your potential trainee to spend the bulk of his time reading the Scripture selections in "A Scriptural Basis for Your Decision." Share the benefits that you have received by doing this study yourself.

FOLLOW-UP APPOINTMENT. Your follow-up appointment should be about one week later. Be sure to allow enough time to work through the six-day reading schedule. It is best, if you can, to nail down the date, day, and time while you are still with the potential trainee.

PRAYER FOR GUIDANCE. After you have established the follow-up appointment, ask if you can have prayer together for God to give guidance in this matter. A prayer containing thoughts that might be included can be found in the *Fishers of Men* booklet.

1. G. H. Trever, "Disciple," *International Standard Bible Encyclopedia,* vol. 2, p. 851.

2. A true church has three basic marks.

(1) The true preaching of the Word (John 8:31,32,47; 14:23; 1 John 4:1–3; 2 John 9).

(2) The right administration of the Lord's Supper and baptism. These should never be divorced from the Word, for they have no content of their own. They derive their content from the Word of God and are in fact a visible preaching of the Word. They should be administered by lawful ministers of the Word, in accordance with the divine institution, and only to properly qualified subjects. That this is true is derived from their inseparable connection with the preaching of the Word and such passages as Matthew 28:19; Mark 16:15,16; Acts 2:42; 1 Corinthians 11:23–30.

(3) The faithful exercise of discipline. This is important for the maintaining of purity of doctrine and guarding the holiness of Baptism and the Lord's Supper. Churches that are lax in discipline are bound to discover sooner or later within their circle an eclipse of the light of the truth and an abuse of that which is holy (Matthew 18:18; 1 Corinthians 5:1–5,13; 14:33,40; Revelation 2:14,15,20).

Louis Berkhof, *Systematic Theology* (Grand Rapids: Wm. B. Eerdmans Publishing Co., 1949), pp. 577, 578.

3. Acts 1:15.

4. Acts 2:41,42.

5. Acts 4:4.

6. Vergil Gerber, *God's Way to Keep a Church Going and Growing* (Regal Books, 1973), pp. 16, 17.

All Scripture quotations are from *The Living Bible,* unless otherwise indicated.

FIFTEEN
THE CHAIN OF COMMAND

A LIFELINE OF CONCERN AND COMMUNICATION

Picture an army composed only of generals and privates. As the general sits in his command tent, studying strategy for the total battle, his field phone rings. The enemy is attacking on the western front. There are no officers in that sector. There are only privates. The general must leave his command tent and rush to the battle so that he can lead his men.

When he arrives on the western front hundreds of privates eagerly await his orders. But the enemy is attacking in full force! He cannot give personal orders to each private. Some wander around not knowing what to do. Before they are aware of what has happened, they are captured by the enemy. Others, on their own, charge into the midst of the conflict. The general shouts, "Come back! The enemy has the high ground. He will slaughter you! Pull back to the ridges where you have sufficient cover. There we can hold the line."

Many of the troops do not hear the general. He is only one voice and the battle is raging. Those who charge ahead are quickly cut down by enemy fire. There is great confusion and in the attempt to run to safety many wounded men are left unattended on the field. The soldiers who were closest to the general heard his command and took up positions on the ridges.

As the battle rages a courier comes from headquarters to tell the general the enemy is now attacking on the eastern front. He must immediately go there and lead the soldiers. What is he to do? The enemy is attacking on all fronts. Soldiers without direction are being wounded and killed. The enemy is overrunning his forces and he cannot adequately defend his positions.

Any war fought like this will be lost in short order! Before the general can ever think of victory he must take time in the command tent to develop strategy for offensive battle. He must have capable leaders on graduated levels in the organization.

The Christian church is an army doing battle against Satan and the forces of evil. This conflict is more intense and devastating than any military conflict has ever been. In this army it is imperative that there be a chain of command. *The chain of command functions as a lifeline of concern and communication. It serves as a channel for the sharing of life within the body of Christ.*

FOREWARNED IS FOREARMED

Every person has his own particular problems. But when you enter a training program to learn to share the gospel, you can *expect special and unique problems.* Capable witnessing Christians are special targets for satanic attack. They are much more of a threat to him than the Christian who is satisfied merely to occupy a pew on Sunday.

Diabolical devices are used especially on new trainees. If Satan can discourage and defeat you before you are able to share the gospel, you will not be nearly so great a threat to him. If he can cripple you spiritually in your process of learning to share the gospel you will be very cautious about ever attempting it again. He will use the *pressure of time, the slowness of mind to learn, the fear of confronting people in a face-to-face situation, family conflicts, physical health* and anything else to discourage and defeat you.

More often than not lay people are better equipped than the minister to help other lay people with problems they encounter in the course of the training program. The chain of command is designed to encourage the more experienced to help the less experienced.

It is more than a cliché to say that *no chain is stronger than its weakest link.* God says in his Word, when one member of the body suffers, all suffer. We generally agree that we are to bear one another's burdens. The problem is that more often than not *everyone's responsibility is no one's responsibility.* The church cannot afford to be the only army that does not care for its wounded!

This lifeline of concern emphasizes the responsibility of the more experienced for the less experienced in the training program—the responsibility of the more knowledgeable person in the program for the person with less knowledge. New trainees must feel free to share their fears and frustrations with trainers, and this means more than sharing the *problems encountered in the learning process.* It should also include sharing *personal problems* related to the total growth of their spiritual life. The sharing of life should also be a reality between trainers and lieutenants, lieutenants and the staff director.

Sometimes this sharing is on a one-to-one basis. Other times it takes place in the visitation team of three; still other times it occurs in the lieutenant group of twelve. Of course, *when anything of a personal, intimate nature is shared it MUST be kept in Christian confidence.*

As this communion of life grows, the unity within the body of Christ becomes more visibly evident. This will enable you to have more spiritual vitality for witnessing. It will also demonstrate the reality of Christ in the lives of his people and thus become a united witness to the truth of our faith (John 17:21).

This line of communication will encourage new trainees to ask their trainers or lieutenants questions which they might not ask the minister. They may be shy or feel the minister is too busy. It provides the minister with a personal line for information to every person in the program.

Our training program is constantly growing out of the personal encounters as the gospel is shared. This line of communication enables trainers to effectively *share new ideas with the leadership* of the program so that all may benefit.

GROWTH BRINGS DIFFICULTIES

As the size of your local E.E. group grows, body life becomes more difficult. To keep this vital, lieutenant groups of no more than twelve people are formed. At specified times during the semester your lieutenant group will stay at the church during the time for on-the-job training. During this time you will pray for the teams out calling. Then you may share your needs and pray for one another in the lieutenant group. If there is time left before the report session, you can practice your E.E. material.

A PROCESS FOR DEVELOPING LEVELS OF LEADERSHIP

As the weak and the wounded are cared for, they become healthy and strong. When you seek to disciple someone to the place where you now are in your Christian life, you will grow, too. When your disciple arrives at the place in his spiritual life where you are now, you will no longer be there. You will grow to a new level of maturity. It is *by this process* that *the army of Christ develops graduated ranks of leaders.*

Let me emphasize again *the chain of command is a lifeline of concern and communication.* It is not to be strict military regimentation, but concern sometimes requires confrontation and communication is not possible without honest praise and constructive criticism. Scripture says we are to submit ourselves one to another (Ephesians 5:21). We are to exhort and admonish one another. Human nature chafes against the shaping process of accountability. But if Christians really care about one another and desire to be made into the likeness of Christ, they will lovingly encounter one another and will listen to the counsel of fellow members in the family of God.

Individuals in the Evangelism Discipleship Training are given additional responsibilities as they prove themselves able to perform them. As you extend yourself into new areas of ministry and responsibility you will discover the gifts God has given you. There are many gifts needed in the ministry of Evangelism Explosion Discipleship Training. Behind and through the "gifts" there is a need for Christlike love for others in the family of God and especially for those who have yet to hear the gospel.

LINKS IN THE CHAIN

The chain of command consists of the following links:

1. Prayerpartners
2. Trainees
3. Junior trainers
4. Trainers
5. Lieutenants
6. Assistant lay teacher/trainers
7. Teacher/trainers (lay and staff)
8. Leadership clinic administrators
9. Leadership clinic teachers

Staff teacher/trainers are certified only in leadership clinics. By "staff" we mean a full-time person on the staff of a local church. The person can be either paid or a volunteer. He must be theologically trained through Bible college or seminary. And he must have experience in ministry, particularly in the teaching and leading of groups within the church.

Notice the reverse order in this chain of command. The staff director is not on top but on the bottom. The more experience and responsibility a person has, the more he is the *servant* of others (Mark 10:43). Now let's look at each of these links in the chain.

1. PRAYERPARTNERS

The qualifications and responsibilities of a prayerpartner are described in detail in the "Prayerpartner" section of the *Prayer in the Forever Family* booklet.

A prayerpartner is a person who shares in your evangelistic activity as a trainer or trainee. He or she prays for you and the people with whom you share the gospel.

God has honored this ministry in a unique way. In the first training semester that prayerpartners were required for all participants at the Coral Ridge Presbyterian Church, the number of professions of faith increased more than 100 percent over the previous training semester. Churches using the prayerpartner program have discovered that trainers and trainees with faithful prayerpartners are more fruitful and less likely to become discouraged and drop out of the training.

Potential prayerpartners should read the *Prayer in the Forever Family* booklet, especially the chapter on prayerpartners. Then if they desire to enter into this ministry of intercession they should complete the commitment card attached to the back cover.

You should have at least two prayerpartners. You can enlist more, but do not have more prayerpartners than you can contact and pray with each week.

Your prayerpartners should be adult Christians, usually over eighteen years of age. They should be members or regular attenders of your local church.

They should *not* be members of your immediate family.

They should *not* be present trainees or trainers in the E.E. program of your church. Selecting adults who are *not* presently in the E.E. ministry helps increase the flow of general information on this ministry to your congregation. It also gives the wider sense of participation that is necessary for a concerted effort in evangelizing your community.

People who are already Christians when you encounter them in witnessing situations may be enlisted as prayerpartners. People your team leads to profess faith in Christ may be enlisted as prayerpartners. When this is done it should be after the seven-day call back is completed, and then only if the new Christian is clear on his relationship to Christ and enthusiastic about his faith.

Preferably your two basic prayerpartners should be a man and a woman. A married couple is excellent. They can intercede together for you and the people with whom you share the gospel. If you enlist a prayerpartner who is married and of the opposite sex, exercise caution not to leave any wrong impression about your weekly contact. This is especially true if either of you is married to an unbeliever. Intercessory prayer should become a vital part of your prayerpartner's family devotions, and this can have a deep impact on their children's lives also.

A prayerpartner must be seeking to walk with Christ and believe that God answers prayer.

He must desire to intelligently pray for you, the people with whom you share the gospel, and the worldwide ministry of Evangelism Explosion. Therefore, he must be willing to talk with you each week so you can give requests and reports on answered prayer. If possible this weekly contact should be in person. Your prayerpartner may come to the church and pray while your team is out calling. Or he may attend only the report session. This will give him an opportunity to hear firsthand what God has done in response to his prayers and gain information for further prayer. If your prayer-partner cannot come to church, then you can have a brief personal contact at another time. Information can be communicated to him by telephone.

The time for sharing answered prayers and giving new requests should usually not exceed fifteen minutes a week. Remember, you should see that your prayerpartner hears what happened with your team and knows the results of the total calling effort for the week.

Use only the first names of the people contacted. Any matter shared with you in confidence in the calling situation must not be shared with anyone else! Be sure to regularly remind your prayerpartner that *all* requests must be kept confidential.

Pray with your prayerpartner each week. After you have reported answered prayers and given new requests, lead in audible prayer. Your prayerpartner might not feel comfortable praying aloud, so do not pressure him or her, but do give opportunity each week. Pray together each week even if the contact is by phone.

One of the purposes of the prayerpartner program is to bring Christians in the same church together in new relationships for a meaningful ministry of intercession. Therefore, it is important that each participant enlist new prayerpartners each training semester. Do not keep the same prayerpartners two semesters in a row.

Benefits. There are many benefits in the prayerpartner ministry. It provides intercessory prayer for the lost and for you as you participate in a witnessing team. It gives effectiveness to follow-up. It provides a personal line of communication about the outreach ministry of your church to those who are not participating in it. The evangelism discipleship training group cannot become a closed clique—an elite group of Pharisees. The prayerpartner program provides opportunity for meaningful involvement in the evangelistic activity of the church for other members who are not able to participate because of physical or mental handicaps.

Though many who begin praying for this ministry will participate as trainees, the prayerpartner program cannot become merely a gimmick to draw them into the calling force. The ministry of intercessory prayer is vital for accomplishing God's work in this world.

Prayer Guide. When you enlist someone to be your prayerpartner, be sure to provide him with a copy of the *Prayer Guide* booklet. Suggest that he first meditate on the material titled "Prayer and Evangelism—Some Biblical Guidelines." A few minutes each day in this will provide orientation for effective intercession for you. Urge him to look up each reference in his Bible as he reads it in the meditation.

Be sure that you read through the "Prayer Suggestions" and check the particular items that you would like your prayerpartner to pray about for you.

Each week contact your prayerpartner with your requests. The list of suggestions should give you some help. Be very specific. Vague, general prayer is little more than a mental exercise. It is basically nothing but wishful thinking. God honors specific prayer because specific prayer honors him. In your own copy of *Prayer Guide,* be sure to write the requests that you want to share with your prayerpartner. Put the date by the request and leave space so that you can note the answer to your prayer when it comes. As you listen to others during the public report session, write in your *Prayer Guide* some of the positive, exciting things that happen so that you can share them with your prayerpartner also. Whenever a request is answered, be sure that you share that with your partner too.

Week by week, as your requests and answers are recorded in writing, you will find your faith strengthened. Seeing how God has responded to your prayers in the past will cause you to be more bold and expectant for the present.

Prayer pact. The main reason we do not attempt great things for God is because we are afraid we might fail. Fear of failure cripples! It prevents an honest appraisal of your personal strengths and weaknesses. It stifles your growth and causes your soul to close up to God and others.

You are weak. This is a fact of life. But God says, "I am with you: that is all you need. My power shows up best in weak people." We should respond to this as Paul did. He said, "Now I am glad to boast about how weak I am; I am glad to be a living demonstration of Christ's power instead of showing off my own power and abilities" (2 Corinthians 12:9, TLB).

God accepts you as you are, in spite of your deficiencies. You must accept yourself as you are before his love and power can make you what you ought to be. When you truly know your weakness, you can draw on God and members of his family for strength. In order to receive this strength, you must be honest and open concerning your need.

Like the parts of a human body, all members of Christ's church depend in some degree on each other. A healthy body is made up of cells that are in a proper relationship with the cells closest to them. The body of Christ will be healthy when you properly relate to a few people with whom God enables you to be open and honest and loving. Attempting to relate to every member of the body of Christ with the same degree of intimate depth will cause pain and frustration.

Growth-producing questions. The *Prayer Pact* booklet raises two growth-producing questions.

1. If the church being what God wants, depends on *me* being what I should be, what needs to be changed in my life?
2. If the church doing what God wants depends on me doing what I should, what should I try to do for the Lord? What would I try to do for God if I were positive I could not fail?

After examining the impact of these questions in the life, suggestion is made that you enter into a prayer pact with someone else. Two or more people can make a pact together. Usually it is best for the pact to last thirty days. The specific length of the pact should be determined when it is entered into. It may be renewed any number of times by mutual desire. For the duration of the pact you agree to do three things with your pact partner.

1. Share your needs as they arise and pray daily for each other.
2. Give yourself without reservation to God and attempt to do whatever he puts in your heart.
3. Renew this commitment before God the first thing each day for the duration of the pact.

Let's consider how prayer pacts can be an effective way of developing growth with other team members, prayerpartners, or new Christians.

Team members. The trainer and trainees in a three-person E.E. witnessing team will find new power for their lives as they enter a prayer pact with each other.

Prayerpartners. After you have prayed with your prayerpartner for five or six weeks you may find it is possible to deepen your relationship by entering into a prayer pact.

New Christians. When people contacted by your team are already Christians or come to Christ through your presentation of the gospel, you may find the prayer pact an effective way to help them grow. This can be determined according to specific needs that are expressed.

Before you attempt to enter a prayer pact, carefully read the booklet. Then give a copy to the person with whom you desire to share the pact. When he or she has read it and understands it, make your commitment to one another and see what God does through your lives.

Dynamic for development. It will be worthwhile to take a few minutes to consider the dynamic that takes place in the membership of the church when the Evangelism Explosion Training Prayerpartner/Prayer Pact programs are properly operating.

Every church is made up of workers and attenders. Some workers are on the staff. This includes the pastor and other paid theological and administrative persons. It also includes full-time and part-time volunteers. The basic function of the staff is to *equip the saints for the work of ministry* (Ephesians 4:12).

A second group of workers can be called *"encouragers."* These are the people who work within the body to make it strong and vital—Bible teachers, choir members, elders, deacons, counselors, ushers, hospital visitors, etc.

The third group of workers are the *evangelizers.* They are the ones who reach out into the community to bring the message and ministry of Christ to people who are not yet Christians. The Evangelism Explosion Discipleship Training Group is part of this group. Others who utilize their gifts of "hospitality" and "helps," etc., are also to evangelize, but they are specially able to minister to unbelievers as bridge-builders. In this group of evangelizers there are a very small percentage who have the gift of evangelist. Most are fulfilling their responsibility in the role of witness.

God has commanded all his people to proclaim the gospel. People with gifts designed to build up the local body from within will not be able to exercise their gifts with maximum effectiveness until they understand and are able to communicate the gospel. Paul told Philemon, "I pray that you may be active in sharing your faith, so that you will have a full understanding of every good thing we have in Christ (Philemon 6, NIV).

Assuming that this is true, E.E. participants can have a meaningful prayerpartner relationship with those who are building up the body from within. As they share and pray together each week, the sense of teamwork grows. For example, if a Bible teacher is the prayerpartner, he will be interested in having a new convert involved in the educational process of the church. He will help the lay evangelist develop him into a responsible reproducing disciple, a part of the force for evangelism in the community. The Bible teacher will not see his teaching as an end in itself, but as a means to the end of evangelizing, bearing much fruit that God might be glorified. On the other hand, the lay evangelist realizes that sharing the gospel, rather than being the end, is only the beginning of the process for developing functionally mature disciples. All the resources of the local church must be used to make this come to pass.

Attenders. Usually the workers form a small percentage of the total membership in the local church. The remainder are *attenders.* Some regularly attend church every Sunday. Others attend only occasionally and still others never attend. They are members in name only.

A small percentage of those who only attend do not work in the church because of *physical or mental limitations.* Christians who have physical or mental limitations can be very effective prayerpartners. In some cases this gives them the first meaningful ministry they have ever had.

Most of the regular attenders are not working simply because they are *spiritually immature.* The usual way we try to make people mature is by scolding them. This arouses feelings of guilt. Scolding usually causes them to rationalize their performance and act even more immature.

The best way to help an immature believer grow to a place of functional maturity is to put him in a vital relationship with a more mature Christian. The prayerpartner program helps to do this. Week by week for four and a half months as a person in E.E. shares with the prayerpartner, the partner gains new insights into the work of God. He begins to identify with the lay evangelist and, as he matures, he too will want to responsibly reproduce.

Some regular attenders have never become workers because they still are *not genuinely converted* or they lack assurance. By enlisting them in the prayerpartner program and maintaining a regular relationship with them this may become apparent. Then it can be dealt with in a spirit of love.

Occasional attenders and those who never attend are quite different. Unless they have physical or mental limitations, they have a definite spiritual problem. If you know such a person, you might get the problem to surface by putting yourself in the dependent role of needing his prayer. Over a period of time, if he is willing to be your prayerpartner, you will gain new insights into ways of ministering to him.

Some churches allow occasional or nonattending members to feel that they are in as good a position as those who are regularly attending and hard at work for God. This should never be!

If the prayerpartner program is what it ought to be, it will, directly or indirectly, add power and personnel to the evangelistic thrust of your church. Many prayerpartners will want to become trainees. Those who cannot become trainees will pray to the Lord of the harvest and he will raise up the trainees of his choosing in the congregation.

2. TRAINEES

A trainee is one who is seeking to master the content of the gospel and practical basic procedure for sharing it with others. He is responsible for attending all classes and calling sessions unless God prevents him. He commits himself to complete all homework assignments before class each week. He is responsible to pray regularly for and with his trainer. He is responsible for enlisting at least two prayerpartners and contacting and praying with them each week. He functions at least as an enlistment scout seeking to find others in the church who are good candidates to be trainees in the next discipleship training program. (Further qualifications and responsibilities for trainees are discussed in this book under Enlistment for Enlargement, practical procedures.)

3. JUNIOR TRAINERS

A junior trainer is a person who has gone through at least one semester of E.E. discipleship training. He may have the basic content of the gospel and some ability to communicate it but needs more experience in actually sharing the gospel. Like the trainee, he is responsible for attending all the basic classes. He is responsible for participating in on-the-job training. The homework is to be completed for the trainee course each week before class. Prayerpartners are to be enlisted, contacted, and prayed with each week. Each is to pray for and with his trainer. In consultation with his trainer he will present the gospel from the beginning of the training program, as he is able to do it well. He will enlist trainees for the next semester.

4. TRAINERS

The trainer is one who has knowledge of the content of the gospel and ability to share it. He is responsible to attend all class and on-the-job training sessions for the semester unless God prevents him. Homework assignments are to be completed before class each week. He is responsible for giving personal attention to the trainee and/or junior trainer working with him. He is to pray for and with them regularly. He is to assist them with any personal or learning problems. If necessary, he can call on his lieutenant or the teacher/trainer to help. When his trainee or junior trainer is absent, he is to check and find out why and supply him with the assignment and any information from the class that he might need.

He is to report to his lieutenant whenever a member of his team is absent. When a trainer knows that he is going to be absent, he should contact his trainees or junior trainers and let them know so that they won't be caught off guard by his absence. A trainer should also notify his lieutenant if he is not going to be present.

A trainer should regularly check with his team members to see how they are progressing. This can be done in the car going to and from calls, after report sessions, in person, or over the telephone at a later time. The best trainers make it a point to meet for about one hour of private tutoring with their trainees between class sessions. This can be made into a *family affair* that brings all of the families involved together rather than fragmenting them. Some use a potluck dinner once a week for this purpose. If this is done, be sure you do not let it deteriorate into an extended time of fellowship with no tutoring. Each week the trainer has his trainee or junior trainer recite the memory work.

When the contact during the calling session turns out to be with a Christian and it is time for the trainee or the junior trainer to present the gospel, the trainer should ask the contact if he may practice sharing with him.

The trainer should encourage his trainee/junior trainer to stay for the report session.

When personal contact is not made with a prospect during the calling time, the trainer should use this time by having the trainee/junior trainer practice his presentation and share any personal problems or questions for help and prayer.

The trainer should set an example of consistent witnessing in his daily life and encourage his junior trainer/trainee to do likewise.

Trainers are to enlist trainees for the next training semester for their own teams and for the program as a whole.

Certification. Before a person functions as a trainer he or she must satisfactorily meet *minimum standards.* This is where certification with E.E. III International comes in. Trainer certification in Evangelism Explosion is *not* certification to be a witness. Rather it is certification *in this specific training program* to train others in this program. All Christians are commanded by Christ to witness and it would be presumptuous for any group to claim the authority to certify a Christian as a witness.

Certification is a way of establishing *minimum standards of excellence* so we can give God our best evangelistic effort. God deserves nothing less than our best. The sacrificial lamb in the Old Testament was to be closely observed for a period of time to see if it had any blemish or tear in its skin. If it was not perfect it was not acceptable. God wants the best we can give him. None of us is absolutely perfect, therefore no method of evangelism put together by men is going to be perfect. But as we are obedient to the Great Commission and go forth with the gospel, the resurrected Christ by his Holy Spirit goes with us. In actual witnessing situations he gives insights that are never received in the classroom. As these insights are shared, every person in the local training program is made more effective. As those insights are shared with E.E. III International and then communicated to others throughout the world, lay evangelists become more effective and the quantity and quality of the spiritual harvest is greatly increased.

For a person to be certified as a trainer in a local Evangelism Explosion program he must meet minimum standards agreed upon by E.E. III International and his local church. These standards include:

1. A basic ability to verbalize the gospel as demonstrated by making a thirty-minute taperecorded practice presentation to another person. This taperecording is evaluated by a standard oral presentation checklist.
2. An understanding of the basic concepts of the gospel. This is tested by a final written checkup.
3. An understanding of the basic principles of communicating the gospel. This also is evaluated on the basis of the final written exam.
4. Experience in actually sharing the gospel. This is evaluated from the participation report form.

No one should seek to be certified until he has completed at least ten actual visitation experiences over a period of not less than two months.

No one is to be certified as a trainer unless he is functioning as a trainer. The purpose and total process for all levels of certification with E.E. III International are covered in the booklet, *Make Disciples of All Nations . . . A Strategy for Local Church-based Evangelization of the World.* This is available free when requested by pastors on church stationery. Write E.E. III International, P.O. Box 23820, Fort Lauderdale, Florida 33307.

Certified trainers in the local church must realize that their training does *not* qualify them to function as a teacher/trainer, leadership clinic administrator or leadership clinic teacher. Further instruction and training of a different nature is required for these responsibilities.

Once a person becomes a certified trainer, he can function as a missionary trainer in certified leadership clinics. He can also minister on a short-term or long-term basis in certified E.E. works in different parts of his own country or other parts of the world.

Other specific requirements for trainer certification are contained in the Learning Kit for Trainees.

5. LIEUTENANTS

Trainers who demonstrate faithfulness and fruitfulness in the discipleship training program over a period of time may be given the responsibility of working with up to three trainers. By *faithfulness* we mean they have been consistent in their attendance and the use of the content and concepts of Evangelism Explosion III Discipleship Training. By *fruitfulness* we mean they have led others to profess faith in Christ, who have become vital members of their local church, enlisting trainees and discipling them to become trainers.

Lieutenants are to attend all class and on-the-job training sessions unless prevented by God. They are to complete any homework assignments given them. They are to pray regularly for and with those in their charge. They are to enlist prayerpartners and contact and pray with them each week. They may alternate on their trainers' teams for on-the-job training. This is especially important for people functioning as trainers for the first time. The lieutenant can monitor their performance in the field and affirm what they are doing correctly and give suggestions to improve other aspects of their witnessing and training activities. Lieutenants are to check with their trainers to see that prayerpartners are contacted and prayed with by both trainers and trainees. They are to check with their trainers after each calling experience and help with any problems or questions which may have arisen. If trainers in their group are absent, the lieutenant is responsible to check and see why and share any information with them that they need from the class. If a trainer from the lieutenant's group is absent, the lieutenant should check with the other members of the trainer's team to see what happened in his on-the-job training. If a trainee is regularly absent, his trainer and lieutenant should seek to make personal contact with him to help and encourage in any way possible. When the lieutenant encounters any problem or question he cannot handle, he should share this with the staff director. If the lieutenant is not able to make contact with his trainers before or after the report session he should contact them in person or by phone during the week. The lieutenant should work with his trainers to encourage and implement enlistment of new trainees in the next semester. Progress on this enlistment should be reported to the church office.

6. ASSISTANT LAY TEACHER/TRAINERS

Assistant lay teacher/trainers must be faithful and fruitful. These terms are defined for assistant lay teacher/trainers in the same way as for lieutenants.

The assistant lay teacher/trainer must be respected by the other members in the E.E. fellowship. He must have the ability to communicate to a group in public.

He must have the ability to receive and act on constructive criticism.

He is responsible to attend the teacher's meeting with the certified teacher/trainer. Usually it is best for these to be monthly meetings.

He is to teach under the supervision of the teacher/trainer as assigned.

He is to participate regularly in on-the-job training and to disciple one trainee.

He is to complete all homework assignments related to his particular responsibilities. When he has completed one semester as assistant lay teacher/trainer, his work is to be evaluated by the responsible person from the recognized leadership of the local church. If it is acceptable, he is then to attend a certified leadership clinic for Evangelism Explosion training to become a certified lay teacher/trainer.

Teacher/trainers, both staff and lay, are certified *only* in leadership clinics. Valuable training procedure and strategy is provided in leadership clinics that is not usually available in local churches. This information is essential for the proper leading and teaching of Evangelism Explosion in the local church.

Attending a leadership clinic gives opportunity for fellowship with Christians of like heart and vision from various parts of one's nation and the world. To properly lead a local E.E. work, it is essential that the leader have a vision for world evangelization. This is provided in the leadership clinics.

7. TEACHER/TRAINERS (LAY AND STAFF)

Lay teacher/trainer is a part-time volunteer position. A layman becomes a lay teacher/trainer by first functioning as a trainee, trainer, lieutenant, assistant lay teacher/trainer, and then after being recommended, attending a certified leadership clinic.

Staff teacher/trainers are usually theologically trained, ordained persons. However, some are lay people who have gone through the full E.E. process (trainee, trainer, lieutenant, assistant lay teacher/trainer, certified lay teacher/trainer) and then have accepted a full-time staff position. If a person does not have formal theological training it is essential that he have this minimum four-semester experience in Evangelism Explosion before he is placed in this full-time staff responsibility.

Many certified teacher/trainers are functioning in local churches throughout the world. Two-way lines of communication between the local churches and the International Center of Evangelism Explosion III in Fort Lauderdale make it possible to increase evangelistic skills, to inform for specific intercessory prayer, and to enlist for missionary work on a short-term or long-term basis throughout the world. With mutually-agreed-upon minimum standards it is possible for certified trainers from one part of the world to move into an E.E. work in another part of the world and help bring in the harvest.

As people trained in Evangelism Explosion share the gospel, they gain *new insights* into ways of being more effective. As these are shared with the International Center and field-tested, they are then *first made available to other certified teacher/trainers.* Maximum information on this evangelistic ministry is provided to those who relate in this reciprocal fashion. We try to provide service for those who need help and to gain information from those who are doing well so that this may be shared with others to improve the quality of evangelistic activity across the world.

As indicated previously, information for all levels of certification with E.E. III International may be obtained by pastors on request.

8. LEADERSHIP CLINIC ADMINISTRATORS

Leadership clinics are conducted in model churches in various parts of the world. A model church usually has a minimum of forty active certified trainers. Its E.E. ministry must be properly related to a total balanced ministry of worship, education, stewardship, leadership training, etc. A ten-year growth history is studied along with the specific strategy for effectively ministering to and evangelizing the community around the church. In the United States the church usually is in a community of approximately 100,000 population.

When these factors exist, the certified teacher/trainer returns to a leadership clinic at the International Center together with a lay person to go through leadership clinic administrative training. This consists of approximately fourteen hours of instruction in addition to the clinic. The clinic itself is analyzed in detail from behind the scenes so that the administrators will understand what they are putting together in their own church. Not until the administrators have been trained, is a date established for an area clinic to be conducted in their church. E.E. III International provides the basic teacher for the clinic, and the local teacher/trainer and leadership clinic administrator are responsible for the administrative aspects of the clinic.

9. LEADERSHIP CLINIC TEACHERS

An increasing number of certified teacher/trainers are demonstrating an ability to teach not only lay people in their local church, but church leaders in leadership clinics as well. E.E. III International is constantly seeking to develop more teachers to conduct clinics in their own churches after being properly certified and also to conduct clinics in churches other than their own.

ONE MILLION FULL-TIME LAY EVANGELISTS!

Through the ministry of E.E. III International new resources for world evangelization are being mobilized. As a fellowship begins in a local church and people are equipped to share their faith, something happens to them. From within the fellowship God lays his hand on a few and gives them a *holy restlessness.* They are not content to function as they have before. They lift up their eyes and see the whitened harvest field. Then, as they are guided by the Spirit to move out, they have behind them strong prayer and financial support. In many cases they have been able to relocate in other parts of the world in an E.E. work in their own denominational group. Thus they are able to move from country to country and be used of God in a significant way.

Will you join us in praying that God will mobilize a mighty army of at least a million full-time lay evangelists in the very near future?

APPENDIX A

SIDE ONE

Assurance Questionnaire Form

ASSURANCE QUESTIONNAIRE 7 0 1 (1 2 3)

I am ______________ of ______________

We're trying to determine people's religious thinking and assist anyone looking for a faith.

I. Will you help us by giving your thoughts in response to five brief questions?
(1) Yes (2) No — ☐ 4

II. Of what religious group or church are you a member? — ☐ 5 ☐ 6

(01) Baptist	**(08) Lutheran**
(02) Catholic	**(09) Mormon**
(03) Christian Church	**(10) Methodist**
(04) Christian Science	**(11) Presbyterian**
(05) Congregational	**(12) None**
(06) Episcopal	**(13) Other**
(07) Jewish	

____
(Please print name of "other" group.)

III. What local church do you attend? — ☐ 7

(1) ______________
(Please print name of local church.)
(2) None

IV. How often do you attend? — ☐ 8

(1) Weekly (2) Often (3) Seldom (4) Never

V. Have you come to the place in your spiritual life where you know that you have eternal life—that is, do you know for certain that if you died today you would go to heaven? — ☐ 9

(1) Yes (2) Hope So (3) No

VI. If you were to die today and stand before God and he said to you, "Why should I let you into my heaven?" what would you say? — ☐ 10

____
(Print person's actual words)
____

(1) Faith (2) Works (3) Unclear (4) No answer

This completes the questionnaire. Your answers are interesting. Thank you for your help.

Gospel & Testimony? (1) Yes (2) No (3) Didn't Ask — ☐ 11

May I have a few more minutes of your time to share with you how I came to know I have eternal life and how you can know it too?

(After presenting gospel, check address and note day and time for follow-up appointment.)

SIDE TWO

Address: (1) Yes (2) No (3) Didn't ask — ☐ 12

NAME (please print) ______________

STREET ADDRESS ______________ Apt. ______

CITY ______________ STATE ______ ZIP ______

Phone ______________ **(1) Local (2) Other** — 13 ☐

FOLLOW-UP APPT. (1) Yes (2) No (3) Didn't ask — 14 ☐
Day ______________ **Time** ______________

Future Visits (1) Yes (2) No (3) Didn't ask — ☐ 15

May I visit you with some friends when we have more time and share how I came to know I have eternal life and how you can know it, too?
Day ______________ **Time** ______________ — Check Address

Letter: (1) Yes (2) No (3) Didn't ask — 16 ☐ Check Address

May I send you a letter which explains how a person can know for certain that he has eternal life?

Future Phone Call: (1) Yes (2) No (3) Didn't ask — ☐ 17

May I phone you in a day or so and share how I came to know I have eternal life and how you can know it, too?
(Get at least first name and phone number.)

Invitation to Worship: (1) Yes (2) No (3) Didn't ask — ☐ 18

We would like to have you worship with us any time you can.
(Give day, time, place of worship)

LITERATURE: (1) Yes (2) No (3) Didn't Offer — 19 ☐
(Print Title) ______________

ATTEMPTED CONTACTS	DAY OF WEEK	TIME of Day: MORNING	AFTERNOON	EVENING	NOT HOME*

Contacted **(1) At home (2) In public (3) By phone** — 20 ☐

Admitted in home **(1) Before survey (2) Before gospel (3) No** — 21 ☐

Results: (1) Profession (2) Rejec. (3) No decision (4) Assurance — 22 ☐

Date ______

Age: (1) Jr. H. (2) Sr. H. (3) 18–21 (4) 25–40 (5) 40+ — 23 ☐

Sex (1) Male (2) Female — 24 ☐

Comments ______________

*** Put "T" Telephone. "V" Personal Visit**

APPENDIX B
Initial Contact Results Report Form

SIDE ONE

EVANGELISM EXPLOSION RESULTS REPORT

Record Code	1	2	3	Date	Month 4	5	Day 6	7	Year 8	9
	7	0	2							

How to fill out this report:

1. Underscore proper item in each section and place its number in the computer box.
2. Complete a separate report form for <u>each</u> person contacted.

Name (please print)

Street Apt.

City State Zip

Phone **Geo. Zone** 15 16

Office Use Only	Prospect I.D. No.	10	11	12	13	14

(1) Local (2) Out of town — 17 ☐

Time of day: (1) Morning (2) Afternoon (3) Evening — 18 ☐

Type of contact: (1) Church visitor (2) Quest—Pub. (3) Quest—door-to-door (4) Survey—Phone (5) Referral (6) Church visitor's Friend/family (7) Sunday school (8) Personal (9) Other (please indicate) — 19 ☐

Sex: (1) Male (2) Female — 20 ☐

Age group: (1) 6–9 (2) 10–12 (3) 13–15 (4) 16–18 (5) 19–25 (6) 26–29 (7) 30–39 (8) 40–49 (9) 50+ — 21 ☐

Marital Status: (1) Single (2) Married (3) Separated (4) Divorced (5) Widowed (6) Not known — 22 ☐

Children at home (1) Yes (2) No — 23 ☐

Names and ages

Occupation/place of employment (1) Yes (indicate) (2) Did not ask — 24 ☐

SIDE TWO

Hobbies/interests: (1) Yes (2) No (3) Did not ask — 25 ☐

Religious affiliation: (1) Baptist (2) Catholic (3) Congregational (4) Jewish (5) Lutheran (6) Methodist (7) Presbyterian (8) None (9) Other (Please print) — 26 ☐

Regular at another local church: (1) No (2) Yes (please print name of church) — 27 ☐

Knows members of our church (1) No (2) Yes (please print names) — 28 ☐

Sure of going to heaven before gospel presented? (1) Yes (2) No — 29 ☐

Answer to God's Why?

(Print actual answer—then classify) — 30 ☐

(1) Faith (2) Works (3) Unclear (4) No answer

Results: (1) Already a Christian (2) Profession (3) Gosp. present.—No decision (4) Gosp. present.—Reject. (5) Gosp. present.—Assur. (6) Gosp. present. for trainee (7) Would not let team in (8) Only friendly visit (9) Personal testimony only. (Follow-up calls must be on follow-up report.) — 31 ☐

Immediate follow-up (1) Full (2) Abbreviated (3) None — 32 ☐

Appointment for follow-up call (1) No (2) Did not ask (3) Yes (indicate) Day Time — 33 ☐

Follow-up tapes: (1) Yes (2) No (3) Did not ask — 34 ☐

"Welcome" booklet given: (1) Yes (2) No — 35 ☐

Follow-up suggestions/comments (1) Yes (2) No — 36 ☐

Team members' names: (Please print)	Team Member I.D. No.		
	37	38	39
( ) Trainer ( ) Jr. Trainer ( ) Trainee ( ) Guest	40	41	42
( ) Trainer ( ) Jr. Trainer ( ) Trainee ( ) Guest	43	44	45
( ) Trainer ( ) Jr. Trainer ( ) Trainee ( ) Guest			

APPENDIX C
Seven-Day Call Back Follow-up Report Form

SIDE ONE

EVANGELISM EXPLOSION FOLLOW-UP REPORT

Record Code	1	2	3	Date	Month 4	5	Day 6	7	Year 8	9
	7	0	3							

Name of new convert

Street Address Apt.

City State Zip

Phone

Office Use Only	Prospect I.D. No.	10	11	12	13	14

Appointment not kept 15
(1) Canceled (2) Stood up (3) Not admitted
Why?

Appointment rescheduled 16
(1) No (2) Yes: When?

Time of contact 17
(1) Morning (2) Afternoon (3) Evening

Answer to God's "Why?" 18
(Please print and then classify)
(1) Faith (2) Works (3) Unclear (4) No answer

Sure of going to heaven? 19
(1) Yes (2) No

BIBLE READING
I. One chapter per day 20
(1) Completed (2) Partly (3) None

II. Underlined & marked questions 21
(1) Yes (2) No

MEMORY VERSE 22
__ John 3:16
(1) Yes (2) No

SIDE TWO

Tapes Loaned 23
(1) At time of profession
(2) Day after the profession
(3) At the time of the follow-up call
(4) Not loaned (5) Other

Tape player loaned 24
(1) Yes (2) No

Tapes listened to 25
(1) All (2) Part (3) None

Bible study groups 26
(1) Offered to take to group
(2) Mentioned (3) Did not mention

"Prayer in the Forever Family" left 27
(1) Yes (2) No

Asked to be prayerpartner 28
(1) Yes (2) No

Considering church membership 29
(1) Yes (2) No
(3) Has not been mentioned

New Christian personal problems 30
(1) No (2) Yes: Explain

New Christian has questions 31
(1) No (2) Yes: Explain

Additional comments 32
(1) No (2) Yes: Indicate

Team members' names: (Please print)

	Team Member I.D. No.		
( ) Trainer ( ) Jr. trainer ( ) Trainee ( ) Guest	33	34	35
( ) Trainer ( ) Jr. trainer ( ) Trainee ( ) Guest	36	37	38
( ) Trainer ( ) Jr. trainer ( ) Trainee ( ) Guest	39	40	41

APPENDIX D
EVANGELISM EXPLOSION—Public Report Board Layout

Suggested format for a chalkboard to be used during report sessions to record results of calling for the week.

Place the total *number* of each appropriate item in the proper boxes.	TYPE OF CONTACT										GOSPEL PRESENTED							GOSPEL NOT PRESENTED					FOLLOW-UP			
TEAM MEMBERS' NAMES	Church visitor	Ques.—Public	Ques.—Door-to-door	Ques.—Phone	Referral	Ch. vis. fam./friend	Sunday school	Personal	Total attempted	Total completed	How many times	To how many people	For trainee	Profession	No decision	Rejection	For assurance	Not admitted	Already Christian	Only questionnaire	Only friendly visit	Only pers. testimony	Immed. full	Immed. abbrev.	Appt. for 1st week	1st week visit
TOTAL TEAMS CALLING ______